Ingolf U. Dalferth

Transcendence and the Secular World

Ingolf U. Dalferth

# Transcendence and the Secular World

## Life in Orientation to Ultimate Presence

Translated by
Jo Bennett

2nd, revised
and translated edition

Mohr Siebeck

INGOLF U. DALFERTH, born 1948; 1977 Promotion; 1982 Habilitation; Professor Emeritus of Systematic Theology, Symbolism and Philosophy of Religion at the University of Zurich; since 2008 Danforth Professor of Philosophy of Religion at Claremont Graduale University in California.

ISBN 978-3-16-156329-4 / eISBN 978-3-16-156330-0
DOI 10.1628/978-3-16-156330-0

The Deutsche Nationalbibliothek lists this publication in the Deutsche Nationalbibliographie: detailed bibliographic data are available on the Internet at *http://dnb.dnb.de.*

Title of the first (German) edition 2015: *Transzendenz und säkulare Welt. Lebensorientierung an letzter Gegenwart*



The book was typeset by Martin Fischer in Tübingen, printed by Gulde Druck in Tübingen on non-aging paper and bound by Buchbinderei Nädele in Nehren.

Printed in Germany.

To the PRT students in Claremont
who fought for their program

## Preface to the 2018 English Edition

This book is the last of a series of studies written in recent years on questions of human life and existence. The translation of the first book of that series was published under the title *Creatures of Possibility. The Theological Basis of Human Freedom* (Grand Rapids, Michigan: BakerAcademic, 2016). The second *Selbstlose Leidenschaft: Christlicher Glaube und menschliche Passionen* (Tübingen: Mohr Siebeck, 2013) has not been translated yet. The third one is the present volume. I am greateful to Jo Bennett who has again produced an excellent translation. She is a master of the art of translation, and I am fortunate to have had the chance of working with her.

I also wish to thank Katharina Gutekunst from Mohr Siebeck for her interest in the translation and the constructive collaboration in the production of the book. Marlene Block has again been of invaluable help. I am grateful to her.

The book is dedicated to the Philosophy of Religion and Theology (PRT) students in Claremont who stood up and fought for their program because they believe in academic excellence and the future of the humanities.

Ingolf U. Dalferth

# Preface to the 2015 German Edition

As long as it is necessary to emphasise that we are living in a secular age, we are not yet living in one. Even in the 21st century, religions play an important role in our world, in the private lives of many people and in the public sphere. It is daily apparent that this is not entirely a good thing. Religions can bring out the best in human beings, but they can also delude them into doing their worst. They paint us a picture of heaven, yet they can make life hell on earth. To them we owe our insights into the harmony of the universe, the power of love and the possibilities of a shared humanity. But time and again, human lives are devastated by the destruction of order, the temptation to hatred, the suppression of freedom and the justification of inhumanity beyond comprehension. We need to pay heed to both, where religion and non-religion are concerned. To live religiously is not good *per se*, and to live non-religiously is not evil *per se*. In both cases it depends on *how* one is what one is and *how* one does what one does. One can live non-religiously and be an exemplary human being, and one can believe one is living a religious life and behave like a beast.

Christians therefore do well to see the secular world and society not purely in negative terms, but to strive for a discriminating view and attitude. In many respects it is an advantage that we no longer live in a society dominated by religion, but in a secular one, in which freedom of religion is held to be a fundamental right. Undoubtedly we may deplore the loss, in Western modernity, of much that is familiar. Yet much which was the stuff of dreams has been gained. No one who has the good fortune to live in a free society which values justice and equality, respects the distinction between state and religion and upholds the fundamental right of freedom of religion can seriously want to forgo all of that. Never have people been able to live as freely by their religious convictions as they can in secular Western society. But never has there been such bitter opposition, backed by appeals to religious conviction, to the modern principles of freedom without which such a life would not have been possible.

Christian theology ought to be adopting a critical attitude to the current swan song of secularisation and the fashionable heralding of a new post-secular religious era. From the very beginning, the Christian faith has made a decisive contribution to the worldlification of the world, the critical appraisal of religion, religions and religiosity and the re-creation of human life in the presence of God. Christians have been and are being persecuted regularly on account of this critical faith. Christian faith is about the orientation to God's presence in all spheres of life, beyond the boundaries of prevalent religious forms and often in distinction from them. Correctly understood, the Christian life orientation[1] moves beyond the alternative between religious and non-religious life. Its point of reference is not any distinction between the profane and the holy in the world; rather, it is the self-mediating presence of God, and the distinction, established by this presence of God within the possibility space of the world, between a life that orients itself to that presence (faith), and a life which does not (unfaith). The philosophical code of this life orientation is the distinction between transcendence and immanence in the practices of life.[2] These signify, not distinct areas of life, but different attitudes towards all areas of life on the basis of an event

[1] On the concept of life orientation cf. I. U. DALFERTH, *Selbstlose Leidenschaften. Christlicher Glaube und menschliche Passionen*, Tübingen 2013, 48–50.

[2] In this book I use 'transcendence' as a shorthand term for 'the transcendence' and 'the transcendent'. Where there is need of a more detailed definition of this orientational concept as it contrasts with 'immanence', it is given in the relevant context.

which can be encoded as the irruption of transcendence into immanence and which can lead to the reorientation of life as it is opened up to transcendence. This philosophical distinction is paralleled in Christian life and thinking in the distinctions between creator and creation, divine and worldly, the ultimate presence of God, unchanging and effective everywhere, and the changing presence in which we live temporarily, whether it be in faith, in which humans live their lives in orientation to the ultimate presence, or in unfaith, in which they do not.

This book is about orientation to this ultimate presence and to the primacy of transcendence within the immanence of a secular world. This primacy manifests itself in life by means of events that are often completely ordinary, but which create an awareness of the distinction between transcendence and immanence by showing that and how transcendence is distinct from immanence, making itself present and interpreting itself *as* transcendence. And since we are unable to orient ourselves by this guiding distinction without making further distinctions, it is about the distinctions by which such a life orientation to the ultimate presence takes place in practice, consciously in faith, and factually in unfaith.

The book deals with material from the following publications: Religion als Privatsache? Zur Öffentlichkeit von Glaube und Theologie, *Theologisch-praktische Quartalschrift 149* (2001) 284–297 (Chapter H); Glaubensvernunft oder Vernunftglauben? Anmerkungen zur Vernunftkritik des Glaubens, in: F. Schweitzer (ed.), *Kommunikation über Grenzen*, Gütersloh 2009, 612–627 (Chapter D); Weder möglich noch unmöglich. Zur Phänomenologie des Unmöglichen, *Archivio di Filosofia / Archives of Philosophy LXXVIII* (2010) 49–66 (Chapter G); Religionsfixierte Moderne? Der lange Weg vom säkularen Zeitalter zur post-säkularen Welt, *Denkströme. Journal der Sächsischen Akademie der Wissenschaften 7* (2011) 9–32 (Chapter A); Ist Glauben menschlich?, *Denkströme. Journal der Sächsischen*

*Akademie der Wissenschaften 8* (2012) 173–192 (Chapter D); Andererseits. Zur Phänomenologie des Entscheidens, *Archivio di Filosofia / Archives of Philosophy LXXX* (2012) 145–159 (Chapter E); Ereignis und Transzendenz, *Zeitschrift für Theologie und Kirche 110* (2013) 475–500 (Chapter B); Ist radikale Negativität möglich?, in: E. Angehrn / J. Küchenhoff (eds.), *Die Arbeit des Negativen. Negativität als philosophisch-psychoanalytisches Problem*, Weilerswist 2014, 37–60 (Chapter F).

I should like to thank the publishers for their permission to use and transcribe these texts and to take their thinking onward. I also wish to thank my publishers Mohr Siebeck for their interest in the subject matter and for their excellent and constructive collaboration.

Ingolf U. Dalferth

# Table of Contents

## B. Event and Transcendence. Three distinct event discourses



## C. Transcendence and Immanence. A fundamental distinction for religious life orientation today

## D. Faith or reason? Critique of a confusion

## E. On the one hand / On the other hand. Decision-making as orientation through the making of distinctions



## F. Wholly other. Negativity as a possibility condition for differentiation

## G. Neither possible nor impossible. Impossibility as a boundary concept and boundary horizon of differentiation



## H. Orientation to Transcendence. The point of making distinctions

# A. Orientation by Distinctions. Christian faith and the secular world

We live in a secular age in which faith in God, the gods or the divine is no longer the norm, but has become just one option amongst others.[1] This is true despite considerable differences between the regions of the world, and despite the fact that the secularisation process varies in different cultural contexts and certainly does not always lead to the dissolution or dismantling of religious affiliations and orientations.

## *1. Secularity, religion and spirituality*

Secularisation – the "worldlification" of the world – can take many forms, not all of which rule out the possibility that people are leading a religious or spiritual life. There is a difference, but no sharp dividing line, between the two. It is true that religion exists only in the diversity of world religions; however, it is not just someone who participates in collective religious practice who lives religiously, but also anyone who reverences the order and diversity of life and is careful to follow the precepts that give life a deeper meaning. And spirituality, too, consists not simply in participation in the conventional pious practices of a religious tradition, but is understood in a broader sense as the search for meaning and for a life that experiences "connectedness to the moment, to self, to others, to nature and to the

[1] Ch. Taylor, *A Secular Age*, Cambridge, MA 2007; H. Joas, *Faith as an Option: Possible Futures for Christianity*, Stanford 2014.

significant or sacred".[2] However, not all religion, religiosity or spirituality equates to consciousness of transcendence, and not all consciousness of transcendence is religious or spiritual. There are 'religions' such as Shintō or Confucianism that consider life to be lived predominantly in the here and now, and there is an awareness of transcendence in numerous cultural communities that neither are nor wish to be religious.

Even in the West, leaving the church is not necessarily the same as loss of religion, but rather the reverse side of a search that turns to other religious forms and a creative, selective and individuating acceptance of unfamiliar spiritual traditions. Those who seek find a great deal. And those who do not (any longer) find what they are seeking in the traditional forms of their religion and culture will seek it elsewhere. But what is being sought? Perhaps it is a search for religion as something with which one can align oneself because one has to make an explicit decision in favour of it. Religion is meaningless if it does not confront me with existential decisions that give me a new view of myself, my world, others and God. In that case it is merely an inherited social custom, which one can dispense with, since it neither demands anything from one, nor reveals anything to one. One does not even need to oppose or criticise it in order to be free of it: one simply ignores it.

[2] Chr. M. Puchalski et al., Improving the Quality of Spiritual Care as a Dimension of Palliative Care: The Report of the Consensus Conference, *Journal of Palliative Medicine 12* (2009) 885–904, here: 887: "Spirituality is the aspect of humanity that refers to the way individuals seek and express meaning and purpose, and the way they experience their connectedness to the moment, to self, to others, to nature and to the significant or sacred." Cf. S. Peng-Keller, Spiritual Care als theologische Herausforderung. Eine Ortsbestimmung, *Theological Literaturzeitung 140* (2015) 454–467.

### 2. Being a Christian as a dual and double-sided decision

This linking of religion, decision and identity is a phenomenon characteristic of modernity. But it has a long prehistory, closely connected with the history of Christianity. Christianity originally began as an eschatological religion of decision, in a twofold sense. According to Christian conviction, God showed himself in Jesus Christ and through his Spirit to be the one who has decided permanently and irrevocably for human beings, even though they are living as sinners, leading a life that ignores God and is remote from him. That is the heart of the Christian message of God's redemptive coming to renew the world out of love for his creatures. Humans, for their part, can decide for or against God's decision by placing their faith in the Christian message of God's decision for them, or by not doing so, either because they do not know the facts of this message, or because they explicitly refuse or reject it. If they do put their faith in it, they do not consider this to be their own decision, but rather to be the work of God, who decided unconditionally for human beings, as became clear in and through Jesus Christ, and who through his Spirit enables them to decide for this decision, demonstrated by their change from unfaith to a life of faith. In their baptism Christians acknowledge God's decision as their unmerited gift, which has freed them from their old attachments and orientations and which opens the door to a new form of life with God and with each other. When they present themselves for baptism, they are deciding for a life of faith and simultaneously against a life of unfaith. God's decision for human beings (Jesus Christ) and his self-mediation of this decision to human beings (Spirit) means that the old life of remoteness from and rejection of God is left behind and the new life in fellowship with God, opened up by God through Jesus Christ and the Spirit, becomes not just possible, but actual (new being). Of his own free will God has made himself our neighbour, so that all human beings can call on him as their good father and are to be considered and treated as children, heirs and neighbours of God. In this new community of God's neighbours there are – as Paul says – no longer Jews or Greeks, slaves or free, men or women (Gal. 3:28), since none of those distinctions are determining factors for the new life in Christ.

God's neighbours' new identity is not their own choice, but a free gift from God. No one can obtain it for themselves, nor does anyone have a right to it, which is why no one has a greater right to it than anyone else. Where it enters someone's consciousness, it is perceived as a gift and a mission from God which is not attached to any prior conditions. One can accept it in faith as it stands, or ignore and refuse it in unfaith. Both responses confirm that this new identity is a gift and provision that does not depend on one's own acceptance or rejection, but precedes them and is what makes them possible at all. It is not something one had always been searching for, but the experience of something unexpected and new, of the improbable possibility that God is becoming neighbour to those who do not care about him. To find one's identity as a neighbour of God, it is not even necessary that one is engaged in a search for it. It can happen against one's own wishes and intentions, as when Paul was converted from being a persecutor of Christians to becoming an apostle of Christ, for instance. Where it meets with a response, it leads to the identity being split into an old and a new self. As Paul writes in Romans 7, the existential tension between the two cannot be resolved in either direction, but can only be endured with the help of God. One is no longer in control of oneself, but, as God's neighbour, one belongs to another's sphere of control, whether one welcomes that in faith or disregards or disputes it in unfaith.

One can acknowledge this new identity by giving thanks for God's gift, being baptised and thus deciding against a life in unfaith and for a life in faith in the Christ-community of the new being. Alternatively, one can reject God's gift and refuse the change of orientation to a life in faith, thus remaining in the Adam-community of the old being. Every human being belongs to this old humanity (Adam) in which everything revolves around self-assertion, self-preservation and self-promotion, which is why a life in faith can only ever exist when one turns away from a life in unfaith. But everyone can in fact belong to the new humanity (Christ), which God opens up to us by making himself our neighbour in such a way that love for God, and for everyone else as God's neighbours, can determine our lives. However, just as the decision for Christ does not in itself constitute the new being, so equally the non-decision for, or the decision against, Christ does not negate the new being. God's gift and thus God's decision for human beings precedes any human decision-making (dual decision). God's decision is what makes the human decision possible in the first place: now we can live a life oriented towards God's love in reliance on God's gift, and can decide against unfaith and for a life in faith (double-sided decision).[3] But God's decision also makes the human decision essential: given God's decision, a lack of an explicit human decision for or against it is nonetheless a decision – in which case it can remain uncertain whether such a non-decision must always constitute a decision against, or whether the acutal life of the one concerned can in fact offer proof of the opposite.

These are the fundamental characteristics of the new being in Christ, as outlined by Paul. The more, however, a life orientation in accordance with the new being in Christ was reduced to one religious form amongst others, becoming, in the Roman empire, the dominant religion into which one was born and within

[3] Deciding for a life in faith and against a life in unfaith are the two sides of one and the same decision, not two different acts of decision. But this double-sided decision is contingent upon and enabled by the prior decision on God's part, without which there neither could nor would be a human decision for a life with God and against a life of disregard for or denial of the presence of God.

which one grew up culturally and socially, the less this dual moment of decision shaped and characterised Christian being and consciousness. Of course it was kept in mind in the church's baptismal practice. However, the practice of infant baptism emphasised the gift-character of faith in Christ and being Christian, and therefore God's decision for the human being, but only to a lesser extent the human decision for God's decision in taking leave of the old and turning to the new life. The church's introduction of confirmation is a reaction to this problem. The debate over the practice of infant baptism and the call for adult baptism are examples of the conflicts that arose from this. While the one stresses God's unconditional antecedent decision for human beings, the other insists on the human responsibility to make one's own decision for God's prior decision. And whereas for the one, membership of the church is the social norm, to be adopted out of regard for the church as an institution, for the other no church membership is legitimate in Christian terms unless it is based on a personal decision. Unless you decide in favour yourself, you do not really belong. And one who explicitly decides against has at least understood that a decision has to be made.

### *3. Religion in late modernity*

The conflict is a paradigm for the way modernity handles religion. The process of modernity has led increasingly to religion being deemed a social and cultural given. One participated in it, one could even participate in it in a purely external manner, without taking any specific decision. It has become a mark of the individual identity, distinctiveness, authenticity, perhaps even the sacrality of the person. Whether one lives religiously or not, one ought to do either from conviction. Just joining in by itself is not enough, but nor is not joining in. One must make a wholehearted commitment for or against. But the price of this pressure to identify oneself is high. When it is a matter of authenticity and one's own identity, even the incidental becomes significant. Nothing can be up for negotiation, everything has to be defended: images in church, crosses on mountain tops or in courtrooms, public holidays, cultic vestments, Latin masses, rites of circumcision and full-body veils. Everything is always pivotal, and one's very self is constantly at stake. No longer is there any distinction between the issue and the person, between the important and the less important.

For many that is just too demanding. But they cannot avoid the pressure to identify by questioning the coupling of religion with identity, but only by becoming indifferent to everything religious. They are not for one religion and against others, nor are they even for or against religion as a whole. All that no longer has anything to do with them and their identity. Everything religious has ceased to be of interest to them and they seek their authenticity and identity elsewhere.

Others hold onto the idea that religion and faith are pivotal to one's own identity, but can no longer find this identity within the bounds of traditional religious forms. They are not abandoning faith and religion themselves, but their institutionalised social forms and organisational membership structures. They are searching for other forms of spiritual life, and they find them easily in the global market of religions, where supply and demand constantly reinforce each other. As Daniel Bell stated, back in the seventies: "Where religions fail, cults appear."[4]

Thus we cannot speak of the end of religion. Even in an enlightened Europe religion is still present in numerous different ways, both in private life and in the public arena.[5] And there is

---

[4] D. Bell, *Die Zukunft der westlichen Welt. Kultur und Technologie im Widerstreit*, Frankfurt a. M. 1979, 201.

[5] Th. Luckmann, *Die unsichtbare Religion* (1967), Frankfurt a. M. 2005; P. L. Berger (ed.), *The Desecularization of the World. Resurgent Religion and World Politics*, Washington, D. C. 1999.

some evidence that trends in the development of fundamentalist movements, as seen not only in Islam, but also in Christianity, Judaism, Hinduism and Buddhism,[6] may actually be caused by the alienating forces of economic, technological, cultural and media-oriented globalisation, rather than by the functional differentiation of society and a politically, legally, morally and scientifically secularising modernity.[7] In order to participate on an equal footing in political and legal affairs, morality and science, and to be recognised in those fields, one can be, but does not necessarily have to be, religious. Each of these spheres has its own logic, its own norms and values and its own guiding principles. A religious orientation cannot be a determining factor, in either a negative or a positive sense, if peaceful coexistence between humans of differing convictions and philosophies of life is to be possible in a plural society.[8]

This has changed the traditional religions themselves, as well. The conflict between religion and the secular world long ago became a conflict within the religious traditions themselves. And in fact, not just a conflict between premodern and modern trends in individual religions, but to an even greater extent a conflict-ridden split among those who are not closed off in a traditionalistic way to social modernisation processes, but actively react to them. Thus there are some who endeavour to establish a positive relationship with these processes and to update their religious traditions in line with modern conditions, while others

---

[6] Cf. C. Six / S. Haas / M. Riesebrodt (ed.), *Religiöser Fundamentalismus: Vom Kolonialismus zur Globalisierung*, Innsbruck 2005.

[7] Cf. B. Kaiser, Der Terror der Entwurzelung. Die Ursache des Neofundamentalismus, *Neue Ordnung 2* (2013) 19–23; M. Mies, Globalisierung und religiöser Fundamentalismus (http://www.was-die-massenmedien-verschweigen.de/aktuell/GlobalisierungFundamentalismus.pdf) (12/8/2014).

[8] Cf. F. W. Graf, *Dient Religion dem guten Leben? Ein Plädoyer gegen jede Selbstverabsolutierung*, Hamburg 2012; idem, *Götter global. Wie die Welt zum Supermarkt der Religionen wird*, München 2014.

adopt a negative, fundamentalist stance and reject the challenges of modernity, not just ignoring them but actively opposing them. The definitive signature of the current religious situation is not the conflict between traditionalists and modernists. Rather it is the conflict between reformers, who are attempting to affirm in a new way the basic insights of their religion under the dynamically changing conditions of late modernity, and fundamentalists, who do not want to engage with the questions posed by modernity, but rather to oppose it actively in the name of their religion and to set up their own construct of their religious tradition. They are both modernisers. However, the former see modernity as a religious challenge with which they are engaging, whereas the latter perceive it as a call to a religious antimodernity, which they are using modern means to affirm.

### *4. Sociological interpretations*

All this has been discussed in detail in recent years.[9] One can, in company with José Casanova and Charles Taylor, question the sustainability of an oversimplifying undifferentiated theory of

---

[9] Cf. J. Casanova, *Public Religions in the Modern World*, Chicago / London 1994; D. Martin, *On Secularization: Towards a Revised General Theory*, Aldershot 2005; D. Novak, *The Jewish Social Contract. An Essay in Political Theology*, Princeton 2005; J. Stout, *Democracy and Tradition*, Princeton 2005; Taylor, *A Secular Age*. An overview of older literature in English is provided by K. M. Schultz, Secularization: A Bibliographic Essay, *Hedgehog Review* (2006) 170–178. For a wider appreciation of the debate as it affects the field of law, cf. H. Dreier, *Säkularisierung und Sakralität. Zum Selbstverständnis des modernen Verfassungsstaates*, Tübingen 2013. For the theological backgrounds to the secularisation thesis, cf. J. Dierken, Immanente Eschatologie? Säkularisierung bei Hegel, Troeltsch und Löwith, in: idem, *Ganzheit und Kontrafaktizität. Religion in der Sphäre des Sozialen*, Tübingen 2014, 219–238.

secularisation and develop counter-narratives,[10] or one can, with Detlef Pollack and others, point to comprehensive and meaningful empirical data that ought not to be ignored.[11] One can adopt Niklas Luhmann's view that, although religion does not necessarily have to play a role in the life of every human being, on a social level it examines a basic problem which no society can evade: religion observes "the un-observability of the world and of the observer"[12] and thus considers the basic prerequisite for all social reality: the improbable possibility of meaning. One can, as Habermas does, turn this around so that one sees, in the traditional elements of religion, not just premodern conflict potential, but normative resources of meaning which can be rendered fruitful through the translation of religious content into a neutral language for use in a plural democracy and liberal civil society.[13] One can take such perspectives, with their focus

[10] CASANOVA, *Public Religions*; TAYLOR, *A Secular Age*.

[11] D. POLLACK, *Säkularisierung – ein moderner Mythos? Studien zum religiösen Wandel in Deutschland*, Tübingen 2003; IDEM, *Rückkehr des Religiösen? Studien zum religiösen Wandel in Deutschland und in Europa II*, Tübingen 2009; IDEM / U. WILLEMS / H. BASU / TH. GUTMANN / U. SPOHN (eds.), *Moderne und Religion: Kontroversen um Modernität und Säkularisierung*, Bielefeld 2012; K. GABRIEL / CHR. GÄRTNER / D. POLLACK (eds.), *Umstrittene Säkularisierung. Soziologische und historische Analysen zur Differenzierung von Religion und Politik*, Berlin 2012; U. OEVERMANN / M. FRANZMANN, Strukturelle Religiosität auf dem Wege zur religiösen Indifferenz, in: M. FRANZMANN / CHR. GÄRTNER / N. KÖCK (eds.), *Religiosität in der säkularisierten Welt. Theoretische und empirische Beiträge zur Säkularisierungsdebatte in der Religionssoziologie*, Wiesbaden 2006, 49–82.

[12] N. LUHMANN, *Die Religion der Gesellschaft*, published by A. KIESERLING, Frankfurt a. M. 2000, 29.

[13] J. HABERMAS, *Glauben und Wissen. German Book Trade Peace Prize 2001*, Suhrkamp special edition, Frankfurt a. M. 2001; IDEM, *Zwischen Naturalismus und Religion. Philosophische Aufsätze*, Frankfurt a. M. 2005; K. WENZEL / TH. M. SCHMIDT (eds.), *Moderne Religion? Theologische und religionsphilosophische Reaktionen auf Jürgen Habermas*, Freiburg i. Br. 2009; M. BREUL, *Religion in der politischen Öffentlichkeit. Zum*

on society, and follow Hans Joas in setting against them the conviction of the "sacredness of the person"[14], which singles out each human being as distinctive, giving fundamental significance to the idea of human dignity. It was in this sense that Durkheim understood "belief in human rights and human dignity as the expression of the sacralisation of the person",[15] which precedes and underlies all social processes.

The results are illuminating. Under pressure from actual secularisation processes, attempts are being made to transform the concept of religion into either a systemic problem at the level of society (meaning), a set of values underlying liberal participatory democracy (morality), a side effect of life-world processes (everyday piety) or a fundamental phenomenon of human personhood (sacrality). One way or another, it is assumed that religion demonstrates its value in the services it performs for society, democracy, human life and the individual. The critical yardstick by which it is judged lies, not within religion itself, but outside it: religion is not the measure of other things, but is measured by them.

What is happening at present against the background of secularisation theory, leaves many philosophical and theological questions open. The ongoing reality of religions in a secular world poses practical organisational challenges, theoretical questions of substantiation and problems of social legitimation. The widespread viewpoint that we live in a secular, or increasingly secularising, world, and that this is the legitimation backdrop against which all religion has to prove itself, is by no means self-evident. It is not immediately obvious that the argumentative obligation should be located on the side of religion, nor

*Verhältnis von religiöser Überzeugung und öffentlicher Rechtfertigung*, Diss. Phil., Catholic Theology, University of Cologne,, 2014, 101–171.

[14] H. Joas, *Die Sakralität der Person. Eine neue Genealogie der Menschenrechte*, Freiburg i. Br. 2011.

[15] Loc. cit. 86.

is it automatically secularity that constitutes the present world, whether as the state in which it finds itself, or as the goal towards which it is moving.

From a theological point of view, therefore, one must not always take up the cudgels on behalf of religion (or even of each religion) in the face of the demands of secularity, nor should one always take issue with and criticise the secular world on behalf of faith. Not everyone who says 'God' speaks for truth, and not everyone who criticises religion has subscribed to non-truth. Paul, Augustine, Luther, Barth, Bonhoeffer, Gogarten, Ebeling and Jüngel remind us that in any case Christian faith is not *per se* in opposition to a secular world, but is actually a contributory factor to it in certain respects. And even if one shares the widespread negative view held by the religious traditions of secular modernity, one should not forget that "no previous era" has made it so possible to "live a life of faith in God as the modern one has".[16]

## *5. The ambivalence of the secular*

Christian attitudes to the secular world are thus thoroughly ambivalent. There is a good reason for this: the ambiguity of the term 'secular'. On the one hand it can mean that which is not religious, while on the other hand it can mean that which is not divine. The non-secular, from which the secular is being differentiated, means on the one hand the religious, and on the other hand the divine. The two contrasts are not the same, but define different ideas of secularity. One can live secularly in the second sense without living non-religiously in the first. But one is not yet

[16] M. STRIET, Glauben in einer entsicherten Welt, in: J. SÖDER / H. SCHÖNEMANN (eds.), *Wohin ist Gott? Gott erfahren im säkularen Zeitalter*, Freiburg i. Br. et al. 2013, 249.

truly living secularly in the first sense as long as one continues to identify oneself as living secularly. The concept of the secular, understood in this way, appears to contain a negative idea of the religious which cannot be edited out without emptying the concept of its content. This does not apply to the concept of the religious. The term 'religious' is neither always, nor in essence, defined in contrast to the term 'secular'.[17] The meaning of the term 'secular', on the other hand, when used in this first sense, always includes a negative reference to 'religious'.

This has consequences that are often overlooked. If what is meant by 'secular' is negated so that we speak not merely of 'non-secular' but of 'post-secular', we end up with two options and not just one, as is often thought. We can understand post-secular as the recovery of the religious – that is to say, the possibility of the religious – at the end of modernity (weak post-secularity),[18] or as the overcoming of the distinction between the religious and the secular (strong post-secularity).[19]

---

[17] Cf. on this subject the studies of the history of concepts by E. Feil, *Religio. Volume I: Die Geschichte eines neuzeitlichen Grundbegriffs vom Frühchristentum bis zur Reformation,* Göttingen 1986; idem, *Religio. Volume II: Die Geschichte eines neuzeitlichen Grundbegriffs zwischen Reformation und Rationalismus (ca.1540–1620),* Göttingen 1997; idem, *Religio. Volume III: Die Geschichte eines neuzeitlichen Grundbegriffs im 17. und frühen 18. Jahrhundert,* Göttingen 2001; idem, *Religio. Volume IV: Die Geschichte eines neuzeitlichen Grundbegriffs im 18. und frühen 19. Jahrhundert,* Göttingen 2007.

[18] Cf. H.-J. Höhn, *Postsäkular: Gesellschaft im Umbruch – Religion im Wandel,* Paderborn. 2007; idem, *Der fremde Gott. Glaube in postsäkularer* Kultur, Würzburg 2008; F. Johannsen, *Postsäkular? – Religion im Zusammenhang gesellschaftlicher Transformationsprozesse,* Stuttgart 2010; Breul, *Religion in der politischen Öffentlichkeit,* 126 f defines the concept of 'post-secularity' too imprecisely.

[19] I have developed this in more detail in I. U. Dalferth, Religionsfixierte Moderne? Der lange Weg vom säkularen Zeitalter zur post-säkularen Welt, *Denkströme. Journal der Sächsischen Akademie der Wissenschaften 7* (2011) 9–32.

Those who are post-secular in the strong sense are not those who, in the wake of the religious criticism and religious abstinence of modernity, have begun to take the possibility of religion seriously again. Rather, they are those who live the way they do without endeavouring to use the antithesis between 'religious' and 'secular' to characterise their lives in any way. Only those who live neither religiously nor secularly, who neither emphasise nor feel they ought to emphasise one or the other to define their lives, have truly left modernity behind them. One is not living truly secularly until one has no need – or believes one has no need – of such a designation.

This is certainly not just the abstract possibility of a future that may be conceivable one day, but a thoroughly present reality – in the lives of individuals and groups within our society, no less than in the self-understanding of nations and national communities. One concrete example of this is the *Consolidated version of the Treaty on European Union* dated 30.3.2010.[20] There is no mention of secularity, but it is in fact put into practice. Religion and religious traditions are referred to only in the past tense, when the Preamble speaks of "the cultural, religious and humanist inheritance of Europe, from which have developed the universal values of the inviolable and inalienable rights of the human person, freedom, democracy, equality and the rule of law".[21] There is also an indirect hint of religion in the

---

[20] *Consolidated version of the Treaty on European Union*, Official Journal of the European Union (30.3.2010) C 83/13-C 83/45.

[21] Loc. cit. C 83/15: "RESOLVED to mark a new stage in the process of European integration undertaken with the establishment of the European Communities, / DRAWING INSPIRATION from the cultural, religious and humanist inheritance of Europe, from which have developed the universal values of the inviolable and inalienable rights of the human person, freedom, democracy, equality and the rule of law, / RECALLING the historic importance of the ending of the division of the European continent and the need to create firm bases for the construction of the future Europe, / CONFIRMING their attachment to the principles

non-discrimination provision, when Article 2 speaks of the values on which "the Union is founded" namely "respect for human dignity, freedom, democracy, equality, the rule of law and respect for human rights, including the rights of persons belonging to minorities. These values are common to the Member States in a society in which pluralism, non-discrimination, tolerance, justice, solidarity and equality between women and men prevail."[22] Apart from that, religion plays no role. It is neither affirmed nor disputed, but is ignored from a political point of view. In the European Union one can be religious or not – neither position is considered of sufficient political importance that it requires addressing in the Treaty on European Union. Secularity is no longer defined by separation from the religious, but by the fact that the antithesis between the religious and the secular no longer plays a political or constitutional role.

### *6. Secularisation as the loss of significance of the religious*

It would appear from the above that the modern secularisation process has achieved its goal. In 1966 Bryan Wilson defined "secularization" as "the process whereby religious thinking, practices and institutions lose social significance".[23] This definition assumes the existence of societies where religious thinking, religious practices and religious institutions were once of social significance, but have now ceased to be significant at all, or are no longer as significant as they once were. It is unclear, however, whether it is intended to imply that religious phenomena are disappearing from the life of society and that religion has no

of liberty, democracy and respect for human rights and fundamental freedoms and of the rule of law, …"

[22] Loc. cit. C 83/17. Cf. also Article 6 C 83/19.

[23] B. R. Wilson, *Religion in Secular Society. A Sociological Comment*, London 1966,14.

future in modern society. Or whether the implication is that they are being transformed into religious phenomena which no longer have any particular social relevance, and that religion will continue to exist, but will no longer play an important role in society. Or whether it is implying that religious phenomena will be changed into, or replaced by, non-religious phenomena so that religions are superseded by non-religious functional equivalents in society. All or some of the above could be intended to a greater or lesser extent. The definition is thus too vague and undifferentiated to be of any real help.[24]

Despite these inadequacies, Wilson's definition offers five important points for consideration:

*1. Relevance for society.* Religious phenomena are considered from the perspective of their social relevance or social significance in a given society. This is a sociological viewpoint, not the first or most important perspective from which believers in a religion would describe what they believe and do. The definition considers the issue from a sociological, not a philosophical or theological perspective.

*2. Differentiation.* It assumes a social distinction between religious and non-religious spheres of life which is not valid for all societies, but is the result of social differentiation in Western (European) modernity. The presence of this differentiation is perceived to be the criterion of a society's modernity. But this fails to take into account that, even if it applies to the way European culture and society have developed, it is not necessarily valid for other cultures or societies. "Instead of viewing European modernity as the only valid model",[25] it would be better to

---

[24] Cf. D. Martin, *A General Theory of Secularization*, New York 1978; K. Dobbelaere, *Secularization: A Multi-Dimensional Concept*, Beverly Hills, CA 1985; Casanova, *Public Religions*.

[25] S. N. Eisenstadt, Die Vielfalt der Moderne: Ein Blick zurück auf die ersten Überlegungen zu den 'Multiple Modernities', *Themenportal*

speak of a 'multiple modernity' or of 'various routes to different modernities'.[26]

3. *Asymmetry*. In addition, it assumes an asymmetry between religious and non-religious spheres, inasmuch as those who live in modern societies can live religiously, but do not have to, whereas they not only can live non-religiously, but must. No one can be a member of present-day society without participating in the spheres of politics, the economy, the law, education, the media and so on. Apparently the same does not apply to religion. This accounts for the widespread view that, in contrast to other spheres of society, not only can religion change, it can completely disappear from society, whereas the non-religious spheres of society can indeed change, but cannot entirely vanish. People will always be political, economic and social beings, but will not necessarily always live religiously. However, the contrary view is also put forward, supported by anthropological or sociological arguments. It is held that, although people are no longer – or are less and less – religious in the traditional church sense, they nevertheless have many different ways of living religious or spiritual lives outside traditional church organisations, whether or not they would describe their lives as religious.[27] Moreover the problem of the improbability of meaning and the difference between indeterminability and determinacy, which religions seek to examine by reference to the fundamental distinction between immanence and transcendence, is also subject to examination in

---

*Europäische Geschichte* (2006), URL: http://www.europa.clio-online.de/2006/Article=113.

[26] Cf. S. N. EISENSTADT, *Die Vielfalt der Moderne*, Weilerswist 2000; IDEM (ed.), *Multiple Modernities*, Transaction Publishers 2002.

[27] Cf. F. STOLZ (ed.), *Homo naturaliter religiosus. Gehört Religion notwendig zum Mensch-Sein?* Bern/Berlin et al. 1997; P. L. BERGER (ed.), *The Desecularization of the World. Resurgent Religion and World Politics*, Grand Rapids, MI 1999.

secular societies, so that, although religion may 'disappear' from people's lives, it cannot 'disappear' from society as a whole.[28]

*4. Societal spheres or practising individuals.* The range of reference of the definition is unclear. It speaks of societal practices and institutions, but makes implicit assumptions about the conduct, attitudes and activities of believers in a religion. Thus, for instance, it is assumed that people in differentiated societies live either religiously or non-religiously or, in certain senses or circumstances, both. It is not assumed (to name just some of the possibilities) that they pursue different religious activities in different spheres of society, or perform different social roles in their religious lives, or carry out their different functions and activities within a life that is religious as a whole. And it is also assumed that non-believers carry out non-religious activities, but no religious ones, while believers do – and are required to do – both.

*5. Transfer.* Finally, it is assumed that there has been a transfer of (the meaning of) things, goods, practices, institutions, rules or ideas from the religious to the non-religious spheres of society. This transfer or change has altered the social relevance of these religious phenomena, but not necessarily their religious significance. They used to be religious and can still be religious in religious contexts, but in non-religious contexts within society they have no further function, having been superseded and replaced by secular alternatives.

From a religious point of view, however, this loss of social relevance is only significant if social relevance is important for a religion or a religious tradition, which is certainly not always the case (hermits, anchorites). Or where the overall social context of life is not determined by the religious, but where there are a host of significant non-religious practices, institutions or ideas besides, so that the transfer does not merely constitute a change

[28] Cf. LUHMANN, *Die Religion der Gesellschaft.*

from one strand or mode of religious life to another. Or where this transfer is understood from a religious perspective more as loss than gain: in other words, if the goal of religious life is not perceived to include overcoming the distinction between the religious and non-religious spheres of society, so that the non-religious spheres are shaped by the moral ideals of the corresponding religion. Likewise, from a religious viewpoint the process of secularisation need not necessarily be described as a history of loss or subtraction; instead it could – or even should, as Charles Taylor suggests – be presented as a history of gain.

The traditional view of secularisation thus operates on three basic assumptions: the differentiation between spheres of social meaning and relevance, the distinction between religious and non-religious practices, institutions and ideas, and the transfer of something from the religious to a non-religious sphere. Where the distinction between religious and non-religious spheres of a society is in dispute, any change can only take place *within* the religious or non-religious sphere, not *from* one *to* the other. And where it is assumed that social significance does not exist in varying degrees, or that we ought to concentrate on events and not on 'things' (in the widest sense), there is no transfer or change in either direction, but only a different allocation of social significance within a society at different times.

## *7. Collapse of the theory of secularisation*

One can only speak of a secularisation process under certain conditions, and these are not always present, even in modernity. But even where they appear to be present, the position is more complicated than the so-called theory of secularisation would suggest. This has been convincingly demonstrated by the wide-ranging sociological, political, historical, philosophical and theological debate surrounding the theory of secularisation during recent decades.[29] It has led to a significant change in the view of the development of modernity which has been standard since the beginning of the 20th century. According to current sociological thinking, the processes of religious change "under conditions of modernity and accelerating change" have demonstrated in a paradigmatic way that the path to modernity can be described as a scenario "in which mankind shifted from the religious mode to the secular".[30] This process is called 'secularisation', and the 'secularisation theory' seeks to explain it sociologically.[31]

The view of modernity presented here derives from the European experience of the founding fathers of sociology, Max Weber and Emile Durkheim.[32] But it was much too rough and ready to be verified with any precision against empirical data from different countries and cultures. The broadly argued theory of secularisation was therefore broken down by José Casanova and successive thinkers into a series of subtheories, including *privatisation* (religion is a private matter, not a public affair), *rationalisation* (religion must earn its legitimacy by justifying itself in the forum of reason) and *social differentiation* (religion is one social subsystem among others), each of which can be verified in different historical situations within different cultures.

---

[29] Cf. in particular CASANOVA, *Public Religions*; MARTIN, *On Secularization*; NOVAK, *The Jewish Social Contract*; STOUT, *Democracy and Tradition*; TAYLOR, *A Secular Age*; SCHULTZ, Secularization.

[30] MARTIN, *On Secularization*, 18.

[31] Cf. H. LÜBBE, *Säkularisierung. Geschichte eines ideenpolitischen Begriffs*, Freiburg i. Br. ³2003; H. LEHMANN, *Säkularisierung, Der europäische Sonderweg in Sachen Religion*, Göttingen 2004.

[32] Cf. K. EDER, Europäische Säkularisierung. Ein Sonderweg in die postsäkulare Gesellschaft? Eine theoretische Anmerkung, *Eurozine* 07–07–2006, 1–15; M. BORUTTA, Genealogie der Säkularisierungstheorie. Zur Historisierung einer großen Erzählung der Moderne, *Geschichte und Gesellschaft* 36 (2010) 347–376.

Today many sociologists are of the opinion that privatisation and rationalisation are not necessary traits of a secular society under the conditions of modernity. Others hold to the view that the theory of social differentiation remains the crux of secularisation theory.[33]

On both sides, however, the term 'secular' is used not only descriptively, but also normatively.[34] Descriptive usages are oriented towards the fundamental distinction between 'secular' and 'non-secular'. Whenever one side of this contrast is being evaluated positively and the other negatively, the term is used normatively. This constantly leads to a lack of clarity and to ambiguities. Thus it is often unclear whether the term 'secular' is being used in a descriptive or a normative way, and where there is a transition from one to the other. However, it is important to take care over this, in order to understand what is meant when the history of modernity is represented as the 'dismantling or decline of religion and the rise or growth of the secular' or when the present is described as the era of the 'return of religion or the gods to a secular world'.[35]

But the normative use, too, has multiple meanings, since the term 'secular' can be used either positively or negatively from different standpoints, achieving a different result from each.

---

[33] POLLACK, *Säkularisierung*; IDEM, Religious change in Europe: theoretical considerations and empirical findings, in: G. MOTZKIN / Y. FISCHER (eds.), *Religion and Democracy in Contemporary Europe*, London 2008, 83–100; IDEM, *Rückkehr des Religiösen?*; MARTIN, *On Secularization*, 18.

[34] The following sections take up ideas from I. U. DALFERTH, Post-secular Society: Christianity and the Dialectics of the Secular, *Journal of the American Academy of Religion 78* (2010) 317–345. The terms 'antithesis', 'contrast', 'distinction' and 'difference' are used interchangeably to indicate differences of meaning.

[35] Cf. F. W. GRAF, *Die Wiederkehr der Götter. Religion in der modernen Kultur*, München [3]2005.

Thus the term 'secularism' can denote any position which judges secularity or the secular to be positive and all that is contrary to them to be negative. But one can also use the term to mean the opposite, that is an areligious or antireligious ideology that is held to be reprehensible. Clearly the normative sense of these terms depends on whether they are used from a secular or non-secular standpoint, in other words, whether those using them take a positive view of the secular or, conversely, of the non-secular. Upon this will depend the evaluation, whether positive or negative, of the same phenomena, facts or developments which are described as 'secular', 'secularity' or 'secularisation'. The shift from a descriptive to a normative use thus results in a view of the history of modernity either as progress and benefit (constructive) or as regression and loss (destruction) and, accordingly, in an optimistic or pessimistic view of the present, depending on whether one is positively[36] or critically disposed towards religion.[37]

## *8. The dialectic of modernity*

So the term 'secular' can have systematically different meanings. If 'secular' is being defined in terms of the vertical antithesis *divine / worldly*, then secularity is understood as *worldliness*, taking as its thematic context the discovery of the transcendence of the divine and the unfolding of the distinction between creator and creation. If, on the other hand, 'secular' is being defined in terms of the horizontal antithesis *religious / secular*, then secularity is

---

[36] Cf. Stout, *Democracy and Tradition*; Novak, *The Jewish Social Contract*.

[37] S. Dobbelaere, *The End of Faith: Religion, Terror, and the Future of Reason*, New York 2004; idem, *Letter to a Christian Nation*, New York 2006; R. Dawkins, *The God Delusion*, New York 2006.

understood as *secular worldliness* and takes as its context the discovery of the worldliness of the worldly as the dismantling or restraint of the religious in society and in human life. The first has been a part of Christianity from its beginnings, the second is a development of modernity.

The historical dialectic of secularisation in modernity is only comprehensible if one pays heed to this dual form of secularisation: vertical and horizontal. In the first, the world is oriented towards the world in distinction from God, and faith is oriented transcendentally towards God. In the second, the distinction is made within the world between the religious and the secular: worldliness is treated as secular and religion becomes a private matter within a secular world. If we link the two distinctions, the process of European modernity can be described as a re-entry of the vertical distinction *divine / worldly* on the side of the worldly, which is thereby differentiated horizontally by means of the *religious / secular* distinction, which, in turn, can take various different forms: *church / world, sacralisation / secularisation, self-transcendence / repudiation of transcendence* and so on. Here the distinction *religious / secular*, whichever form it takes, is always a distinction drawn *within the worldly* and is not to be confused with the vertical distinction *divine / worldly*. It does not lead out beyond the worldly, but remains within it.

Conversely, theological thinking is distinguished by the fact that it conceptualises the re-entry of the vertical *divine / worldly* distinction as being on the side of the divine: it symbolizes that difference as being between *creator* and *creation*, and it then specifies the distinction thus symbolized through successive self-application in a cascade of progressively differentiated determinations.

Thus, just as *creation* can be defined as that which owes its existence to the self-differentiation of its creator, and which only exists because God differentiates himself from it in such a way that he is perpetually related to it through his self-differentiation, so the *revelation* of the distinction *creator / creation* is identifiable in the creation as the self-revelation of the divine in the world. If the re-entry of the *divine / worldly* distinction on the worldly side characterises the process of secularisation, it follows that the re-entry of this distinction on the divine side characterises the process of the self-revelation of the divine in the world. They are parallel developments. The discovery of *worldliness* as the reverse side of the discovery of the transcendence of the divine (the *divine / worldly* distinction) and the discovery of *secular worldliness* as the discovery of the worldliness of the worldly through the differentiation of all that is religious (the *religious / secular* distinction) are just one side of a process. The other, corresponding, side is the discovery of the divine as the inescapable ground and horizon of the distinction between the divine and the worldly (the *creator / creation* distinction) and the discovery of the possibility of a positive theological view of the secular worldliness of the world in the light of the *creator / creation* distinction. Not only the religious, but also the secular life is a life lived within a creation that owes its existence to the creator. And not only the secular but also the religious life is a life lived within the world that is worldly and not divine.

### *9. The differentiation between the divine and the worldly: worldliness*

The two distinctions, *divine / worldly* and *religious / secular*, are thus not merely different: they are related to each other in a specific way, inasmuch as the second, which serves as a more precise definition of the first, presupposes and is dependent on it. Only within the sphere of the divine can the worldly be partitioned into *religious* and *secular*. However, this raises the question, from where does the distinction *divine / worldly* emanate: from the worldly or from the divine, or from neither, or from both but in different ways? Whichever the answer, it is striking what a minimal role the *divine / worldly* distinction plays in the political, legal and philosophical debate surrounding the so-called theory of secularisation. It is no different even when this theory is broken down into its subcomponents: *privatisation* (religion is a private matter, not a state affair), *rationalisation* (religion must earn its legitimacy by justifying itself in the forum of reason) and *social differentiation* (religion is one social subsystem among others), each of which must be judged separately. Even then the *divine / worldly* distinction is not employed. Yet for the religious traditions of Judaism, Christianity and Islam, the critical and fundamental difference consists, not in a distinction between the religious-ecclesial and state-political *in the world*, but in the distinction between *God* and the *world*, the *One* and the *Many*, the *First* and the *Whole*. The world is created, not divine. Neither the world, nor anything in it, is to be equated or confused with God, the creator. Rather, the latter makes himself the One and the First by differentiating himself from the Many in such a way that, through his differentiation, he unites the Many in a single whole.

Viewed thus, 'the disenchantment of the world' (M. Weber) begins at the point where three intellectual manoeuvres connect: the transition from polytheism to *monotheism* (gods / God), the *discovery of the strict transcendence of the divine* and the corresponding *strict worldliness of the world* (transcendence / immanence), and the understanding of God's relation to the world as *creation* and not as an emanation or participation (creator / creation), and hence not as the differentiation process of the divine, but as the self-differentiation of the One from the (thereby constituted) Whole, to which the One does not belong, but to which it is contrasted. The idea of monotheism taken in isolation is not adequate to explain this development, as hellenistic cosmotheology in its various versions (Platonic, Aristotelian, Stoic) shows (*one cosmos, one godhead*). What is far more decisive is the differentiation between the one *creator* and the one *creation* (*one God, one world*). Not until then was the world 'de-deified' or 'disenchanted', in other words, understood and experienced from a thoroughgoing worldly point of view. At the same time, the transcendence of God began to be conceived of, not merely as a concomitant effect of worldly immanence, but as a condition of the very possibility thereof, and thus in creational terms.

This development resulted in a series of further fundamental differentiations which represent absolute distinctions and cannot therefore be resolved into polar antitheses that are distinguished by degrees. These include the distinction between *infinite* and *finite*: there is no external comparative relationship between the infinite and the finite. Or the distinction between *God* and *idol (false god)*: God may not be equated or confused in any way with a created reality. Wherever that happens – wherever, in other words, something created is deified or revered as divine – this constitutes idolatry and superstition. Or the distinction between *faith* and *superstition*: this distinction, too, does not describe or classify, it is normative and evaluative. It cannot be used descriptively (in the context of the religious sciences), but purely critically (in a theological context), from the perspective of those whose faith is truly in God and not just in an idol.

### *10. The differentiation between the religious and the secular: secular worldliness*

Likewise, the second major differentiation, *religious / secular*, can be formalised in a variety of ways: following the logic of the relevant sphere, for instance, as the distinction *holy / profane,* or institutionally as the distinction *church / state* or *religious / political.* Here, *secular* can be designated from a religious standpoint as everything that is not located on the religious side of this antithesis (*church/secular*: church activities vs. state activities; *clerical/secular*: the monastic life of religious clergy vs. the non-monastic life of secular clergy; *church/worldly*: church music vs. worldly music [secular sonatas]). Alternatively *secular* can be formulated in a political-legal sense as the antithesis between *confessional* and *secular*. This contrast was established with the rise of the nation states in the aftermath of the Wars of Religion in Europe, and is used to consolidate a series of different developments within a single package. Putting it simply, these are: the move from confessional strife to secular peace in the 16th and 17th centuries (political motive); the move from a monopolist state economy to a free market economy in the 18th and 19th centuries (economic motive) and the move from an authoritarian religious past to a liberal modernity in the 19th and 20th centuries (cultural motive).

In the light of each of these changes the secular is construed with a different emphasis, as is the religious. From the perspective of the first change it is held that secular political powers must not interfere in religious affairs ('religion is a private matter'[38]). From that of the second, it is recognised and made legally possible for a plurality of confessions, denominations or religions to coexist within the borders of the same nation state ('religion is plural', 'religion exists only in the plurality of the historical religions'[39]). From the third perspective, only what is defensible according to public standards of neutral and universal reason

[38] Cf. Th. Jefferson, The Virginia Statute for Religious Freedom 16 January 1786, Record of the General Assembly, Enrolled Bills, Record Group 78, Library of Virginia, in: W. W. Hening (ed.), *Statutes at Large of Virginia*, vol. 12 (1823) 84–86.

[39] F. D. E. Schleiermacher, *Über die Religion. Reden an die Gebildeten unter ihren Verächtern* (1799), KGA 1,2, 185–326.

can be taken seriously ('religious faith is pre-scientific and cannot be held rationally'[40]).

### *11. Secularism and fundamentalism*

Where these different assessments of religion as *private, plural* and *pre-scientific* are combined, secular positions intensify into *antireligious secularism* and thus into an ideological world view.[41] Religion is perceived as an atavistic relic of a past epoch, an unbridgeable gulf opens up between reason and religion, and questions as to the future of religion and its significance for the present receive purely negative answers. Religious convictions are attributed to a pre-scientific past and have nothing to do with a modern world and a society guided by reason.

In recent years movements such as *Radical Orthodoxy* have risen up in opposition to this ideological perspective, responding with a counter-ideology. Secularism, secularity and all talk of a secular world are censured indiscriminately as modernist ideology.[42] Secularism, it is said, has dominated Western culture in Europe since the Age of Enlightenment, but its roots can be traced back to the beginnings of Scotism with its far-reaching cultural impact.[43] Scotism misled Western thinking in general, and Western theology in particular, into breaking away from the Platonising world-view of the Church Fathers, Augustine in par-

---

[40] S. HARRIS, *The End of Faith: Religion, Terror, and the Future of Reason*, New York, 2004; IDEM, *Letter to a Christian Nation*, New York 2006; DAWKINS, *The God Delusion*.

[41] Cf. R. SCHRÖDER, *Abschaffung der Religion? Wissenschaftlicher Fanatismus und die Folgen*, Freiburg i. Br. et al. 2008.

[42] J. MILBANK, *Theology and Social Theory*, Oxford ²2006; PH. BLOND, *Post-Secular Philosophy*, London 1997; J. K. A. SMITH, *Introducing Radical Orthodoxy: Mapping a Post-secular Theology*, Grand Rapids 2004.

[43] J. MILBANK / C. PICKSTOCK / G. WARD (eds.), *Radical Orthodoxy: A New Theology*, London 1999.

ticular. It furthered the tendency to replace a realist outlook on the world with a confused nominalism; it propagated a misleading doctrine of a unitary idea of being of God and the world; it defended the view that political authority was centred in the will of the people and not in the will of God; and it resulted in a problematic marginalisation of theology in the academic institutions of the West. It is easy to see how *Radical Orthodoxy* censures modernist secularism by using equally sweeping and generalised arguments, but from a non-secular perspective rather than a secular one.[44] Charles Mathewes has rightly emphasised that, in their critique of secular modernity the advocates of *Radical Orthodoxy* proceed from exactly the same premises, adopt the same approach to problems, cultivate the same style of argumentation and conform to the same thought categories as the advocates of secularism and secular modernity whom they criticise and attack.

This is the pattern of argument followed by many religious reactions to modernity and by most fundamentalist rejections of modernism and secularism. They all take their stand in the anti-secular camp of the *religious / secular* contrast, and they all blur the distinction between vertical and horizontal secularity by identifying their own religious viewpoint with God's viewpoint. They ignore a series of important changes of perspective in the history of European culture and become entangled in contradictory perspectives. It is one thing to define the secular, as classical Christianity did, from a religious point of view as *that which is not religious*, but it is quite another to define the religious from a secular point of view as *that which is not secular*. The religious focus of the first definition (secular = not religious) and the secular focus of the second definition (religious = not secular) do not belong to the same perspective, but to different perspectives, so

---

[44] Cf. W. J. Hankey / D. Hedley (eds.), *Deconstructing Radical Orthodoxy: Post Modern Theology, Rhetoric and Truth*, Farnham 2005.

they cannot readily be brought together or counter one another, like with like. Similarly, it is one thing to reject the non-religious (secular) view of religion as *that which is not secular* from a religious point of view (religious focus), but quite another to do so from a non-secular (i. e., secularly construed, a 'religious') point of view within the secular perspective (non-religious focus). In the latter case, modern secularism is attacked from precisely the point of view which it has itself created, by excluding normatively from its world view religion and everything religious as pre-modern and non-secular. This is exactly what fundamentalism does: it reacts to modern normative secularism on the latter's own terms, and in so doing it turns the religion it is defending into an anti-ideology to a modern secularist ideology. Fundamentalism is not a return to religion as it was before it had been marginalised by modern secularism, but is rather the protest of the marginalised against modernity on modernity's own terms.

What is happening here is, from a theological point of view, a fundamental misconstrual of one's own position. It fails to recognise that the vertical secularity of the Christian faith seriously calls in question the binary distinction between *divine* and *worldly* as a distinction within the creation, so that all intra-worldly differences between *secular* and *religious* (in whatever sense) are located on the side of the worldly rather than the divine. Instead, it seeks to elevate the worldly contrast between *secular* and *religious* into a dominance of the religious over the secular by identifying the religious (in the sense of the horizontal antithesis) with the divine (in the sense of the vertical antithesis). It thus falls prey to precisely the religious criticism that it seeks to defend, because the latter has replaced an enchanted world with a view of the world as a creation that is not in any sense, not even partially, to be identified with the divine.[45] What religious

[45] Cf. R. A. Markus, *Christianity and the Secular*, Notre Dame, IN 2006.

fundamentalism is defending is nothing but a version of the secular modernity it is attacking.

### *12. The ambiguity of the concept of post-secularity*

Whilst the term 'religious' is not comprehensively defined in contrast to the term 'secular', the meaning of 'secular' does appear to include the negation of 'religious'. It follows that it is impossible to speak of the 'secular' or 'secularity', without making reference to the religious. Even those who propagate the idea of a secular era remain fixated on religion.

This is apparent when the catchword 'post-secular' is used to overcome the critical attitude to religion that is typical of modernity with a post-modernity that is more sympathetic towards it.[46] But this approach focuses on just one possible reading of the 'post-secular' figure of thought. The picture changes when one applies the operator 'post', not just to 'secular', but to the whole contrast of meaning inherent in 'secular vs. religious', so that one does not just mean the overcoming of a secular modernity, but the overcoming of a modernity that has defined itself as secular by its dismissal of a religious pre-modernity. 'Post-secular' is then not an indicator for the recovery of the religious within the secular world of modernity, but for a dismissal of the antithetical relationship between the secular and the religious. Only then are we living, not just in a secular age, but in a truly post-secular world. For a post-secular world only exists when there is a post-secular society, and that only exists when the state no longer perceives or defines itself as secular. What does this mean?

---

[46] M. King, Towards a Postsecular Society, *Network, the Science and Medical Network Review* (2003) 7–11; idem, Art and the Postsecular, *Journal of Visual Art Practice 4:1* (2005) 3–17.

As a basic principle, the starting point has to be the separation between the *state* (the political sphere) and *society* (the totality of all socially differentiated spheres), a separation which has been well-established since the 19th century. From that point on, the relationship between *state and church* or between *state and religion* has no longer been able to serve as a paradigm for defining the relationship between religion and society as whole. This is because the former is a relationship between different subsystems of society (religion and state), whereas the latter, in contrast, is a relationship between society as a whole and one of its subsystems (religion and society). One must therefore adopt a different way of thinking through the meaning of 'secular', by relating it specifically to society, the state and the life of the individual.

When considering the difference between state and society, we can distinguish, in the development of European modernity, four typical groupings of *state, society* and *individuals.* In what is an obvious oversimplification, I have called these state types: *religious*, *tolerant*, *secular* and *post-secular*.

*1. Religious states* prescribe which religion is to be believed in and practised by its citizens.[47] This can be for religious reasons, because of a conviction that this religion alone is true and in conformity with the will of God, as was the case in mediaeval Europe. Or it can be for political reasons, as in the European nation states of the 16th and 17th centuries, where, to ensure the unity of the state and the unification of a culturally diverse populace, it was insisted that one religion, and only one, was officially recognised as mandatory for everyone: *one state, one religion* (*or church*).

Such a state is religious, because it prescribes a specific religion as mandatory for its citizens. One can only be a citizen of such

---

[47] Antireligious states, which make atheism mandatory, or which prohibit all or specific religions for their citizens, belong to this type as well.

a state in the full sense of the word, if one is Catholic, Lutheran, Calvinist, Jewish, Muslim, Buddhist, Hindu or whatever (depending on the individual state). Here no distinction has yet been made between *state* and *society*. Likewise, the separation between *state* and *church* is a purely legal separation between the political and religious spheres within a stratified society which not only distinguishes between God and the world in principle (vertical secularity), but also within the world between religious (sacred, clerical, ecclesiastical) and non-religious (profane, secular, political) spheres and activities. For *citizens* of such a state, both sides of the distinction are mandatory: no one can be a citizen of such a state without being a member of the relevant church or religious community as well. In practice, however, the form of such a state can vary. It may have the character of a theocracy (union of church with state) or of a state church (union of state with church).

2. *Tolerant states* do not specify which religion is mandatory for their citizens. But they assume that every citizen will practise a religion more or less intensively, as was typically the case in the European nation states of the 19th century.[48] Of course, there may be a majority religion which receives certain privileges (for instance – well beyond the 19th century – the Anglican church in Great Britain, the Reformed Churches in Switzerland, the Lutheran churches in the Scandinavian countries and the Roman Catholic church in Poland, Italy or Spain). But other religions are tolerated, provided they adhere to certain rules, and citizens can practise them without jeopardising or forfeiting their civil rights. Thus, in this type of state, rather than a specific religion being prescribed as mandatory, various religions are tolerated: *one state, a variety of religions (or churches).*

---

[48] Cf. C. D. Classen, *Religionsrecht*, Tübingen 2006; I. U. Dalferth / C. R. Famos (eds.), *Das Recht der Kirche. Zur Revision der Zürcher Kirchenordnung*, Zürich 2004.

Such a state is tolerant, since, although it expects that its citizens will practise a religion, and perhaps prefers them to practise a particular religion, it accepts that they will decide of their own free will which religion they wish to confess and live by (freedom of religion). Within the social context of such a state a distinction is drawn, not just between *state* and *religion*, but also between different religions, churches, confessions or denominations. This promotes the separation between *society* and *state* (the political system) and paves the way for a differentiated social system and a secular state. In this type of state, *individuals* can practise one or other religion, or indeed none at all, and although there may be instances where this leads to disadvantages in terms of social acceptance and standing, individuals need not be afraid that their religious or non-religious orientation could jeopardise their civil rights. This kind of state increasingly views religion as a private and not a public (i. e. politically relevant) matter. And the greater the understanding and implementation of all that this principle implies for freedom of religion, treatment of atheists and other non-believers, social stability and the political acceptance of the state, the closer a tolerant state comes to being a secular state.

*3. Secular states* (as distinct from antireligious states) do not merely allow their citizens a choice between a religious or non-religious way of life. They prohibit themselves by law from interfering with their citizens' religious or non-religious convictions and practices, and adopt an explicit and legally binding neutral stance to all matters that have to do with religion. Secular states do not prescribe a single religion, nor do they (merely) tolerate different religions; rather they accept the fundamental right of every citizen to live a religious or non-religious life, as they wish.[49] That applies regardless of whether they insist, in

[49] Cf. Classen *Religionsrecht*; M. Germann, Kirchliche Institutionen im modernen Verfassungsstaat, in: A. Arndt / U. Barth / W. Gräb (eds.), *Christentum, Staat, Kultur: Proceedings of the Congress of the*

addition, that citizens have a duty to justify their agreement to coercive legislation, not just from a religious point of view and thus privately, but publicly and with reasons that are reasons for all.[50] In other words, secular states are neutral, not simply as regards which religion its citizens practise, but also with regard to whether they practise a religion at all, or whether they lead a non-religious or antireligious life. In this type of state no one is required to adhere to a religious or a non-religious view or way of life; instead, everyone has the right to choose their own lifestyle: *one state, many religions and non-religions.*

Such a state is not merely tolerant, but defines itself as neutral in respect of the option between religious and non-religious lifestyles. It is restricted by law from enacting any pro- or anti-religious legislation. And it differentiates systematically between the descriptions adopted by religious groups and traditions using their own language, terminology or symbolism (Christian faith, church, Christmas, Easter) and its own neutral legal terminology for these social realities (religions, religious communities, festive seasons, holidays etc.). *Society* is thus increasingly clearly differentiated from the state and other social spheres (law, economy, science, religion, media, private life etc.), and not only are individuals permitted to practise the religion of their choice, or no religion at all; their right to do so is enshrined in law.

*4. Post-secular states* are differentiated from secular states in that they no longer define themselves as neutral towards the religious or non-religious. They do not adopt any position with regard to the religious or non-religious lifestyles of their citizens; instead, they refrain from emphasising their neutrality or from explicitly pointing out that they neither adopt nor represent *any* position on religious questions. To refer to the topic of religion

*International Schleiermacher Society in Berlin, March 2006,* Berlin 2008, 411–432.

[50] Cf. Chr. J. Eberle, *Religious Conviction in Liberal Politics*, Cambridge 2002.

in any way has become irrelevant for them. That does not necessarily imply that religion and faith are unimportant or that they are ignored, suppressed, under attack or viewed with a greater degree of suspicion than other societal spheres, organisations or activities. Rather, it means that the state no longer gives any prominence to its relationship with the religious system, nor does it expressly emphasise it when describing its relationships with the other social spheres or subsystems by insisting that it is 'neutral' or 'secular' with regard to religious questions.

This post-secular indifference is only possible under two conditions. Firstly, the state, i.e. the political system, must have learned to differentiate clearly between its relationships with society as a whole, with the other subsystems of society such as the economy, the law, science, religion and so on, and with individual citizens and their practices, activities, views of life and lifestyles. Secondly, it may no longer lay special stress on its relationship with religion in comparison with its relationships with the other subsystems of society, but must treat the former simply as one relationship amongst others. This has nothing to do with the rationalisation or privatisation of religion, i.e. the requirement to justify religious or non-religious convictions rationally, to give them moral legitimacy, or to limit the place of religion to the private life of the individual while denying it any public role. Whether religious or non-religious convictions can be justified from a rational or moral standpoint is a question to be addressed to the people who hold such convictions, and is not the concern or responsibility of the state. And whether a religion is afforded a private or public role is a matter for society, not the state. It is not a question of any political role played by religion, but of the recognition of the fact that, in the aftermath of the differentiation of society, it must be accepted that there has been a differentiation of various 'public spheres'.[51]

---

[51] Cf. I. U. Dalferth, Öffentlichkeit, Universität und Theologie, in:

A post-secular state is thus indifferent, not simply neutral, with regard to religious or non-religious issues. There may be many religions and non-religions in a society, but the state sees no reason to define or accentuate its relationships with them in any particular way. There is just as little need of legislation that there should be no law for or against a religion as there is of legislation that there should be no law for or against sport or gardening or music making. Should it become necessary and should problems arise, these can be dealt with pragmatically within the framework of other legislation. But the state gives no preference to its antithetical relationship to religion beyond defining and determining its function in society: it is no longer a secular state since it does not define itself, either in a positive or a negative sense, by reference to religion. In a post-secular *society* religion can exist or not, but this contingent fact carries no greater weight, for the political or any other subsystem of society, than does any other social reality. Ultimately, *individuals* in post-secular societies can live either religious or non-religious lives, and such a society may or may not have a religious subsystem with the appropriate religious public sphere. But none of the non-religious subsystems defines its relationships with the others either in religious terms, or by expressly dispensing with a religious stance. If there is religion, then that is a contingent fact. But it is not something to which either the society as a whole, or any of its social subsystems, would require or necessitate a particular positive or negative stance to be adopted. Either there is religion or there is not. The society is no more affected by this than by the existence or non-existence of any other social fact.

---

E. Arens/ H. Hoping (eds.), *Wieviel Theologie verträgt die Öffentlichkeit?* Freiburg / Basel / Wien, 2000, 38–71; idem, Religion als Privatsache? Zur Öffentlichkeit von Glaube und Theologie, *Theologisch-praktische Quartalschrift 149* (2001) 284–297.

### *13. Trajectories of secularity*

If we take the four types of state and society sketched roughly above and place them in chronological order, from the standpoint of the fundamental distinction between 'religious' and 'secular', the following picture emerges:

1. At the level of the *state* or political system, the development is from the *religious* via the *tolerant* and *secular* to the *post-secular* state. However, the crucial change is the one *from the religious to the secular state*, while the tolerant state represents merely a transitional position. For the citizen there is no significant difference between the secular and post-secular state in principle (although this is by no means necessarily the case in practice).

2. At the level of the *individual*, on the other hand, the crucial step change is the transition from a *tolerant* to a *secular* state, in which individuals with various religious or non-religious views are not merely tolerated but have a right, enshrined in law, to confess and practise their religious or non-religious convictions within statutory limitations. The further transfer from a secular to a post-secular society, in contrast, marks no significant change at the level of the individual life, since nothing is now possible which was not possible before, or at any rate not in principle. In other words, there is nothing which, in principle, a post-secular individual could do that a secular individual could not, even if the specific circumstances of their lives may be very different. Each of them can live in a religious way or some other way.

3. Finally, at the level of *society* there is a development from a (relatively) undifferentiated society which does not distinguish (or at any rate not systematically) between different subsystems, to a society which does this quite clearly and which therefore distinguishes itself unambiguously from its subsystems and does not give preferential treatment to any of the latter when it defines and characterises itself. In a post-secular society the political system (the state) has ceased to label itself as either religious or

secular, so that it does not define itself either explicitly or implicitly by reference to religion. So long as a state describes itself as secular, however, it rejects any form of religious self-definition, but in so doing it defines itself *negatively*, so that the *rejection of a religious stance becomes a significant element of its self-definition.* It is one thing not to identify itself with a religion, quite another to repudiate any such identification, and yet a third to have no need to repudiate any such identification or profess explicit neutrality towards religious, non-religious or antireligious orientations or life concepts. Only the third example represents a society that is not merely secular, but indeed post-secular.

While, therefore, it makes little sense to speak of 'post-secular individuals' – apart, perhaps, from so-called 'apatheists'[52] – it makes perfect sense to refer to a post-secular world and post-secular states and societies. But post-secular societies are not societies where the flood of secularisation has come to a halt, so that people can once again practise whichever religion and live by whichever faith they want. Rather, they are societies in which the state no longer defines itself as secular. The real point of the term post-secular is consequently not to be found at the level of the individual life, but at the level of the state and society: *states* can be secular or non-secular (pre- or post-secular). *Societies* are post-secular insofar as their political systems have become indifferent to questions regarding what is religious or non-religious. But at the level of the *individual life* the differentiation between secular and post-secular is not a relevant distinction, since everything required for a freely determined religious or non-religious life is to be found in both a secular and a post-secular

[52] "An apatheist is a type of atheist who, rather than not believing in any gods because the arguments for them are weak, simply doesn't care about the existence of any gods and goes about life as if none existed," in: http://atheism.about.com/library/glossary/general/bldef_apatheist.htm; cf. Dionysios Thriambos, Apatheism, Allognosticism, and the American Religious Landscape, in: http://hermetic.com/dionysos/apatheist.htm.

society – provided that the distinction between 'religious' and 'secular' is understood in the social differentiation sense and does not get mixed up with the topics of privatisation and rationalisation.

### *14. The one-sidedness of the secularity debate*

The development we have sketched in broad outline above makes it clear that there are good reasons to abandon the established pathways of the philosophical and theological debate over secularisation and secularity and break new ground. These debates are conducted, almost without exception, within the context of the *religious/secular* distinction, whereas the *divine/worldly* distinction, far more fundamental from a theological point of view, is conspicuous by its absence or at any rate by the underestimation of its significance. Yet it is this distinction above all that is theologically relevant – in Christianity no less than in Judaism and Islam. It is a question of the importance for human life of the fundamental differentiation between creator and creation, not of the defence of religion and its traditional privileges and vested rights in a secular society.

The theological secularity debate is thus on the wrong track as long as it focuses on the fundamental *religious/secular* distinction and the problems this highlights. It needs to switch its focus to the fundamental *divine/worldly* or *creator/creation* distinction in order to present the real point of the Christian faith in a manner that has current validity. Otherwise, for all their time-diagnostic insights, social relevance and politically explosive nature, discussions about religion, irreligion, religious criticism and antireligion will miss the existential point of the problem, namely that where faith and religion – and equally where unfaith, indifference or rejection of religion – are concerned, it is not a matter of arbitrary private preferences with no wider significance, but of the *truth of the human life*. That is the question which is and should be under debate, not the pros and cons of religion or non-religion in a secular world. How should we live so as to live in a truly human way? How can we do this? What should we focus on in order to be content with nothing less than we could be? What should we orient ourselves by, so as not to be led astray? And how can we do this together with others who seldom understand the genuinely human in precisely the same way as we do?

There is wide-ranging discussion of these questions, and not just in the religious domain. However before we gather and attempt to interpret undifferentiated empiricist data about lived religion, religiosity, spirituality, atheism, scepticism and secularity, and before we begin to question or defend traditional concepts of the religious and the secular, we need to achieve clarity regarding the subject matter and the guiding interest of the discussion. What are the questions and challenges to which religious or non-religious attitudes and actions, convictions and rituals, organisations and institutions are seeking to give an answer? What is it all about, and what is the life-world cause to which the pros and cons of the stated positions are reacting and responding? What is under discussion when questions are asked about the role of religion and faith in a world that is perceived, or perceives itself, as secular?

### *15. From the future of religion to the truth of life*

Here is my answer: what is at issue is not the future of religion, but the truth of life, in other words, the question as to what makes a human life – every individual human life, each in its own way, despite all its paltriness, inadequacy, impairment, duplicity and confusion – true and good and right. A life may be to a greater or lesser extent successful – according to its own standards or those of others – but that does not determine whether or not it is true and good and right. No life is as it could and should be. Each squanders possibilities that could have been important, and not one fulfils all its promises. The question as to the truth about life takes as many forms as there are human lives. But there can be no doubt that it is a meaningful question. Each of us is familiar with experiencing the differences between actuality and possibility, what is and what could be, wish and intention. These are the differences between the happy coincidences and misfortunes, achievements and disappointments, unexpected successes and unanticipated failures which are the source of our dreams, longings, desires, efforts and hopes to live differently. Our lives could be different: they could be better, more upright and truer. This is what we want, if it is at all possible; and since we cannot want it for ourselves without wanting it for others, we challenge ourselves and others to be as good, upright and true as we can be.

This is always more than we can achieve with the means and possibilities available to us. We may see what is not good, upright and true, and we can and should try to avoid it, to put a stop to it and eradicate it. But we cannot guarantee to bring about the goodness, uprightness and truth of what we do. We cannot even foresee everything that this might embrace. We are familiar with lack and deficiency, but not with abundance and fulfilment, because the latter require an excess that constantly oversteps the bounds of what we can see, do and accomplish. What makes our life true, good and upright cannot therefore be anything in our own life. It cannot be something that we are or do or can become of ourselves. Rather, it can only be something which is given to us in such a way that it does not share in the same ambivalences out of which it is intended to lead us. If it is intended to do this – if indeed it is intended to make human life something into which it cannot make itself – then not only can it precede human life as a beginning or principle, it must in point of fact have a transformative effect on it and within it. It must be a provision that transforms and determines our life – not apart from us, but also not purely through us – in such a way that our hope for a life of truth, goodness and uprightness is not disappointed.

### *16. Orientation to the ultimate presence*

In this sense there is a conclusive reorientation of life only with recourse to a life-enabling and life-determining *pre-gift*, which does not allow itself to be drawn into a life or thought process without being permanently distinguished as that process's absolute ground of possibility and prior determination of reality. Without this pre-gift, life processes are impossible (difference between being and non-being); without it, possible life processes are not real (difference between possibility and reality), and without it, real life processes cannot become true and good and righteous (difference between truth and falsehood, goodness and badness, righteousness and unrighteousness). It is not just a matter of understanding the natural bases of human life (the fundamental *human/non-human* distinction: what marks out the animal nature of the human being as a living being amongst other living beings?) and how human life is enacted in its social forms (the fundamental *human/human* distinction: what marks out the sociality of the human being in community with other humans?), but why it is not as it could and should be (the fundamental *human/inhuman* distinction: what is the essence of humanness and why is it not achieved?), and how it can become and will become what it could and should be, (the fundamental possible/actual distinction: how can human beings live as humanly as they could and should?). Or, as Adorno has asked: how can there be right and true life amid the false and untrue?

It is not that one can distil true life from the false. Such attempts culminate at best in the 'perhaps' and usually in the 'nowhere'. Rather, one orients oneself by that which is orienting one before one orients oneself by it: by the truth that makes one true, whether or not one orients oneself by it; by which one can only orient oneself if, and to the extent that, it becomes a life event; and which does not become an event without giving one's life, and everything else, a new and different horizon of meaning which allows one to see and perceive in everything more than that everything intimates. Where this truth arises, life becomes transparent to a transcendence into which it can only pass over because the transcendence itself has passed over into it. Presence thus becomes filled presence, and life acquires greater value and meaning.[53] It is not that we ourselves attribute this fresh meaning to our life, but that in its light we understand ourselves and everything else from a new and different perspective, so that we are able to live a new and different life.[54]

Philosophically and theologically, accordingly, it is a question of fundamental issues associated with a life orientation that aligns the human life, not with penultimate circumstances, but with *ultimate presence* – with a presence, therefore, which must be given if something is to be able to represent something for someone. This presence, as unconditional pre-gift, is the basis for every sign-act – that without which nothing could be possible or become real. There is recourse to it wherever something takes place, and indeed also where nothing takes place, although something could. Without it nothing either is or could be. It is the presence which initially makes possible changing temporal presents and which underlies each of them. Only in this presence are there

[53] Translator's Note: The German word 'Gegenwart' usually refers to the present time, but can signify spatial presence (e.g. 'in God's presence'). Here the German text benefits from this double meaning. I have opted for either 'present' or 'presence' in each instance, but it should be borne in mind that sometimes both meanings are wrapped up in the term 'Gegenwart' in the original text.

[54] Cf. I. U. Dalferth, Verbum Efficax (in print).

passages of time in which events are earlier or later than others, or simultaneous with others. Only in this presence is there orientation in time, as distinct from past, present and future. Only in this presence are there sign-processes, in which something can represent something for someone. This also applies to every attempt to express that presence itself. The ultimate presence cannot be discussed or described as something using a sign-process unless it is also the basis of this sign-process. It cannot be described without simultaneously being that which enables the sign-act: without it, it cannot be described, however it is described. Hence it cannot be captured in a description, nor can it be replaced by a description without remaining distinct from this act as its unconditional basis and non-negatable premise. There is no way of going beyond it, either backwards or forwards: it is the ultimate presence, to which everything refers back, because without it there could be no forward or backward reference.

It goes without saying that it is difficult to orient ourselves to this ultimate presence. It does not readily catch the eye, since it is not encountered as a given among givens and cannot therefore be perceived with the aid of experiential distinctions, but is that which is always and everywhere part of things, wherever the possible and the real are to be found, or where anything at all can be experienced. Without it there would not only be nothing to catch the eye, but also no one whose eye could be caught. The idea of orienting ourselves to this present / ce is by no means self-evident. Before we become aware of it, that which is most self-evident must become non-self-evident: that we ourselves and others exist. This only becomes non-self-evident when one recognises that it could not be otherwise. It occurs when people whose presence we took for granted are no longer there (experiences of loss and death), but also when people enter our lives whose presence we had not anticipated, or when things take place of which we would never have dared to dream (experiences of happiness). These contingent, non-self-evident experiences, both positive and negative, would not exist if there were no ultimate presence. However, they are not revealed automatically, but only when this presence makes itself so self-evident that there is a revelation of the non-self-evidence of all that we had held to be self-evident, but also of all that becomes non-self-evident to us. It is not simply a question of exchanging the self-evident for the non-self-evident and thereby replacing one contingency with another, but of gaining an insight into the contingency of the contingent when the non-contingent is differentiated from the contingent. Only when this takes place – in other words when ultimate presence reveals itself in the temporal horizon of experience with the aid of a specific other in a way that can be understood – can we orient ourselves by it. Such an orientation requires our own activity, but, given that this too avails itself of the pre-gift of ultimate presence, it is rooted in another, precedent activity to which it owes its existence. Hence we can only give our life reliable orientation when we orient ourselves by that which orients life from the outset by making it, against all probability and despite all improbability, right and good. Orientation of life by this truth-event is orientation by that which orients life from the start, and where this takes place, life becomes transparent to the transcendence to which it owes its existence.

## *17. Orientation by differentiation*

The double formula of *event* and *transcendence* captures this. Both concepts are problem formulae whose sense is determined by the contrasts within which they are found. In the case of event, these contrasts are the differentiations between *being* and *non-being, being a possibility* and *being a reality*, *being* and *becoming, being earlier* and *being later, being false* and *being true.* In the case of transcendence, the contrast is the self-differentiation between *transcendence* and *immanence*.[55] In both instances these differentiations can only be elucidated by expanding them into further differentiations. When differentiating, one cannot proceed without deciding on the further differentiations with which one will give substance to the two sides of one's initial differentiation. There is always more than one possibility, and the choice depends on the problem one is seeking to solve and the interests concerned. When trying to explain, one must ensure that one's differentiations are sufficiently descriptive. When seeking to orient oneself, however, one must focus one's efforts at differentiation on exploring the horizon of meaning and one's own position within this horizon.

With orientational differentiations the issue is not primarily the use of these differences to describe a given reality or to provide a metaphysical basis for such descriptions, but to orient oneself within the dynamic reality of life and the world in a way that is intelligible and reliable. The important criterion is not adequate description and theoretical knowledge, but real-life relevance and practical wisdom. Knowledge is built up on the basis of differentiations that stand the test of reality, since different phenomena can be explained as instances of an underlying principle (law). Wisdom, by contrast, is gained through differentiations which help us to orient ourselves in life. All orientation therefore refers back to relationships with a double effect. These use specific differentiations to structure a problem or field of reference (*ordering* function of symbolic representation), and they position the one who is seeking to orient himself to a specific relationship with this context of ordering determined through differentiation (*positioning* function of self-reflexive localisation). Only one who can *position* himself in relation to an order can use it to orient himself,

---

[55] Cf. I. U. Dalferth, The Idea of Transcendence, in: R. B. Bellah / H. Joas (eds.), *The Axial Age and Its Consequences*, Cambridge, MA / London 2012, 146–188.

and only one who is familiar with an *order* and its differentiations can use it to position – and thus to orient – himself.

This context is sometimes overlooked. One who pronounces judgement on others without recognising that he is also pronouncing judgement on himself has not understood the dialectic of orientation. This also applies to the conscious orientation of one's life to ultimate presence. If this presence is to become an orientational point of reference at all, not only can one orient that which is other by it – in so doing one places oneself in a relationship with it (and vice versa). Being able to orient ourselves in this way is a hallmark of human life, but we can only do it because and to the extent that the possibility is opened up to us by the ultimate presence itself. The need to orient ourselves is a fundamental imperative of our life. The ability to orient ourselves is one of our outstanding capabilities. Being able to orient ourselves consciously to ultimate presence, however, is a possibility that reveals what is essentially human about our human life: our creative passivity as beings of possibility who can become more than we can make of ourselves because we live out of an experience through which we become what we cannot make of ourselves – God's creatures and God's neighbours.[56] For the possibility of conscious orientation to the ultimate presence is not within our capability, but opens up only as it is meted out to us as an option for life orientation. It is a possibility that must first become *my* possibility. But no one can live without making a practical response to the possibility of this possibility, since everyone who lives, lives in the presence of ultimate presence. Human life is therefore always lived in one of two ways: either it does not orient itself to ultimate presence, thus restricting itself to its own possibilities, or it does orient itself to ultimate presence and thus begins to discover and live out its human potential.

---

[56] Cf. I. U. Dalferth, *Creatures of Possibility: The Theological Basis of Human Freedom*, Grand Rapids 2016.

### 18. *Transcendence and event*

When we speak of *event* and *transcendence*, it brings to mind this possibility of orientation to ultimate presence which we experience or which comes our way. This orientation becomes possible for us through our experience of life (event), in that the latter takes from our present the illusion of clarity and discloses it as the immanent sign of a transcendent presence, to which it owes its existence (transcendence). Our present and our whole life thereby acquire added value in terms of meaning, the disclosure of which emanates from the event which calls in question the seemingly straightforward meaning of everything taken for granted in the life world. With the aid of the orientational differentiation between transcendence and immanence, this added value unfolds as an increase in the meaning of our life.

The double formula of *event* and *transcendence* thus presents for debate an *orientational differentiation,* not the description of life phenomena, not even those of actual religious or non-religious orientation of life. *Event* and *transcendence* are orientation formulae for identifying our attitude to phenomena, but they do not describe them. Accordingly, the philosophical development of these formulae is a question of working out a second-order regulative-orientational differentiation (a critical *idea* therefore), with the aid of which the multiplicity of actual first-order orientational differentiations and their widely differing symbolisations and historical semantics in the religious and non-religious life of human beings can be subject to a critical-constructive *re-lecture* so as to enable a thoughtful and open attitude towards the enactment phenomena and orientation strategies of one's own life and the life of others. It could be other than we think, believe or assume to be the case. This is not just because we have not yet adequately recognised the reality of the world and of life (though that is also true[57]), but because we lack the necessary wisdom to direct our lives so that we are able to react in a truly human way to and within this constantly changing reality.

The distinctions and ideas that require philosophical and theological development are therefore not primarily to be identified in the phenomena, but function as fundamental critical thought differentiations, which, in view of our rapidly changing knowledge of the world, are intended to help determine how we can, must or should orient ourselves in the complexities and uncertainties of life so as to live a human life in community with others. It is not the clarification of the differentiation between human and non-human (human / animal) in the context of nature that is the chief problem: that is a matter for the (natural and life) sciences. Nor is it the differentiation between humans and other humans (human / human) within the social sphere: that is a matter for social research. What is rather to be clarified is the differentiation between the human and the inhuman (human / inhuman) and hence the image of the human being and the human mode of life that we hold to be incumbent upon ourselves and others. It is a matter of the clarification, always controversial, of what it could and should mean to live a human life, and of the judgement, constantly under dispute, as to what human beings can and should orient themselves by in order to live out their humanness in a truly human way.

The fact that the proposed distinctions can be understood and developed in more than one sense, since their versatility makes them useful for differentiating between different ideas in different contexts, is just one point to bear in mind when

---

[57] J. Schellenberg rightly emphasises that in every sphere, our knowledge is still in its early, not its final, stages. Cf. J. Schellenberg, *Prolegomena to a Philosophy of Religion,* Ithaca 2005; idem, *The Wisdom to Doubt: A Justification of Religious Skepticism,* Ithaca 2007; idem, *The Will to Imagine: A Justification of Skeptical Religion,* Ithaca 2009; idem., *Evolutionary Religion*, Oxford 2013.

working out the details of the orientation of one's life to ultimate presence. This is particularly true when dealing with the orientation of religious life. Unless an effort is made to orient thinking, it will not be possible to move beyond the level of an abstract comparison of positional religious convictions and across-the-board areligious or antireligious criticism. However, in the face of the dangerous tensions between increasingly fundamentalist religions and a progressively secular life-world, the solution is not to be sought in a project of *faith-informed thought* that replicates and codifies the ideology-conditioned contrasts of life in terms of thought. Rather, we should move beyond these contrasts towards a *thinking faith* that is aware of the vital nature of a specific contingent localisation of human life, while conceiving of that life in its relation to the self-mediating and self-disclosing presence of the divine, so that we make this presence, not ourselves, the reference point of our life orientation. The truth of faith does not come into play if we present it in the form of a mere dogmatism or expound it as a 'like it or lump it' doctrinal system mandatory for others as well as ourselves, but only if we recognise and acknowledge, in day-to-day living (life of faith) and in its reflective illumination (theology), the way in which this truth gains precedence – unconditionally and non-compulsorily – within all our experience, awareness, comprehension, deliberation, and analytical thought. The truth of faith precedes faith in both life and thought, not only because it is the truth of faith that makes our life of faith possible, real and true, but also because without that truth there would be no subject for theological thought to consider. True faith constantly refers back anaphorically to that to which it owes its existence, thus pointing the way cataphorically to a new understanding of everything. And in so doing, it holds back in relation to others in such a way that it does not focus on itself, but on what it refers back to, on the basis of which it understands itself and everything else: the presence of the divine in a worldly world.

# B. Event and Transcendence. Three distinct event discourses

In their study *New Phenomenology in France* Hans-Dieter Gondek and László Tengelyi put forward the thesis that "the event-character of everything that is" is the key to understanding the most recent developments "in the New Phenomenology in France".[1] The contradiction between the intellectual and empirical tendencies in the determination of what is given to consciousness "is resolved by the self-givenness of the given appearing as an event which befalls consciousness, in that it establishes itself by itself. The empirical concept of the given, which transforms it into something positive, no longer debatable and often represented as unquestionably self-evident, is thus overcome in just the same way as the intellectualistic idea of a transcendental constitution."[2] That is all very well. But it applies only to the understanding of 'event' that they delineate, and this in itself throws up problems with which 20th century philosophy and theology are all too familiar.[3] The concept of event, therefore, does not offer the solution, but rather highlights the problem which the ongoing discussion will have to address.

This discussion will not clarify anything unless consideration is given to the various discourses which discuss event. No ready parallels can be drawn between these discourses; rather, they are

---

[1] H.-D. Gondek / L. Tengelyi, *Neue Phänomenologie in Frankreich*, Frankfurt a. M. 2011, 671.

[2] Ibid.

[3] Cf. I. U. Dalferth, *Radical Theology: An Essay on Faith and Theology in the Twenty-First Century*, Minneapolis, MN 2016.

to be appreciated first and foremost in their dissimilarity before interfaces and connections are sought. There is not just one notion of event, but a range of different notions, and these refer, not to the same problem in different contexts, but to different problems. To elucidate this I shall, in what follows, outline three concepts of event by reconstructing three event discourses, the *ontological,* the *semiotic* and the *theological.* These discourses are closely connected, but cannot be related back to each other or to a common source. I have called them the event discourses of *being, meaning* and *existence*, and I shall discuss them in that order with varying levels of detail.

### *1. The everyday world of events*

Our everyday world is a world of events, since we live our lives in time. But in time nothing stays the same. It changes, as we know from experience. These changes are not just changes we initiate by our actions, but are also those that befall us and that we suffer. They affect us, but they are not of our making. Thus we draw an ontological distinction, at the meso-level of our everyday world, not just between *actions* and *events*, but also between *things* and *events* and between *things* and *persons.* We can *communicate* and *interact* with persons (subjects), whereas we *make use of* things (objects). Both – things and persons – can change. Whilst, however, all changes are events, not all changes are actions concerning which it makes sense to enquire as to reasons, motives, intentions or actors – unless, that is, one lives in a Leibniz-world in which there are no events, but only the actions and interactions of the infinite Creator and finite creatures. And since events are always, after all, modifications of the state of the world, but are not in every case changes to things, we live in a world in which we have no alternative but to distinguish between *things* and *events*. What does this mean?

### 2. Events of being

There are five points to my answer:[4]

1. Both things and events are objects of potential predication and naming (they can be identified, described or named in one way or another). But only things can be identical at different times; events cannot. It is true that one can, at different times, refer in an identifying way to events such as, for instance, the French Revolution. But such references are themselves events; no event at one time can be identified fully with an event at a different time.

2. For things, as for events, which are actual and not merely possible, one can name a time at which they did not yet exist. But only things *come into being* or *originate*, whereas events *occur* or *take place*. Only things can change, whereas events make way for other events. Events begin, take up a certain amount of time and then give way to other events, but they do not change. Things, on the other hand, can change, with each change being an event that cannot change.

3. Both things and events can have temporal duration, but only events – not things – have temporal components (phases). If an event has temporal duration, there is no point in time when it is wholly present. Every thing, by contrast, is wholly present at each point in time when it exists, albeit differently at any given point. We must therefore distinguish between a *thing* and its *history*. Its history is a sequence of events, that is, a process of temporal duration that is unalterable and could only be fully present at the point when it could no longer be present at all.

4. While things, in contrast to events, do not have temporal components, they always have spatial extent and thus have spatial components. Two things with the same spatial extent cannot

[4] Here cf. I. U. DALFERTH, *Existenz Gottes und christlicher Glaube*, München 1984, 136–138.

therefore be in the same place simultaneously. Two events, on the other hand, can of course occur simultaneously at the same place without needing to be identical.

5. It is not things, but events, that require explanation. Only where something changes, where something comes into being or passes away, where something different appears and what has been up to now is replaced by something else, does the question 'Why?' arise. If our world were a world of things or facts, there would be nothing to explain. In order to understand it, a description of it would suffice. But it is a world of events, so that if we want to understand it, explanations are required.

### *3. Aporias encountered when explaining the world*

Now it is one thing to explain events that occur in the world, but quite another to want to explain the world. The world is not an event in the world, and the totality of events is a reflective concept we form for ourselves, but not the actuality in which we live.[5] As a concept of reflection, the world is the sum of the possibilities of our lives, actions and suffering. We cannot choose it freely, but simply discover ourselves to be in it. It is the possibility space of our lives, and each possible explanation leads us, not beyond this space, but deeper into it.

Thus the existence of our world would appear to be neither in need of nor capable of explanation. Only that which could either not exist or exist differently is *in need of* explanation. And only that for which there can be at least one ground distinct from itself is *capable* of explanation: that which encompasses in

[5] The "new realism" propagated by M. Gabriel in *Warum es die Welt nicht gibt* (Berlin 2013) as the new age that follows 'postmodernism' is thus by no means as new as he suggests.

itself every ground which can be adduced for it is not open to any explanation.

But is the world such that, not only could it be different, it could in fact not exist? And is there something (that is not already part of the world) that could be adduced as a basis for the fact that it exists and that it is as it is? Both questions can justifiably be asked. Firstly, all explanation is subject to the *principle of homogeneity of explanation and that which is to be explained*: the experiential can only be explained by the experiential, the worldly only by the worldly, so that explanation *in* the world is possible, but not explanation *of the* world. Secondly, while it is true of each *specific* world that it could in fact not exist, it is not true of *world as such*. The fact that there is anything at all is a separate issue from that which actually exists. Only the latter requires explanation, not the former. World as such is not a potential object of explanation, but the necessary horizon of all explanation. One who explains is doing physics; one who is doing metaphysics cannot explain and should not want to.

### *4. The Leibniz-world*

Leibniz, however, thought differently. For him it was not inconceivable that there could actually be nothing, "For nothing is simpler and easier than something."[6] For him that provided sufficient reason to ask, "*Why is there something rather than nothing?*"[7] He was convinced that nothing that could also not exist can exist without sufficient reason for existing and for being as it is. This conviction was based upon his understanding of

---

[6] G. W. Leibniz, *Vernunftprinzipien der Natur und der Gnade*, in: idem, *Hauptschriften zur Grundlegung der Philosophie. Volume II,* translated by A. Buchenau, published by E. Cassirer, Hamburg $^{3}$1966, 423–434, here: 428.

[7] Ibid.

the truth *praedicatum inest subjecto*, which he developed in the two principles of his metaphysics: the *principium contradictionis (seu identitatis)* and the *principium rationis sufficientis*. The first excludes the self-contradictory, and thus impossible, from the circle of truths worthy of consideration, restricting it to that which cannot not be (necessary truths) and that which is, but could also not be (contingent truths). The second states, for each contingent fact, that in view of the possibility of its not being, it only is because there is a sufficient reason for the fact that it exists and that it is as it is.

Leibniz never gave satisfactory reasons for this principle, considering it to be self-evident. In his fifth letter to Clarke, Leibniz pointed out that no one had ever cited a convincing case where it did not apply, nor was any such citation likely.[8] Perhaps that is precisely why this principle has been so frequently and variously misunderstood as a misguided attempt to eliminate contingency from the world. However the principle is intended, not to conjure away contingency, but rather the opposite – to *safeguard the contingent*. Only *where God is concerned* does it mean that "nothing happens without its being possible for one who has enough knowledge of things to give a reason sufficient to determine why it is so and not otherwise".[9] *Where we are concerned,* however, it means precisely that we can never adequately explain the contingent. Everything has an explanation – for God, not for us.

This is good news, not bad news. Leibniz's *principium rationis sufficientis* means that humans can live in the contingent in

---

[8] G. W. Leibniz, Fifth paper, § 129, in: H. G. Alexander (ed.), *The Leibniz-Clarke Correspondence*, Manchester 1956, 96. Cf. R. McRae, The Theory of Knowledge, in: N. Jolley (ed.), *The Cambridge Companion to Leibniz*, Cambridge 1995, 176–198, 192–197.

[9] Leibniz, *Vernunftprinzipien*, 428; Leibniz, Principles of Nature and of Grace Founded on Reason (1714), in: G. H. R. Parkinson (ed.), *Leibniz: Philosophical Writings*, London 1973, 195–204, 199.

reliance upon God without having to 'master' it by means of endless attempts at explanation. Leibniz's optimistic view of the world did not result from an illusion that everything can, after all, be explained to us in the best possible way. On the contrary, it was founded on his knowledge that we *cannot* explain everything, nor do we have to, but can confidently leave such explanation to God.

At this point, however, two chasms yawn, threatening to devour Leibniz's metaphysical optimism. One concerns his *idea of God*, the other his *understanding of the world.*

### *5. The aporia of the idea of God*

On the one hand, Leibniz wanted to affirm that we can confidently entrust to God whatever we cannot explain. But he also wanted to establish that our optimistic view of the world is based on our trust in God by seeking to demonstrate both that it is impossible to think that God does not exist, and that the nature of God enables us to trust in him. Firstly, for him God is the "ultimate […] ground of things",[10] since for everything that is he knows the sufficient reason that it is, and that it is what it is. Secondly, this ultimate ground of things does not form part of the range of contingent things (substances) that require explanation. Rather, he is "a necessary being … that holds the ground of his existence in himself",[11] and therefore neither needs nor is capable of explanation. But either God is necessary, in which case he is unable to explain the contingent; or he explains the contingent, in which case he cannot be necessary. If, however, he is not necessary, then he himself requires explanation, if he exists; and if he is impossible, since the thought of a necessary being is non-

[10] Loc. cit. 429.

[11] Ibid.

sensical, then recourse to him cannot explain anything. Hence, even if the two normative principles of the idea of God (*ultimate sufficient ground of everything contingent* and *necessary being, that holds the ground of his existence in himself)* are individually coherent (which is doubtful in both cases), then they are not consistent with each other (which is not indubitable).

Leibniz confirms that his attempt to integrate the idea of God into the overall context of his ontology succeeds only insofar as he defines the idea of God in a doubly ambiguous way: as the *necessary ultimate ground of the contingent* and as the *self-ground of the realisation of his own necessity*. Both are aporetic definitions. It is one thing to explain a contingent by means of another contingent, but quite another to want to 'explain' the explanatory context of the contingent as a whole by recourse to something non-contingent. If the world is in need of, but not capable of, explanation, then recourse to God is of no help. And if it is not in need of explanation, then it offers neither trigger nor starting point for talking in terms of explanation by God. Leibniz's ontotheological method therefore calls in question the idea of the world or the idea of God or the explanatory context between the two, thus proving to be an aporetic attempt to integrate the contingency of the world and the necessity of God.

If we wish to escape this aporia, then God and the world cannot be distinguished from and related to each other from the perspective of necessity and contingency. Within the cognitive horizon of the Leibniz-world this modal distinction must be applied either to *both* or to *neither*. This means that we have two opposing options. One seeks to rescue the Leibniz-world by conceiving of the world, like God, as necessary. The other seeks to dismiss the Leibniz-world by conceiving of God, like the world, as contingent. The first is exemplified paradigmatically by 20th century process philosophy, the second by Hans Blumenberg.

Hartshorne, for instance, argues that the world is just as little in need of an explanation as God, since, like him, it is impossible for it not to exist. Admittedly this does not apply to any specific world, but it does apply to the world as such. We must therefore distinguish between the necessity of a *world as such* and the contingency of any one *specific world*. Likewise, God's relationship with the world must then be differently perceived and thought through, both as regards the world as such and also as regards any one specific world. This is not possible unless God himself is conceived of from the differential perspective of necessity and contingency, in other words (according to Hartshorne) as *dipolar*.[12] The *Leibniz-world* is thus rescued by holding the world *and* God to be both necessary *and also* contingent, so that the traditional distinction *between* world and God is incorporated into the idea of the world and the idea of God. The consequence is that the relationship between God and world is not an explanatory relationship, and God is conceived of, not as the ground, but as the logical implication (entailment) of the world. This means, however, that the idea that the world is explained by God, or that God is disclosed through the world is relinquished: there is no world without God (and vice versa). For this very reason, no contingent condition of the world can be adequately explained by recourse to God. God is there, but that explains nothing.

### *6. The aporia of the idea of the world*

Blumenberg arrives at his relinquishment of an explanatory context between God and world from precisely the opposite direction: God is just as unnecessary as the world and just as little in need of explanation. But the distinction between God

[12] CH. HARTSHORNE, The Dipolar Conception of Deity, *Review of Metaphysics 21* (1967) 273–289; IDEM, *Creative Synthesis and Philosophical Method*, Washington, 1983; IDEM, *Omnipotence and Other Theological Mistakes*, Albany 1984; D. W. VINEY, Hartshorne's Dipolar Theism and the Mystery of God, *Philosophia 35* (2007) 341–350.

and world can therefore no longer be conceived of in principle. Either God himself is a special case of that which requires a worldly explanation, or he is ontologically superfluous within the horizon of metaphysical attempts at explanation.

If this is so, the principle of sufficient reason must of course be relinquished as a principle. This is precisely what Blumenberg suggests, since for the *principium rationis sufficientis* he substitutes the *principium rationis insufficientis,* switching from the Leibniz-world to the life-world and seeking to relocate discourse concerning God from the sphere of metaphysical explanation and justification to that of life-world enactments.

These changes reflect the way in which the modern thought focus has shifted from God to humans. For Leibniz the *principium rationis sufficientis* means that humans can live confidently in the contingent, since they can depend on God and do not need to explain everything themselves. For Blumenberg on the other hand, the *principium rationis insufficientis* means that human beings cannot explain everything because they are deficient beings. The "principle of insufficient reason (*principium rationis insufficientis*)" is thus, according to him, "the corollary of the anthropology of a being who is deficient in essential respects".[13]

Both Leibniz and Blumenberg take the contingency (inescapable for us) of our event world seriously. Leibniz, however, regards it as something that we do not *have to* explain, since it is explained by God, whereas Blumenberg views it as something that we *cannot* explain, since it is inexplicable. We are compelled to live with this contingency without even being able to hope for an explanation. We live, not in a Leibniz-world of sufficient reasons, but in a life-world of insufficient reasons. This weakness is our strength: "not to need a reason is the exactitude of life itself".[14]

---

[13] H. Blumenberg, An Anthropological Approach to the Contemporary Significance of Rhetoric, in: idem, *Wirklichkeiten in denen wir leben. Aufsätze und eine Rede*, Stuttgart 1981, 104–136, 124.

[14] H. Blumenberg, *Höhlenausgänge*, Frankfurt a. M. 1989, 168.

For Blumenberg, therefore, recourse to the life-world is not a search for ultimate grounds, but quite the contrary, the uncovering of the ultimate groundlessness of everything taken for granted in the life-world. Correspondingly, he understands phenomenology, not as transcendental contingency control, but as a heightening of the consciousness of the contingency of everything taken for granted in the life-world.

Nevertheless, there is still a problem, since Blumenberg continues to be determined by the programme from which he wants to free himself: in substituting for the *principle* of sufficient reason the *principle* of insufficient reason, he is suggesting that both situations revolve around reasons or grounds, albeit one around sufficient grounds, the other around insufficient grounds. But the difference between the life-world and the Leibniz-world is much more fundamental. The life-world does not (yet) lack grounds. It is the universe of the self-evident and is not in need of grounds, since everything goes without saying, just as it is. The Leibniz-world, on the other hand, cannot lack grounds: it is the universe of necessary and contingent, but in all cases sufficiently grounded, truths. Blumenberg confounds the two in a manner fraught with consequences, inasmuch as he stages the exodus from the life-world as if it were a farewell to the Leibniz-world. But to remove self-evidence from the self-evident is by no means the same as replacing the necessary by the contingent. Nor is the relinquishment of sufficient reasons the same as the insufficient relinquishment of reasons. And the loss of trust in God as the ultimate ground of explanation is certainly not the same as the loss of God's significance for the conduct of our lives. The fact that we are deficient beings and, as such, incapable of ultimate explanations, does not mean that we can dispense with grounds as a matter of principle; and the fact that life itself does not need ultimate grounds does not mean that it is not in need of God.

Nevertheless, without God the Leibniz-world disintegrates into a mere multiplicity of world perspectives with no hope of any ultimate unity and connectedness. The life-world, on the other hand, whether with or without God, turns out to be forsaken already, and the sense of the loss of all that we take for granted is in no way assuaged through recourse to God. The Leibniz-world without trust in God lacks what the life-world also lacks: the groundless validity of the self-evident. But it is only in the Leibniz-world, not the life-world, that this implicit lack can be overcome through recourse to God. Trust in God is no substitute for the shattered self-evidences of the life-world, and the search for ultimate grounds is not the right way to recover them. God explains neither himself nor everything else for us, but even if either were the case, this would not stabilise our situation in the wake of the shattering of everything taken for granted in the life-world.

On the contrary, this shattering of the life-world's self-evidences brings to the fore a problem that was concealed in the Leibniz-world. The implications of this problem, with the switch to the life-world and the stress on its contingency, have not yet been thought through. In the Leibniz-world there are *no radically new events*. The *principle of sufficient reason* states not just that we can only know imprecisely that which God knows fully, but that what we experience in life as an event is in truth the realisation of potentialities inherent in each monad's individual being from the outset. Since each monad is defined by that which distinguishes it from the totality of all other monads (and this presupposes what Leibniz rigorously defends: that there is only *one* world), nothing occurs in the life process of a monad that would not actualise a possibility that exists for it from the outset. *With every event we become what we are*, but for us there is no possible event that would in fact be radically new, in the sense that it would open up an entirely new possibility. We only become different by becoming what we can be, because we are who we are. But we do not become anything that we could not have become from the outset, since otherwise we would not be who we are. In the Leibniz-world, therefore, there are *no new events*, but only actualisations of predetermined possibilities.

Thus the Leibniz-world is more strongly reminiscent of its mediaeval antecedents than is sometimes realised. Nothing can come into being, the possibility of which is not paradigmatically predetermined in the ideas of the divine Mind. The possible can only be realised in the world process; it cannot be changed by it.

For God, what may look to finite beings like a new event is never anything but the contingent realisation of a possibility belonging to the totality of the possible that defines the identity of this monad as distinct from all others. In truth there are no new events, merely actualisations of predetermined possibilities.

Admittedly, that only applies from God's perspective. With the loss of the centering idea of God during the 19th century and the replacement of classic substance ontology, with its distinction between *thing* and *event*, by a systematic event ontology in the 20th century, a different problem arises. That becomes apparent, not only in the event metaphysics of Whitehead's or Hartshorne's process philosophy in the first half of the 20th century, but also in the event ontology of Alain Badiou's mathematical philosophy at the beginning of the 21st century.

### *7. Sense-events*

According to Badiou, besides being there is event; besides the complexity of a situation, which becomes, through knowledge, the determinacy of a particular situation, there is the event that effectuates the truth – the true meaning – of a situation as compared with its self-understanding. The truth-event is thus always a sense-event, and, in relation to the situation in which it occurs, it is always entirely new, underivable and unpredictable. No analysis of the real and the possible, however exact and complete, can elicit that which occurs as event. It is true that the situation – the historical situation, at any rate[15] – includes the *place* where the event occurs, the *event site* (*site événementiel*), but not what occurs there. The event site is present in the situation, but it does not re-present anything: it exists *"on the edge of the void"*.[16] It is not therefore the facts of a situation that precede the event, but the emptiness of the void. The event has no ground of being; rather it becomes the ground of meaning for something else. It arises as something new and underivable which inaugurates, within a given situation, a new sequence of sense-incidents, not derivable from that situation. The event is the principle of the new, since it is, in principle, new.

With his event figure Badiou takes up Heidegger's ideas from the 1930s, which have only recently become more readily accessible. In his studies on event, Heidegger made constant fresh attempts to emphasise that, "Event expresses the explicitly self-clearing inceptuality of the beginning". It is the beginning of the beginning, not a mere beginning. "Being does not start and stop, nor does it exist 'perpetually' in the duration of beings. Being begins, and does so essentially: it *is* the appropriating beginning."[17] This appropriating beginning is not silent, but *speaks* itself in an original way so that "event" becomes "conception".[18] Event aims for conception and only thus does it set speech and thought in motion.[19]

Heidegger's analyses seek to illuminate this frame of reference in detail, but here it is sufficient to draw attention to the following basic configuration. Occurring is the fundamental characteristic of being. It means that there is nothing *from* which what is becomes, but rather, on the contrary, that being is the occurring

[15] Cf. A. Badiou, *Das Sein und das Ereignis*, Zürich 2005, 203.

[16] Loc. cit. 200–204.

[17] M. Heidegger, *Das Ereignis* (GA 71), Frankfurt a. M. 2009, 148.

[18] Loc. cit. 301.

[19] Loc. cit. 300: "Speech is only thinking speech if it has received the appropriating event from the beginning."

beginning, to enquire into which is senseless in the strictest sense. The question of the origin of being can only be answered by reference to being as origin, so that it does not lead beyond being, but only ever refers back to it. *Here* is where what is begins, and there is nothing before or behind this Here.

This is what Badiou takes up, when he allows event – admittedly in contrast to being! – to arise from nothingness, from the gap, the vacuum, the void. The event has no preceding genealogy: quite the opposite, it liberates a truth-procedure which, in fidelity to this event, establishes a new sequence of meanings in the world. Following the event there exists a new chain of phenomena; the event, however, is not a phenomenon in a preceding chain of phenomena.

Whereas Heidegger adheres strictly to the singular (*the* event of being as a *singulare tantum*), Badiou, in distinguishing between being and event, speaks of a *type*, for which there is more than one *token*. He is not interested in *the* original incipient beginning which precedes and underlies everything, but in the constantly recurring underivable beginning, in which it is possible to see through a complex of being (a situation) to its true meaning so that an excess occurs which gives rise to the formation of a new sequence which Badiou describes as "a continuous exploration of the situation, one that is subject to the imperative of the event itself".[20]

The gap from which something new eventuates is unforeseeable and can occur anywhere. It manifests itself in the irreducible semiotic difference between the symbol and the symbolised. The event does not actualise predetermined possibilities of the situation in which it occurs, but liberates a possibility that was not possible there previously. The fact that the French Revolution is to be named thus cannot be deduced from the occurrences

[20] A. Badiou, *Ethik. Versuch über das Bewußtsein des Bösen*, Wien 2002, 91.

signified thereby. But to identify it thus speaks its truth in such a way that connections become possible that were not possible before. Heidegger's singular event of being (*singulare tantum*) thus becomes, in Badiou's analyses, the sense-event of the singular that can occur, unforeseeable and unannouncable, and that determines the particular situation to be what it truly is. Here – according to the theorem of the point of excess[21] – it is true that the representation of a situation always exceeds its presentation, in other words, 'says' more than it 'is'.[22] It is one thing that something is present; that it is present *as this*, is quite another. *In* the situation this is not represented, which is why re-presentation of *one* as *this* is always more than the presentation of the many represented as *this one*.

Non-derivability from the situation, excess of meaning in naming the truth of a situation, and fidelity to the event in a truth-procedure through which an event finds meaningful expression, are accordingly the decisive characteristics of the event for Badiou.

A critique of his conception of event focuses on all three points. He is accused of underestimating the extent to which the new is negatively conditioned by what precedes it, thereby making the new incomprehensible and inexpressible. And he is charged with eliminating the distinction between truth-event and ideology by determining the event solely from the perspective of the participants in the new community of those who hold to the truth-procedure and, through whose fidelity to the event, the latter produces effects in history.

The first charge highlights a problem that originates from a truncating understanding of the category of event. For Heidegger event was the original expression of the self-clearing inceptuality

[21] Loc. cit. 104: "the one-multiple composed from its subsets, whose existence is guaranteed by the power-set axiom is essentially 'larger' […] than the initial multiple."

[22] Badiou, *Das Sein und das Ereignis*, 101–111.

of the beginning, which means: the event of beginning is always, at the same time, the beginning of the *expressibility* of the event, in which the latter not only *can be* expressed, but *is expressed* in such a way that it can determine all subsequent speech and thought. For Badiou, in contrast, the event liberates a truth-procedure through which meaning is ascribed to it in the first place. The event becomes speakable through those that speak it; and this *speaking* of event is different from its *occurring.* Not until it is named as that which gives a specific name to the situation in question is it possible to relate to the event as a specific event, in fidelity to it. But it *does not name itself,* meaning that it does not find expression *as something.* Hence one can only say of it what those affected say of it, but that, in turn, cannot be critically measured against anything else. Heidegger's event is the original expression of being, whereas Badiou's events are silent *per se,* even if they provoke speech and only *in so doing* become phenomena in the life-world.

### *8. Master, Hysteric, University Discourse, Mystic and Analyst*

Žižek was one of the first to address the questions raised with perspicacity. Badiou's truth-event "cannot be reduced to, or deduced from, any (previous) situation; it emerges 'out of the void.'"[23] It can only be described in subjective language – the language of the participants and those affected. For the generally accessible language of knowledge it is nothing.

But then the question is: How are we to "draw a demarcation line between a true event and its semblance"?[24] How can the subjects constituted by the event protect themselves

[23] S. Žižek, *Die Tücke des Subjekts,* Frankfurt a.M. 2001, 184. Cf. the related critique by A. Hollywood, Saint Paul and the New Man, *Critical Inquiry 35* (2009) 865–876.

[24] Žižek, *Tücke des Subjekts,* 187.

from understanding themselves merely from the perspective of a *supposed* event, rather than one *that really happened*? Any cross-checking against the perspective of others is excluded. "There is no neutral, enlightened public opinion that is impressed by the event, since the truth can only be recognised by the potential members of a new community of 'believers', with its shared viewpoint."[25]

Drawing on the psychoanalytical distinction between *Master* and *Hysteric* and Badiou's extension of this dyad by the addition of the *University Discourse* and the *Mystic*, Žižek attempts to provide an answer based on the thinking of Lacan. Badiou, Žižek considers, elevates "the figure of the master: … who *names the event*" and, through a significant Master, "reconfigures the symbolic field by reference to the new event". Lacan, on the other hand, positions himself on the side of the Hysteric, who "questions the naming of the event by the Master" and "insists … on the gap between the event and its symbolisation / naming", asking: '*Why is this particular name the name of the event?*'"[26] Whereas Master and Hysteric both make reference to one event and are only arguing as to whether it is 'really' that which the master names it, "the perverse agent of the University Discourse disavows that there was the event of an act in the first place."[27] He tries to explain away "the realm of consequences" or to attribute it to another cause. "Love? It's nothing but the result of a series of stimulus responses in our neural network!' etc.)."[28] The Mystic essentially does "the exact opposite of the perverse University Discourse: if the latter seeks to isolate the symbolic chain of consequences from its foundational event, the Mystic seeks to isolate the event from the network of its symbolic consequences. He insists on the ineffability of the event and disregards

[25] Loc. cit. 190.
[26] Loc. cit. 226.
[27] Loc. cit. 227.
[28] Ibid.

its symbolic consequences".[29] Lacan, in contrast, gives fourth position, alongside Master, Hysteric and University Discourse, not to the Mystic, but to the Analyst. This is another *"discursive* position", one which does not explain away the event, but reinforces the gap emphasised by the Hysteric "as a positive and productive one". "It asserts the real of the event as the 'generator', the generating core that is repeatedly encircled by the subject's symbolic productivity."[30] This does not mean that the event is disavowed, but that it is retained as "the *unnameable* real"[31] that eludes every grasp, but constantly generates new denominative possibilities. At the same time, to insist, with regard to each naming of truth by a significant Master ('It is that and nothing but that'), that no naming truly captures the entire situation – would be sheer totalitarianism. "When truth pretends to grasp / name the entire situation, we end up in the catastrophe of Stalinism or the Maoist Cultural Revolution with their thoroughgoing 'totalitarian' destructive rage."[32]

Žižek's thinking distinguishes a true event from a merely putative one, in that what is labelled an event retrospectively (anaphorically) by those involved is characterised by its repeated engendering of new consequences which are not exhausted in its naming but in fact enable new namings. This means that no naming of truth captures *everything*, but leaves precisely "the Real", that is to say the event as such, uncaptured. It is not that the "Real" remains unabsorbed in any truth-naming, but rather that beyond the named truth there exists the generative reality of the event.

The latter, however – and this is the decisive point – is silent. It is not the event that engenders its naming, rather, it is that

[29] Ibid.
[30] Loc. cit. 227 f.
[31] Loc. cit. 230.
[32] Loc. cit. 229.

which, in its retrospective naming by others, is determined to be a truth-event without being absorbed in this determination. The event *takes place* (otherwise there would be nothing in terms of which one could understand oneself), but it *is silent*. Hence it can only be understood according to its naming by others. These namings cannot be measured against the event, but only against other namings, which in themselves are no less arbitrary or equally legitimate. And since no event can be expressed and named in one way alone, an event only ever finds expression in the potential or actual dispute over namings. This dispute cannot be decided by reference to the event, since that is silent, not expressive but non-expressive, and thus only ever understandable in the way that it is named and interpreted – that is contentiously. Which of these conflicting namings prevails and becomes culturally determinative is not a matter of truth but of power. If the balance of power changes, there is typically also a change in the normative naming of an event and in that which, in its aftermath, is held to be either self-evident or problematic – this can be clearly seen in the dispute surrounding the use of the category 'Reformation' to determine the unity and plurality of the Reformation(s) of the 16th century.[33] But it is a wide-ranging problem that makes it plain why today's cultural processes are played out essentially as a semantic dispute over namings and the power of naming. Anyone who can persuade others to see what happened in the light of his or her naming of it determines what is held to be either self-evident or not self-evident, and in accordance with which self-evidences, 'facts' and values one orientates oneself and one's life, judgements and actions. It is significant that namings today are critically assessed almost solely on the basis of their societal impact, conflict or conformity with

[33] Cf. B. Hamm / B. Moeller / D. Wendebourg, *Reformationstheorien. Ein kirchenhistorischer Disput über Einheit und Vielfalt der Reformation*, Göttingen 1995.

the interests of specific social groups with their own conventions of political language or morality, rather than on the basis of their 'correctness', 'accuracy' or 'truth'. In other words, they are not judged according to whether they distort and miss the point of the event they name, or conversely correspond with and clarify it. The event is silent and not self-interpreting. The dispute over its correct naming and interpretation thus remains external, even if the dispute would not exist without the relevant event.

### *9. Speech-events*

At this point the hermeneutic theology of the previous century took a different line, at any rate with regard to the foundational and singular event designated 'word of God' – although not in the sense that it sought to treat this designation as referring to an indisputable original event of the Christian faith. Rather, it understood the religious and theological dispute with and within Christianity, not as an external dispute regarding the naming of an opaque event, but as a dispute, both internal and external, surrounding the interpretation of a self-interpretation, in itself strained and contentious, of what it called 'word of God'.[34] It took the self-speaking moment of Heidegger's concept of event seriously and spoke not only, as Badiou did, of event, but of *word-event* or *speech-event*. This means, amongst other things, that event itself appears as something that communicates itself in a specific sense-form and with a specific sense-content. It is not an opaque referent of retrospective interpretation, but interprets itself, so that it does not merely *take place*, but does so in such a way that it makes itself *comprehensible – in a specific manner*. It is

[34] Cf. DALFERTH, *Radical Theology*; I. U. DALFERTH / P. BÜHLER / A. HUNZIKER (eds.), *Hermeneutische Theologie – heute?*, Tübingen 2013.

not simply a self-giving of the given (as emphasised by Jean-Luc Marion or Michel Henry),[35] but a comprehensible self-interpretation of that which gives itself.

As such it is not only comprehensible *per se*, but *quoad nos*, i.e. in the eyes of those who understand it *as something*. Just as music happens, not on the instrument, but in the ear of the listener, it follows that the speech-event takes place, not *per se*, but at the point of those who experience it as a specific event: *the comprehending experience of the event is its comprehensible occurring*, and vice versa. That is to say: it is not that the event first takes place and is then interpreted; rather, it takes place *as* interpretation, or more precisely, as *self*-interpretation in, with and as part of the external interpretations which are considering the event post festum and from which, as self-interpretation, it is to be repeatedly and critically distinguished. This critical self-differentiation of the self-interpretation from the external interpretation cannot, however, be accomplished *per se* in any given situation, for there both interpretations always converge in the unity of an occurrence. The two are only distinguishable in a change of situation and in the process of an act of symbolisation and interpretation to others within a growing discourse which relates anaphorically to what has gone before and opens itself cataphorically to what is to come. In order to articulate the singular intelligibly, one must say it not just once, but repeatedly and in fresh ways. Only repetition makes it clear that one is not speaking of a special case of something universal, but rather of something singular.

---

[35] J.-L. Marion, *Étant donné. Essai d'une phénoménologie de la donation*, Paris 1997; M. Henry, Nicht-intentionale Phänomenologie und Gegen-Reduktion, in: R. Kühn / M. Staudigl [eds.], *Epoché und Reduktion. Formen und Praxis der Reduktion*, Würzburg 2003, 87–107, 95–107; idem, *Auto-donation. Entretiens et conférences*, Paris 2004.

Thus it is only possible to decide between the self-interpretation and the external interpretations once the speech-event has been repeated in other situations: it is not the event, but only its repetition that makes it possible to distinguish its self-interpreting occurrence from the mere imagination, dream or fantasy of what has been spoken of. Truth-events are only meaningful as speech-events that interpret and communicate themselves intelligibly as something specific, by repeating themselves when they continue to be spoken of in a specific way. Whether we are considering a self-interpreting speech-event or merely a supposed event cannot be discerned from an event *per se*, but only becomes apparent from its repetition in other situations during the process of its thematisation in new life situations.

When we see it in this light – as Heidegger does – the speech-event is the self-repeating beginning which renders itself comprehensible, in distinction from what is other, as something specific and thus not as an opaque something or a dark nothing, but as that which articulates and defines itself over and over again and which interprets itself to us in an intelligible way. To occur means to render itself comprehensible as something specific, and thus not merely to give itself, but to *interpret* itself – repeatedly – as that which gives itself. That cannot happen without a deconstruction of those articulations which define the event unsatisfactorily, incorrectly or (in context) one-sidedly, abbreviately or ambiguously. As a speech-event it must itself be the critic and reviewer of any external definitions, whether more or less apposite. To do this the event must not lie back in the past so that it can only be brought to mind by a process of recall, but must be the permanent critical companion of its articulation. *Without repetition* there can be no distinction between faithful recourse to an *event* and reference to a mere *supposed* event. It is not the retrospective historical safeguarding of an occurrence, but the critical repetition of it that proves the truth of a speech-event. One who seeks to safeguard the truth of an event must continue to speak critically of it by making a distinction between what one says and that of which one says it, and by trusting that what one speaks of as event is repeating itself.

### *10. Ways of naming the event of transcendence*

For all that, and whatever other names or descriptions it may attract, as free self-repetition an event is first and foremost *transcendent*. No name is such that the event would not ever differentiate itself from that name by generating other ways of naming.

This transcendence can be understood in at least five different ways which can be variously combined: psychoanalytically as *the real*, phenomenologically as *excess*, hermeneutically as *that which is self-interpreting*, theologically as *a passively experienced change in the mode of existence*, and ethically as an active *reorientation* of life.

*1. The real*: Following Lacan, the event is defined psychoanalytically as *the real*, that is to say the *generative beyond of all ways of naming*, the referent that is not generated by these namings, but to which they point without ever being able to grasp it. It is the residue that is not taken up, either into the symbolic or the imaginary. It cannot therefore be either symbolised or imagined 'as such', but is the permanent 'beyond' of the symbolisations and imaginations which it enables and generates. It is the fundamentally inexpressible, unfathomable and uncontrollable, which one can only ever thematise by reference to its consequences, because, as the unfathomable generative ground, it precedes all its namings without allowing itself to be apprehended as such.

*2. The excess*: Taking his cue from the thought traditions of negative theology, Merold Westphal has narrowed this down phenomenologically. He defines this transcendence as *excess*, *as permanent excess of meaning*, in other words as that which can always be more, and also other, than what is ever understood and apprehended: "an other can rightly be said to be wholly other if it enters my experience on its own terms and not mine, if it *permanently exceeds* the forms and categories of my transcendental ego and *permanently surprises* my horizons of expectation."[36]

*3. The self-interpreting*: That, however opens up the abyss of the total otherness of an event in comparison with its definitions, an abyss which renders God and the devil indistinguishable. This is why hermeneutical theology has described the excessive beyond of all namings more precisely: as a *speech-event which interprets itself for others in a specific way*, and which has therefore occurred not just once, originally, (as a historical 'revelation'), in which case it would merely mark the historical point of reference for retrospective namings, but which functions as the permanent creative critic, reviewer and progressive determinant of these contingent ways of naming (which is, in other words, present as the 'word of God').[37]

*4. The radically new*: If we consider these three elements, the *real*, the *excess* and the *self-interpretation* together, we have, from a theological point of view, three key characteristics of the *radically new* in history. This is something that requires to be named, although it is not exhausted by any of its namings or definitions. It is something that moves beyond each of its namings in a double sense, both by being present through an other *before* and *independent of* any naming (real), and by moving *beyond* every external naming (excess). And it is something *radically* new because it does not simply represent another instance in an already existing sequence (although it can indeed always be regarded as such). Rather, through its self-interpretation it initiates and defines a new sense-sequence, without, as a sense-generating,

---

[36] M. WESTPHAL, *Transcendence and Self-Transcendence. On God and the Soul*, Bloomington, IN 2004, 3.

[37] Cf. DALFERTH, *Radical Theology*, 150–159.199–211.

self-interpreting event, becoming an element of this sequence or commingling with the sequence as a whole.

5. *Existential event*: It is not one event amongst many – this would be to misunderstand it, even if it allows itself to be understood as such. Instead, it is what binds together the Many into One in a new way (and thus initiates a new sequence of experiences in one's life). No new element is added to the existing experiential world; rather, a new realm within which to experience everything is opened up. To put it another way, the radically new is not an ontological event in the world (event of being), nor is it a semiotic event in the life-world (sense-event). It is in fact that *existential event* which binds together not only the Many into One, but also Everything into something New. It does this by adding everything to a new whole in a very specific way and thereby drawing a distinction between it and the Old (that is, it opens up a new complete view of all the experiential sequences of life that is different from the old complete view). These overall views can be measured according to how a life is to be judged in terms of God's making himself present within it: whether as a new life oriented towards God's presence, or as the old life that ignores it.

The modal distinction between the old and the new covers not just some aspects, but *everything*, since it is anchored, not in the phenomena of the world, but in our relation to and manner of dealing with these phenomena. It denotes, not an event of being, but an *existential event*, which changes the mode of human existence before God from a life that ignores God (old life) to a life that does not ignore him (new life), in which everything is determined by the call and gift of that which this new life describes, retrospectively and anaphorically, as the self-mediation of God in his word ('word of God').[38] This singular existential event changes the horizon within which life is lived, experienced

---

[38] Loc. cit. 207–211.

and understood, and within which a universal discourse with a new semantic evolves. Nothing is understood in the same way as before; rather everything is mapped according to the perspective of the 'Word of God', of the self-interpreting speech-event of the creative presence of God, into a new and comprehensive context of meaning related to the transformation of the mode of human existence before God, since it is there that this revolution in existence occurs and recurs.

### *11. The event of the Word of God*

Reference to this event has two basic preconditions. Firstly, the identity of what happened back then and of what is happening here and now is preserved by means of the repetition – in the same way – of this self-interpretation-for-others-as-something-specific. The *identity* of the occurrence can be deduced from the *mode* of the recurrence: what is occurring is indicated by how it occurs. As a rule, however, both are clear, not in their enactment, but in their retrospective contemplation: a posteriori, in other words. Secondly, the first occurrence and the critical constant recurrence of the speech-event are explicated theologically – i.e. with a retrospective interpretation – as a self-interpreting event of the 'Word of God' (as it is called). This is not the descriptive title for a special phenomenon, but an abbreviated theological formula for the interpretative event in which – from the point of view of those affected – God makes himself comprehensible to human beings in a particular way and through particular events *as their God*, in other words as their creator, thus simultaneously defining them and everything else in a new way, in other words as his creations. As a once-only distinction as part of a once-only event this would be meaningless or arbitrary. But on the one hand, the fundamental distinction between creator and creature relates to everything, so that it does not denote a distinction within the world, but rather a distinction between different understandings of world and existence. And on the other hand, it would be entirely abstract if it were not actualised and explicated in a branching series of consequential distinctions which work out this understanding of world and existence, based on the event of this fundamental distinction, as a new orientation context for human life.

This indeed is the task of Christian theology, which, by thinking through the orientation grammar of practical Christian living, contributes to the formation of a new universal discourse (one which extends to everything) with a new semantic. If the term 'Word of God' – when used within the context of Trinitarian theology – means God's original comprehensible self-communication to the other in order to open up to that other a living fellowship with him, then this applies in *exactly the same way* to the *first occurrence in history* (in the story of Jesus Christ) as it does to the *critical constant recurrence in history* (in the communication of the gospel). This is what binds all that is distinct from God into the unity of a new context determined by God (the creation), in which one speaks no longer of the world but of the creation, not of human beings but of creatures made in the image of God, not of God but of the Creator, Redeemer and Consummator, and not of life but of the new or the old life.

Theologically, therefore, the term 'Word of God' functions, not as the name of an event (such as the 'French Revolution') or as a questionable descriptive title for a book (the Bible), but as a concentrated basic metaphor with multiple definitions, which interprets the overall event of creation as a self-interpreting event of God's self-communication – from the *verbum aeternum* (second person of the Trinity) through the *verbum personale* (Jesus Christ) and the *verbum efficax* of sermon and sacrament to the *verbum externum* (proclamation of the gospel) and the *verbum internum* (Spirit-effected assurance of the truth). All these *verba* are not the names of different events which can be considered individually, but aspects of the one occurrence of the one 'Word of God', so that they unfold a singular event of universal dimension.[39]

The singularity of this event is not that of the enumerable One, from which the Many is formed. The speech-event of the Word of God is not one event of being among many, nor is it one sense-event alongside others. If it were, it would be merely the special instance of a universal, but not singular. So it does not enter our field of vision until it is understood, not ontologically as an event of being or semiotically as a sense-event, but as an existential event.

### *12. Existential event*

By 'existential event' I mean here the non-compulsory change of mode of one's human existence before God, the existential reorientation of one's life, which in theological terms, by virtue of the radical nature of the new beginning this signifies, can be encoded by the Johannine image of new life from God (ἐὰν μή τις γεννηθῇ ἄνωθεν, οὐ δύναται ἰδεῖν τὴν βασιλείαν τοῦ θεοῦ [Jn 3:3]), that is, new birth through the Spirit (τὸ γεγεννημένον ἐκ τῆς σαρκὸς σάρξ ἐστιν, καὶ τὸ γεγεννημένον ἐκ τοῦ πνεύματος πνεῦμά ἐστιν [Jn 3:6]), as a change from the *old to the new life.*

Questions of mode have a bearing on the *way in which* humans lead their lives. This question merits attention for a number of reasons. Ever since Kant it has been clear that the answer to the question of whether something exists contributes nothing by way of the answer to the question of what it is. The statement 'Britta is an unemployed sales assistant, the mother of 3 children

[39] Cf. I. U. Dalferth, Understanding Revelation, in: I. U. Dalferth / M.Ch. Rodgers (eds.), *Revelation*, Tübingen 2014, 1–25.

and a conservative voter' is not in any way further defined by the detail 'and she exists', which simply states that there really is such a person as the Britta thus described.

In fact, neither the what-question nor the existence question provides the answer to *how* Britta lives – rationally or irrationally, confidently or despairingly, in faith or with no interest in God. The question of mode coincides neither with the question of determination nor with the existence question, but calls for independent answers.

Likewise, the question of mode can be posed from two angles, from the point of view of the What and of the That of a human life: How do human beings live their lives? How do human beings exist so as to fulfil their lives? The first question focuses on the manner in which they conduct their lives and thus, treated normatively, on the moral question of the good life (as distinct from the bad life): How should humans live so as to live in a truly human way? The second question focuses on the manner of their being or existence, and thus on the existential question as to the right life (as distinct from the wrong life): How must one exist in order not to lead a life that is wrong before God and humanity?

Both questions presuppose that one can live (be) in one way other another, and can exist (be there) in one way or another. Just as ethical reflection has as its theme the question of the good life (How *should* we live – as humans amongst humans, as human beings amongst other living beings?), so in the same way, theological reflection has as its theme the question of living aright (How *can* we exist – before God, with God, through God?)

The answer, according to New Testament theologians such as John or Paul, is: human beings exist before God either in orientation to God's presence (that is, believingly, i. e. in faith) or by ignoring, disregarding or denying him (that is, unbelievingly, i. e. in unfaith). Differentiation between modes of existence is a theological orientation distinction and is as little suited to sorting phenomena or classifying human beings as is the distinction between right and left in spatial terms.[40] Just as the existence predicate contributes nothing to the definition of something, in the same way the detail of the mode of existence contributes

[40] It follows that culturally and socially prevalent distinctions such as those between Greeks and barbarians, Roman citizens and non-Romans, or Jews and Greeks are irrelevant 'in faith' or 'in Christ'. As Paul emphasises: "For there is no distinction between Jew and Greek; for the same Lord is Lord of all." (Rom. 10:12). For "now that faith has come … there is neither Jew nor Greek, there is neither slave nor free man, there is neither male nor female; for you are all one in Christ Jesus." (Gal. 3:25–28). None of these social descriptive differences is simply removed or abolished. But 'in faith' – that is, in the faith-filled process of existence in God's presence, as was revealed in Jesus Christ and is now through the Spirit decisive for life in Christian community – they have no further function in orienting Christian life. No one who exists in faith (that is in acknowledgement of God's presence) as a neighbour of God among God's neighbours, can apply these descriptive cultural distinctions to exclude others from those who are also to be perceived as God's neighbours and are therefore to be treated according to the law of love. A. Badiou, *Saint Paul: The Foundation of Universalism,* Stanford, 2003 is absolutely right to see in this the starting point for "Christianity's potential universality" (57). All with whom God stands in such a relationship that they are able to have faith in him are equal before God and are, in their respective otherness, to be treated as equals before God. The Christ-event reveals that God's generosity allows anyone to receive this opportunity, even if, as the Spirit-event makes clear, none of us realises it of our own accord. This makes Christianity the religion of human beings' radical equality before God – even though Christians of every epoch and cultural stamp have constantly rejected and contravened this insight, and are still doing so. From a Christian perspective, human beings are equal because God makes them equal and not because they share a common range of characteristics – if indeed it is sufficiently clear that they do – which distinguishes them from other living beings. Cf. I. U. Dalferth, Religion, Morality and Being Human. The Controversial Status of Human Dignity, in: P. Jonkers / M. Sarot (eds.), *Embodied Religion*, Utrecht 2013, 143–179. The distinction between Christians and non-Christians is thus based solely on whether or not one is aware of this principle of equality before God and is seeking to live by it in a radical spirit of shared humanity.

nothing to the description of a life: How one exists changes nothing about who and what one is. And what one does is, to be sure, evidence that one exists, but in itself reveals nothing about how one exists. The term 'believe' is therefore construed here, not substantivally or verbally, but modally or adverbially – i. e. not to say that 'Britta believes', but rather that 'Britta lives *believingly*' or '*in faith*' or '*in a faith-filled manner*'.

Seen in this light, faith and unfaith denote possible ways – the only two possible ways, in fact – of existing before God. (Where God is concerned there is no neutral position.) Anyone who lives, lives either in faith or not. No one is born into a position of faith. Rather, everyone who lives in faith comes from a position of unfaith. But no one who is living in unfaith begins to have faith of their own accord. It follows that all who have faith know, or can and should know, that they do not have themselves to thank for it.

Both modes of existence are therefore possibilities, but not options between which one can choose. It is only *in faith* that one is able decide for or against unfaith, whereas one never decides *in favour of faith*, since in unfaith the decision is impossible and in faith it is unnecessary.[41] It is no accident that the life of faith involves confessing that one owes this change to the faith mode of existence, not to one's own reason and strength, but to God himself and to God's Spirit. It *befalls* a life and cannot be initiated methodically or brought about deliberately; it affects not just one aspect of human life, but the whole of it, including everything one can experience, do or suffer.[42]

---

[41] This, then, is the sense in which one confesses what one has become and is becoming.

[42] Hence a conversion is not a change to some of one's convictions, but a revolution in one's life, leading to a new attitude to everything. Everything that follows looks different, even if life continues with very little alteration.

### *13. Transformative transcendence*

This change in the mode of existence is therefore not an ontological event of being which binds Much into One (thus continuing a sequence of experiences or opening up a new sequence of experiences). Nor is it a semiotic sense-event which uses the One to denote, and thus reconfigure, the Much. Rather, it is an event of existential reorientation which binds not just *Much* into One, but *All* into a *New*.

Every sense-event is transcendent as regards the situation in which it takes place. It is not part of the sequence of what happens in a given situation, but opens up a new sequence in which the meaning and the truth of this situation are expressed. The existential event, on the other hand, is not merely situation-transcendent, as sense-events are. Rather, it is radically transcendent, since it discloses the truth of not just one situation but all possible situations of human life before God. It can take place at any point during a life. However, it does not form part of the sequences which together constitute our experiential world, but qualifies this world in a fundamental way. Hence the old life is not simply what preceded this event, nor is the new life simply what comes after it. Rather, from the standpoint of this event it is possible to discern retrospectively what was pointing forward and leading to the new, and equally what was obscuring and hindering it. And conversely, looking forward to what is to come, what is being opened up and released by the new can be distinguished from the after-effects of the old which are impeding or preventing the growth of the new.

The distinction between new and old functions as the operator of a differentiating view of all that is past, present and future. However, it is not itself an instance of the life experiences that it critically qualifies. As the difference operator it stands *in front of* the brackets containing the experiential sequences which make up our lives, but is not itself an experience within those brackets:

we do not have to experience something new to live in the new, and when we live in the old we are not experiencing what is old. It is not the experiences that are new, but the mode of existence of those who have them. And it is not the experiences that must change to become new, but the manner in which one exists before God: no longer *etsi deus non daretur [as if there were no God]*, but open to his presence.

The change in mode of the existence in which this takes place is thus not one experience among others, but a radical break which has two aspects. In its negative aspect it *disrupts* a life story and *dislocates* or *decentres* those who consider themselves to be the subjects of their life stories: all that seemed self-evident has lost its self-evidence. At the same time, in its positive aspect, it gives life a new orientation covering past, present and future – in constant reconnection with the existential change of mode to which one owes one's new life, knowing that it is not due to one's own efforts.

This event is therefore only properly recalled when one makes it clear that it is not the memory but the event itself that recalls the event – if indeed it is recalled at all. It is not the memory that is transformative, but the event recalled.

### *14. Event of being, sense-event and existential event*

It is clear that the ontological concept of event summarised at the start differs from Badiou's semiotic notion of event and from the concepts of speech-event and existential event outlined above. It is one thing to live in a world of events, quite another to live in a world of meaning, and yet a third to re-orientate our lives from the ground up in the light of a speech-event that communicates its own meaning. The second and third cannot be reduced to the first, since we are not dealing with the explanation of what has happened (event of being), but with self-understanding and self-communication in the world (sense-event) and with the reorientation of one's life in relation to God (existential event).

Only those who see, in the events of life, *more* than can be grasped empirically as fact are living in a world of meaning. Human beings cannot help but live in such worlds of meaning. Parents see more in their children than mere biological organisms, psychological systems, social cases or human resources. They see human beings with names and faces, without whom their own lives would not be what they are, since life is made up of experiences. Parents who lose this way of looking at things will fail to do their children justice. But parents who retain this viewpoint always see more in their children than is evident at a given moment. Unless we consistently attribute to others the added value of meaning, we are not living in a meaningful human world. Only this kind of world, however, is more than an abstract collection of events. It is a real-life world – a world in which humans can live together in a human (though also in an inhuman) way.

After all, if we pay heed to the fact that humans are not merely *living with* humans, but are living with them *before God*, and that a life may or may not heed this very point – bearing in mind that it is never heeded without having previously been unheeded – then it becomes clear that each human being can live his or her life, not just morally as a good or bad life (in terms of life with others), but also existentially as a life that is right or wrong, new or old (in terms of existence before God). It is essential not to confuse the two: morality and faith have less in common than is sometimes thought. This may not be to everyone's liking. But it is so, nonetheless.

# C. Transcendence and Immanence. A fundamental distinction for religious life orientation today

## *1. The essence of the distinction*

The term 'transcendence', together with its counterpoint, 'immanence', is a fundamental philosophical – and by derivation also theological – *orientation concept*. It does not stand for anything (it is not the name of a particular phenomenon called 'transcendence'), nor does it define anything (it is not the determinant predicate of some phenomena as distinct from others: 'these are transcendence phenomena – those are not'). In its philosophical and, to a large extent, its theological usage it tends to function as "a concept of reflection that explicates meaning, an elucidating tool",[1] with the aid of which we interpret particular sense phenomena of human life in such a way that we can orient ourselves more reliably in understanding, thinking through and dealing with the unmanageable complexity of life.[2] We do this by using 'transcendence' and 'immanence', not as self-contained names or concepts, but as a contrasting pair, *immanence/transcendence*, with the aid of which we orient ourselves in life in a particular way.

---

[1] Th. Rentsch, Transzendenz und Sprache. Der Mensch im Verhältnis zu Grenze und Sinngrund der Welt, in: idem, *Transzendenz und Negativität. Religionsphilosophische und Ästhetische Studien*, Berlin / New York 2011, 201–216, 204.

[2] Cf. I. U. Dalferth, The Idea of Transcendence, in: R. B. Bellah / H. Joas (eds.), *The Axial Age and Its Consequences*, Cambridge, MA / London 2012, 146–188.

The essence of this orientational differentiation consists, not in distinguishing between phenomena, but in structuring our relationship with phenomena in a particular way. It is not a matter of the (different types of) appearance, but of the *appearance of phenomena for us at all.* The orientational differentiation *immanent / transcendent* cannot be used to sort or classify phenomena. Rather, it says something about how we relate to the way phenomena appear to us. It is the *for us* of their appearance that is in the forefront, and not *as what* they appear. When we relate to something, we orient ourselves by how that thing presents itself when it appears to us *as something.*

Where the orientation function of the *immanence / transcendence* antithesis is concerned, on the one hand, the two different sides of the antithesis are not individually debatable, while on the other hand, the distinction between them cannot be resolved or levelled without destroying its power of orientation. Exploring 'transcendence' or 'immanence' separately is just as misguided as seeking to understand them as the two poles of a continuum. To do this is to confuse the logic of a distinction with its application. We can distinguish between *left* and *right* in spatial terms in relation to our current position, but nothing is left or right *per se.* Whether any particular object is to our left or our right depends on our current position. But that does not mean to say that the object is located on a left-right continuum, but that, through our orientational differentiation, our *right / left* relationship with something changes with the conditions under which and the place from which we apply this distinction.

So figures of differentiation such as *right / left* (in spatial terms) or *transcendent / immanent* (in relation to the world or to life) lose their orientation function when one attempts to 'dedifferentiate' them, whether by tracing each side back to something they have in common so that they merge, or by using each one separately to describe particular phenomena, resulting in the disintegration of the dual orientation into two descriptive classification concepts. Obviously these differentiations do not occur in a vacuum; they draw on much that preceded them. But if one were to attempt to dismantle or eliminate either difference, they would no longer be distinctions by which one could orient oneself. We orient ourselves in the world and in our lives by differentiating, that is by paying heed to relevant differences or drawing important distinctions. We can and must correct and revise our distinctions if they are not fulfilling their purpose and are leading us astray – either literally or figuratively. But we destroy their orientation function if we nullify the distinction they draw. What is decisive for orientation is not the subject of the distinction, but that and how the distinction is drawn. It is the act of distinction, and not primarily what is being distinguished between, that reveals how we are orienting, or seeking to orient, ourselves in our current context.

### *2. The hermeneutic of an orientational differentiation*

The task of a *hermeneutic of transcendence* is accordingly not an esoteric hermeticism of the life beyond, nor is it the interpretation of some eschatological doctrine of the mysteries of another world; rather it is the explication of the sense structures of human life in this world. It concerns itself, not with the life beyond, but with this life, or more precisely with the way in which, in various spheres of human life in this world – in feeling, thinking and activity, in cosmological, epistemic, ethical, aesthetic, religious or theological discourses – reference is made to a life beyond, different in each case, which qualifies this life in a particular way. What is decisive in this regard is not *what* something is, but what it is *for us* ('for-reference'). However, nothing can be *for us*, unless we can understand it *as something* ('as-structure'). We can only do this because and to the extent that it is accessible to us *through something* as something granted and accessible ('through-character'). And it is evident from the discourse and practical contexts of our life in what a wide variety of ways this takes place. In our shared life in the world, questions are posed *for us* which we seek to answer with the aid of the distinction between *transcendence* and *immanence*. But we cannot do this unless we seek to understand *transcendence* and *immanence* (and thus ourselves too) *in a specific way* or *as something specific*. How we understand them varies according to the different practical and discourse spheres *through which* questions are raised and within which *transcendence* and *immanence* function as an orienting fundamental distinction. The use of *transcendence* and *immanence* in the singular must therefore not be allowed to obscure the fact that the semantic of this orientational differentiation varies according to the problem constellations of the cosmological, epistemic, ethical, aesthetic, religious or theological discourses in which it is actually being used.

In what follows I will concentrate on the *theological use* of this orientational differentiation. Transcendence is not an inherently theological term. But it is used theologically, albeit interpreted by a special semantic, in which the 'transcending' is expressed, not primarily by the human being, but by God, and 'transcendence' means the divine sphere (the divine life), while 'immanence' means the world (the life of creatures). Likewise, in theological usage *transcendence* is one side of a contrasting pair, of which the other side is *immanence*; in theological terms this contrast is interpreted through a cascade of interconnected distinctions such as *creator / creature*, *redeemer / sinner*, *consummator / new creation*, *eternal life / earthly existence* and so on. It is precisely these distinctions that are orienting for Christian life and thought, rather than the individual concepts distinguished between. To put it another way: the respective aspects of the *transcendence / immanence* antithesis only function as orientation when they are taken together, so the pair must be treated together.

*Transcendence* comes from *transcend*, and the Latin *transcendere* means: *step over, move beyond, surpass.* In order to understand the logic of moving-beyond, we need to examine three groups of problems: the distinction between *Here* and *There*, the moving-beyond from *Here* to *There* and the demarcation line between *Here* and *There.* I will restrict myself to eight points.

### 3. Here and There

There can be no transcendence unless one draws a distinction between a *Here* and a *There*, a *Now* and a *Then*, a *Like This* and a *Like That*, between two *places, conditions, periods of time, modes of being* or *spheres*: the one in which one is (immanence), and the one into which one is moving or on which one is focused (transcendence). The two places or modes of being are functionally separate from each other and are interrelated, but the differential relationship between them is not symmetrical. It is only from the perspective of immanence that we can distinguish between immanence and transcendence. But only within the realm of transcendence is there an immanence, from the perspective of which a distinction can be drawn between immanence and transcendence. Why?

### 4. A complete alternative

Differentiation between *immanence* and *transcendence* marks a *complete disjunction*: there is nothing that cannot be localised in this way. While the negation of immanence (non-immanence) is transcendence and the negation of transcendence (non-transcendence) is immanence, the negation of both (neither immanent nor transcendent) is an impossible operation which fails to identify any possible place in which one could find oneself.

Meanwhile the affirmation of both (immanent and also transcendent) is only possible if one is each at different times, in different respects or in different ways. This can only be achieved without contradiction if the difference between the two positions is communicated dialectically with recourse to time, to different perspectives on the same thing or to the integration of the antithesis at a higher level.

It is thus impossible to distinguish between immanence and transcendence without positioning oneself in what has been distinguished between. There is no third position that would be distinct from *immanence* and *transcendence*; rather, one always proceeds from one side of the distinction drawn – even when, and in fact precisely when, drawing the distinction. We can adopt Spencer Brown's terminology and call this side the *marked space*, and the other side the *unmarked space*.[3] For us *immanence* acts as the *marked space* (immanence perspective); this means that 'immanent' is the position from which we relate to that which we distinguish from it as being 'transcendent': *immanence (immanence / transcendence)*. If, on the other hand, we conduct a thought experiment in which *transcendence* is the position from which the distinction is being drawn (transcendence perspective), then 'immanent' is differentiated from transcendence by drawing the distinction *within* transcendence: *transcendence (immanence / transcendence)*. In the first instance the subject of the transcending is localised in immanence (the *marked space*) and the movement of transcending is construed as *self-transcending in immanence*, that is, it is understood as *self-trans-ascendence*.[4] In the second instance, in contrast, the subject of the transcending is localised in transcendence, so that

[3] Cf. G. Spencer Brown, *Laws of Form*, Toronto 1973.

[4] Cf. J. Greisch, Das Spiel der Transzendenz: Trans-Aszendenz, Trans-Deszendenz, Trans-Passibilität, Trans-Possibilität, in: I. U. Dalferth / P. Bühler / A. Hunziker (eds.), *Hermeneutik der Transzendenz*, Tübingen 2015, 61–82.

the *marked space* of the observer (immanence) and the *marked space* of the subject (transcendence) are defined as opposites and the movement of transcending is described as the moving-beyond-self of the transcendent *in* its transcendence towards the immanent, and is therefore construed as *self-trans-descendence.*

## 5. Transcending

Transcending is understood as a *movement* leading from the *marked space* into or towards the *unmarked space.* This movement can be understood not simply as the succession of events in time that take place in an "earlier than … and later than" arrangement. There must also be a moment of identity, without which the sequence of the elements distinguished could not be perceived as, or determined to be, movement. This moment of identity does not necessarily correspond with that which moves (i. e. which shifts from *Here* to *There*), but can also consist in the context within which it moves (and within which therefore *Here* is distinguished from *There*). The movement presupposes a *horizon of reference*, under the conditions and in terms of which the distinction is drawn between transcendence and immanence. This horizon of reference is defined by the place from which the movement is undertaken.

Since everything is either immanent or transcendent and there can be nothing which is neither the one nor the other, we have two contrasting possibilities. Some maintain that it is only within immanence that it is possible to distinguish between immanence and transcendence: the process of transcending establishes a distinction within immanence. But this is impossible, others maintain, unless a distinction is drawn within transcendence between immanence and transcendence: without the self-differentiation of transcendence there can be no distinction within immanence, since there is no immanence; the first is the necessary condition for the second, since without the first the second may perhaps establish a *difference*, but not a difference *within immanence*.

The first is the voice of a half-hearted secular modernity which has not been conclusively thought through: a world that is purely and exclusively immanent is an impossible concept. The other is the voice of a theological tradition which is tantamount to a reversal of the distinction between the *marked* and the *unmarked space*. This represents a thoroughgoing counterproposal to the first approach. As a result, theological discussion of transcendence and immanence cannot be understood as the continuation and deepening of the non-theological transcendence discussions, but at best as a complete sea change.

### 6. *For and by*

The transcending movement is attributed to someone who, or something which, performs it (the *subject of the transcending*) and/or observes it (the *observer of the transcending*). Unless the process of transcending has a subject and/or an observer (which may or may not be identical), there is no distinction between immanence and transcendence, either in immanence or in transcendence. Putting it phenomenologically: the distinction *between* immanence and transcendence is always a distinction *for* or *by someone* who accords this differentiation orientational significance because, where he or she is concerned, there is a distinction between a *marked* and an *unmarked space*. In an immanence context this 'for-reference' is normally applied to humans, who are, accordingly, understood to be *transcending, that is, self-transcending beings*. In a transcendence context, in contrast, the distinction is applied – by us, from an anthropological perspective! – to whatever or whomever is designated 'ground of the world' (in cosmological terms), 'the Other' (in ethical terms), 'existential ground of meaning' (in hermeneutical terms) or 'God' (in theological terms). This God is understood *as the being who makes immanence possible*, that is, as the *creator* who allows for a creation distinct from himself by the very fact that he distinguishes himself from it as its creator.

### *7. The ambiguity of self-transcending*

Not only have both models been implemented in many and various ways throughout the history of thought, they have typically been linked.[5] Human self-transcending to the divine would be a purely immanent matter and would be exposed to all the objections of religious criticism if the distinction between immanence and transcendence in the finite life were not grounded in a distinction between transcendence and immanence in the divine life. For one thing, the transcending movement which characterises many areas of human life besides religion does not lead beyond immanence. However, it cannot be addressed as such, because it is itself what posits the distinction between immanence and transcendence in the first place, while remaining a purely 'immanent' proposition. For another, the transcending movement within the divine life takes place as a self-differentiation of the transcendent from the immanent. This, similarly, does not lead beyond the transcendence of the divine life, but establishes within that life a fundamental difference, in which something other than what is divine becomes possible.

The concept of self-transcending thus becomes systematically ambiguous, since it is always necessary to state precisely on which side of the distinction the movement is taking place: on

---

[5] Cf. the contributions in J. Sirovátka (ed.), *Endlichkeit und Transzendenz. Perspektiven einer Grundbeziehung*, Hamburg 2012.

the side of the immanent (human self-transcending) or on the side of the transcendent (divine self-transcending ). Neither movement leads beyond the horizon of its differential position. Rather – and this applies to all types of transcending – each in its own way leads deeper into that position. Thus, to transcend oneself means that, *in focussing on the other, one distinguishes oneself from what, where, how or who one is not*. Where this takes place within the shared horizon of immanence, that which is fundamentally other can only be defined negatively: as non-immanence (negative transcendence). Where, on the other hand, it takes place on the transcendent side, there is no fundamentally other. Rather, self-transcending is conceived of as the establishment of the difference between immanence and transcendence, that is to say, as the differentiation of the transcendent from itself. And this self-differentiation establishes, within the horizon of transcendence, the distinction between transcendence (the place where the difference is established) and immanence (the place established by the differentiation).

## 8. *Vertical and horizontal transcending*

This distinction is not to be confused with the distinction between *vertical* and *horizontal* transcendence. This is a distinction on the side of immanent transcending which, on closer examination, is untenable. Thus we speak of a *vertical difference* between the transcendent and the immanent when we are distinguishing, from an immanent perspective, between the experiential world (immanence) and a 'world above' or 'world beyond' (transcendence). In contrast, we speak of a *horizontal difference* when we are distinguishing between two positions, conditions or stances within immanence which can be formalised in various different ways: as categorial transcendence (categories / transcendentals), as epistemic transcendence (subject / object of cognition), as alteriological transcendence (I/other), as ethical transcendence (subject/other subject), as religious transcendence (this world/new world) and so on. Each involves the formalisation of the distinction between immanence and transcendence within a different context of meaning, but does not refer to something different in principle. These various conceptions of transcendence have an orientation function wherever this distinction is made *by someone* or *for someone*, who, with the aid of this distinction, locates him- or herself (and everything else) within what is thereby distinguished.

### 9. *Absolute and relative transcendence*

The perspectives of the distinction between transcendence and immanence are not exactly symmetrical in both directions. Immanence is the correlate of transcending, but transcendence is only the correlate of immanence where the latter had already been established as the correlate of the transcending. Only where there is transcending, is there a transcendence/immanence distinction. From the immanence perspective, on the one hand, 'transcendence' signifies that which, in the process of transcending, one marks off as other. From the transcendence perspective, on the other hand, 'immanence' signifies that which, in the process of transcending, is established as other than transcendence *within* the transcendence perspective.

This gives 'transcendence' a double meaning: firstly it signifies that which is *other than immanence*, and secondly it means the *context* within which the distinction between immanence and transcendence is drawn. I shall call the first *relative transcendence*, and the second *absolute transcendence*. This must always be borne in mind when distinguishing between immanence and transcendence. It is thus impossible to speak of absolute immanence in this sense, since immanence owes its existence to an operation that cannot be carried out within it unless it already exists. Whereas the transcendence perspective is shown to be the perspective of absolute transcendence by being the necessary condition for differentiating between relative transcendence and immanence, the immanence perspective, on the other hand, always presupposes the reference to transcendence. To distinguish between transcendence and immanence *within* immanence (re-entry of the difference) presumes the *outside* distinction of immanence from transcendence. Setting this distinction within transcendence, on the other hand, distinguishes absolute from relative transcendence and it is not until this distinction is made that immanence is established. It is only in transcendence that it is possible to distinguish between transcendence and immanence. In immanence this distinction is always posited and drawn upon. Hence there is indeed absolute transcendence, but no absolute immanence.

### *10. Borders and limits*

One way or another, we accept that there is a demarcation line between the *Here* and the *There*. If we accept that this line can be crossed, it is understood as a *border*, not a *limit*. *Borders* such as a state border can be crossed and viewed from the other side, whereas *limits* such as the horizon cannot. If the demarcation line is understood as a border, not a limit, the distinction between *Here* and *There* remains an internal border within 'immanence' or 'transcendence'. Strictly speaking, however, immanence cannot be described like this, since the distinction does not lead beyond it so as to define it through an external contrast, but merely deepens it through an internal contrast. We distinguish between *Here* and *There*, but we can no longer construe this as a distinction between immanence and transcendence, since that distinction would have to be presupposed to allow us to speak in this way, rather than being deferred until the point of distinction between *Here* and *There*.

So the *metaphor of the border* and the *metaphor of the limit* open up quite different conceptual possibilities which must not be confused if the orientational differentiation between transcendence and immanence is not to become a dreadful muddle. The border metaphor implies an external contrast between immanence and transcendence, while the limit metaphor implies an internal border from one side. The first assumes that the other side is a 'beyond', while in the second the limit is a self-limitation in the 'here and now' (whether the here and now of immanence, or of transcendence). The term 'transcending', accordingly, oscillates between two meanings: *moving beyond immanence* or *becoming immanent* (in the case of the border) and the *extension of immanence* or *differentiation of transcendence* (in the case of the limit). That is to say: if the demarcation line between *Here* and *There* is conceived of so that the *There* is, or can, be an immanent *Here*, then transcendence is simply another location within immanence, or conversely, immanence is simply an internal distinction within transcendence and the absolute demarcation line is understood as a *limit* which can shift but cannot be overstepped. If, on the other hand, it is considered that the *There* cannot become an immanent *Here*, but remains in a marked space, distinct from every *Here*, then transcendence is understood as the beyond of immanence and the demarcation line as a *border* which either cannot be overstepped (so that one always remains in the *Here* of immanence) or can only be overstepped in such a way that one is no longer *Here*, but *There*, without being able to say, at the location of this There, that one is Here.

That sounds paradoxical, but it makes it clear that to be on the transcendence side in this sense means that one is no longer differentiatingly in the *Here* or the *There*, and thus no longer participates in the orientation practices of immanence: *transcendence is the place where the orientation practices of immanence no longer apply*. Conversely, this means that from the transcendence perspective there is no possibility of a *There* that could not be a *Here*. If the distinction between *Here* and *There* depends on the distinction between relative immanence and transcendence taking place within absolute transcendence, then the *Here and There* distinction is always pegged into the realm of absolute transcendence. Every *Here* or *There* is a *Here* in absolute transcendence. But it only makes sense to speak like this if the distinction between immanence and transcendence is established within absolute transcendence, making it possible to distinguish between *Here* and *There*.

In theological terms, only a self-transcending God can be a creator, and only humans who can transcend themselves can see themselves as creatures and behave as creatures – or not. But a self-transcending God can never transcend into something other than himself, so that his transcending can only be understood as deepening and intensification, not as a moving beyond his divinity. Only in God, that is within God's horizon, can the distinction between immanence and transcendence be established, so that every *Here* and *There*, from whatever side, is a *Here* in God. This is precisely why God can be present as an absolutely transcendent God on both sides of the distinction established by him, in the immanent and the transcendent, without invalidating or surrendering his transcendence as God, whereas a self-transcending human can never move beyond or leave the realm of immanence – either by vertical or by horizontal transcending.

## *11. Loss of transcendence in modernity?*

With the aid of these distinctions we acquire a more differentiated picture of the supposed loss of transcendence in a secular world. In recent years Charles Taylor has sought to demonstrate comprehensively that we no longer live in a disenchanted world, but in a secular era.[6] Like many others, he starts from a profound contrast between *now* and *then*. Between 1500 and 2000 the place of transcendence in the world underwent a complete change.[7] Given that its place had classically been in the sphere of religion, encoded in such antitheses as *sacred/profane* or *religious/secular*, it follows that for many people today it is no longer an issue. In the "modern western world" religion is "often pushed to the margin …, after having been at the centre of society throughout the whole of human history".[8] Taylor offers three arguments to support this thesis. In "contemporary democracies" religion is "no longer at the centre of public life; they are, generally speaking, either officially or semi-officially, 'secular'.[9] "In a large proportion of such societies many people do not practise religion; they do not go to church and frequently describe themselves as non-believers."[10] And while "in the past its was extremely difficult to be an unbeliever, today the situation is quite the opposite: For some people in certain environments it is faith that is more difficult, since it is considered an eccentric and implausible option."[11]

### 12. *The dual role of the Christian faith*

There is much that is correct in this point of view, but one ought not to romanticise the religious past. The Christian faith has thus far never taken itself for granted; indeed, the past 2000 years

---

[6] Cf. CH. TAYLOR, *A Secular Age*, Harvard 2007.

[7] CH. TAYLOR, Ein Ort für Transzendenz? http://www.michael-funken.de/informationphilosophie/philosophie/taylortranszendenz.html (5/26/2012) 1–7, 1.

[8] Ibid.

[9] Ibid.

[10] Ibid.

[11] Ibid.

of its history show that it is at least partly responsible for the development described. Without going into historical details, I will highlight just two points:[12]

Firstly, while some historical forms of the Christian faith have been focussed around intra-mundane distinctions between *sacred* and *profane* or *religious* and *secular*, this is by no means its intrinsic or central position. Rather, from the very beginning it has made an important contribution to dismantling and eliminating these differences, to a thoroughgoing disenchantment of the world and the worldlifying of the entire cosmos as creation and thus the place of God's presence: God is God and the world is the world. It owes its existence to God, but it is not divine, whereas God is divine precisely because he is or can be present everywhere in the non-divine world without becoming worldly.

Secondly, the modern volte-face against this Christian view of the world as creation has resulted in the world no longer being understood as meaningful creation, but as infinite universe. The world is what it becomes as nature and culture, whereas God is not, or at any rate not in the sense that when seeking to understand the world one can or must refer to God. The world is to be understood without considering it as creation.

While the first step worldlifies a cosmos pervaded by spirits and similar forces, turning it into creation, the second secularises the creation by eliminating the creator so that it becomes a senseless universe. But the second process is not simply a continuation and intensification of the first. The transformation of the cosmos idea into the idea of creation takes place in the orientation to the fundamental difference between transcendence and immanence, which is understood as the self-differentiation of the divine creator from the created world: as creator, God is

---

[12] Cf. in more detail I. U. Dalferth, Post-secular Society: Christianity and the Dialectics of the Secular, *Journal of the American Academy of Religion 78* (2010) 317–345.

rigorously differentiated from the world, but nonetheless always and everywhere present – albeit not always and everywhere in the same way. The transformation of the created world into an evolutionary universe, on the other hand, takes place by eliminating or rejecting this fundamental difference by means of two processes: negatively by the rejection of every worldly distinction between *sacred* and *profane* or *religious* and *secular* as representative of the vertical differentiation of divine transcendence from worldly immanence, and positively as a new formulation of the distinction between transcendence and immanence as a horizontal differentiation in the categorial, epistemic, ethical or alteriological sense. Every beyond to which meaningful consideration can be given in the world is a beyond *in* the world and not a contrast to the world. The world is worldly and nothing but worldly, but the worldliness of the world is enacted dynamically as a permanent self-transcendence which, however, never leads beyond the world, but merely changes it.

Thus, Christianity is doubly implicated in the increasingly radical process of worldlifying the world: as the driving force behind the *worldlifying of the world into creation* through faith, and as the discontinuation point for the *worldlifying of the creation into a secular world* in contradiction to the Christian view of the world as creation. Where the former is concerned, Christian faith in God has, from its beginnings, acted to adopt and carry forward the culmination of the Jewish prophetic tradition in Jesus, in contradistinction to polytheistic religious practices and by outdoing traditional cosmotheological thinking as the embodiment of the disenchantment of the world into creation. As regards the latter, since the advent of modernity the Christian attitude to the created world has increasingly become the trigger for the worldlifying of creation into the universe, since Christians have not consistently upheld the fundamental distinction between the divine and the worldly in the creation concept, but have rendered it problematic in two respects. On the one hand, there were attempts to suggest that the created world's relation of transcendence with the creator can be deduced *from the created world* itself by treating teleologically interpreted natural phenomena (the beauty and order of nature), the natural structures by which the cosmos is ordered (laws of nature) and historical events and developments (the rise of Christianity, the expansion of Europe's power, the Lisbon earthquake) as signs of God's will and presence. It was said that world order, as seen in nature and history, follows a divine plan, making the transcendent God immanently present as architect, guarantor and controller of the cosmic and social world order.[13] On the other hand, despite the overturning of the enchanted world, distinctions such as *sacred / profane*, *monastic / secular* and *church / state* were re-established *within* the created world and presented as analogies for the fundamental orientating distinction between divine transcendence and creaturely immanence. Together these two approaches had disastrous consequences.

For one thing, this created a basis for perceiving every phenomenon that negated or disrupted world order (evil, wickedness) as calling in question the goodness of the divine order and as an argument against God's goodness (the theodicy problem). For another, the attempt to explain world order from a natural rather than a divine perspective (modern science) was classed, not just as secular, but as anti-God, and was misconstrued as questioning the createdness of the world – whether or not that was what was intended. In the *Great Debate* between naturalistic and theistic explanations of the world and its structures, this dispute around an unnecessary alternative has continued to the

---

[13] Cf. H.-M. Barth, *Atheismus und Orthodoxie. Analysen und Modelle christlicher Apologetik im 17. Jahrhundert*, Göttingen 1971; A. von Scheliha, *Der Glaube an die göttliche Vorsehung. Eine religionsgeschichtliche, geschichtsphilosophische und theologiegeschichtliche Untersuchung*, Stuttgart 1999; P. Michel, *Physikotheologie. Ursprünge, Leistung und Niedergang einer Denkform*, Zürich 2008.

present day.[14] Thirdly, the criticism, dismantling and rejection of the intra-mundane distinctions *sacred / profane*, *monastic / secular* and *church / state* in the course of modern secularisation movements in social philosophy, social theory, law and politics was likewise perceived as contesting the distinction drawn by creation theology between divine and worldly. The attempt to affirm the distinction between divine transcendence and worldly immanence *in the world* (by setting church and state over against each other) or practically (by comparing and contrasting clerical or monastic forms of life with the professional lives of other Christians) has thus contributed decisively to the undermining of the very thing it intended to encourage: the orienting of life on the basis of the fundamental distinction between God as divine and the world as worldly.

### *13. Three theological transcendence discourses*

It is therefore worth reading Christianity critically against the background of its own history and in the light of Christian faith, lest we fall victim to the misconception that we ought to defend something that is not to be defended. The distinction between transcendence (divine) and immanence (worldly) is fundamental for life orientation in the Christian faith. But here we are not referring to a repetition (re-entry) of this distinction on the immanence side (in whatever form), that is, not the various horizontal distinctions of anthropological self-transcending, but purely a repetition on the transcendence side in the

[14] Cf. E. H. Ecklund / J. Z. Park / K. L. Sorrell, Scientists Negotiate Boundaries Between Religion and Science, *Journal for the Scientific Study of Religion 50* (2011) 552–569; E. H. Ecklund, *Science vs. Religion: What Scientists Really Think*, Oxford 2010. There is a consistent disregard for the fact that only a fraction of scientists and social scientists in the USA see any conflict between religion (faith) and science.

form of divine self-transcending, which Christian thinking has encoded as creation, redemption – resurrection / incarnation, communication of the gospel / faith – and consummation. It is not a human capability for self-transcendence, but God's actual self-transcendence that is the decisive point of reference for Christian life orientation.

In order to be able to reconstruct the transcendence orientation of the Christian faith in adequate theological terms, therefore, we need to distinguish between three transcendence discourses, which focus in turn on *being* (ontological transcendence), on *being human* (anthropological transcendence) and on *being God* (theological transcendence).

The first of these (ontological transcendence) focusses on the *fundamental creation-theological distinction between transcendence (creator) and immanence (creation)*. It only exists where it is established from the transcendence side, and on the immanence side it is only ever discovered or experienced as established or given: it is not we who make ourselves into creatures, rather we discover our createdness as we become attentive to the self-differentiation of the creator from the creation. Since this does not obtrude itself upon us at any point in our experience of the world and of ourselves, we can only become aware of this fundamental creation-theological distinction where the creator reveals himself intelligibly in his self-differentiation from creation in the creation. The theological code for this is the *self-revelation of God*, who conceals himself as creator in the creation, as redeemer on the cross and as consummator in the future and who reveals himself *sub contrario* in these different ways. Seen in this light, revelation is in fact God's very concealment,[15] and this is precisely the necessary condition for being able to recognise the fundamental creation-theological

[15] Cf. I. U. Dalferth, Understanding Revelation, in: I. U. Dalferth / M. Ch. Rodgers (ed.), *Revelation*, Tübingen 2014, 1–25.

distinction between transcendence and immanence and to orient ourselves by it.

The second transcendence discourse focusses on the *horizontal transcending* or *self-transcending of humans* on the immanence side (anthropological transcendence). No transcending movement on this side is a moving-beyond; each is a deeper penetration into immanence. Human beings are human by the very fact that they reach out beyond themselves – epistemically, alteriologically and in the realms of ethics, aesthetics and religion. All these self-transcendings widen and deepen immanence; they do not move beyond it. They take place in the *Here* of immanence and do not attain the *There* of transcendence.

The third transcendence discourse focusses on the *kenotic self-transcending of the divine* on the transcendence side. Ontological transcendence is the necessary condition for anthropological transcendence: only where there is humanness as a worldly phenomenon of immanence can there be human self-transcending. But such an immanence is only present where divine transcendence differentiates itself from worldly immanence, and in so doing brings about such immanence. When the transcendent God himself differentiates himself from himself, he confronts himself in the repetition of this distinction (the God / God's Word, God / logos or Father / Son distinction). In this way he differentiates himself, not simply from what he is not, because it cannot be (the impossible), but also from what he is not, even though it can be (the possible) and from that which thereby becomes actual, even though it also could not have been (the contingent).

### *14. The priority of transcendence over immanence*

In intensifying the difference between the divine and the worldly by emphasising the transcendence of the creator and the immanence of the created world to an incommunicable fundamental contrast which cannot be bridged via any emanation stages, the Christian faith became a critic, both of the mythical forms of religion with their view of the world as a battleground of spirits, demons and similar forces and of Hellenistic philosophical cosmos theology with its tendency to reduce the divine to a cosmological ordering principle. This led to the quashing of each iteration of the fundamental difference between transcendence and immanence on the immanence side (even though the distinction was softened and blurred again before long). For this fundamental difference was understood from the outset, not as a human proposition or orientational convention, but as a divine proposition and hence as truth.

As such it must surely have been established *for someone*; in other words, it must not merely distinguish the divine and the worldly without confusion and without separation, but must clarify, *by whom* and / or *for whom* this distinction was established. The answer to this came through the iteration of this distinction not on the immanence side, but on the transcendence side. God himself establishes this distinction by differentiating himself from himself (God / Word of God; absolute transcendence / relative transcendence) and by repeating this distinction in the distinction between himself and all that he is not (transcendence / immanence) within the sphere of his divine transcendence (absolute transcendence [transcendence / immanence]) in such a way that he can also appear on the side of the immanence that he himself has established without jeopardising or losing his divine transcendence. Given that the transcendent God repeats himself eternally as himself in his Word within the horizon of his transcendence, he can repeat this repetition temporally in the immanence of the world, from which he distinguishes himself as its transcendent creator, in such a way that he can be recognised and understood in his transcendence in the world of human beings.

To put it another way: it is not human self-transcending on the immanence side that opens human beings up to the beyond of the divine transcendence. On the contrary, this takes place by means of a fivefold iteration on the side of divine transcendence: (1) in the eternal distinction of God from himself in his Word (first distinction between *God and God* by the self-repetition of God in his Word: absolute transcendence / relative transcendence), (2) in the differentiation of the world from himself and his Word in the creation (second distinction between *God, God's Word and the world* in the self-differentiation of God in his Word from all non-divine reality and possibility: absolute and relative transcendence / immanence), (3) in the temporal presentation of the Word in the immanence established thereby (third distinction between *God's Word and the story of Jesus Christ* in the self-presentation of the Word in the story of Jesus Christ: self-interpretation of the divine transcendence in worldly immanence), (4) in the communication of this self-interpreting self-presentation of God's Word in the story of Jesus Christ through the gospel (fourth distinction between *God's Word, Jesus Christ and the gospel:* self-communication of the divine self-interpretation in Jesus Christ through the gospel), and (5) in the human understanding of the gospel communication of this historical self-presentation of the self-differentiation of God from himself and creation through the Spirit in faith (fifth distinction between *Spirit, gospel and faith:* faith as the understanding and appropriation of the truth of the gospel from the self-presentation of the divine transcendence in the immanence of the world).

The whole process covers what Christian theology calls the *self-revelation of God* – the recognition of God as God through God's Spirit, at the place where the human being is. The differentiation between divine transcendence and worldly immanence takes place in faith as it relates to the presence of the Word through the Spirit *through God himself for human beings*. It takes place *for the human being,* to whom the fundamental creation-theological distinction between God and the world is thereby revealed as that to which he owes his existence and which he has not established himself. And it takes place *through God* in such a way that the whole process happens on the transcendence side and thus cannot be understood as a blueprint originating from immanence, since it is this process which makes possible all immanent processes, and not they which make it possible.

### *15. The impossibility of negating creation within the creation*

The crucial point is that this whole process of differentiation which is part of the fundamental distinction is carried out, not on the immanence side, but on the transcendence side. If this fundamental distinction is ignored or disputed, one does not maintain an immanent standpoint. Rather, once transcendence is negated, one's standpoint loses its immanent character as well. Nietzsche gave eloquent acknowledgement to this in his *Twilight of the Idols* in the chapter "How the 'true world' finally became a fable" as the final stage of his brief "history of an error": "The true world is gone: which world is left? The illusory one, perhaps? ... But no! *We got rid of the illusory world along with the true one*!"[16] Only in the relation of transcendence is there an immanent world. Without it all that remains is a world, and certainly not a creation.

However, the relation of transcendence, and with it the immanent character of the world, is not to be overcome by negating on

[16] F. NIETZSCHE, Wie die „wahre Welt" endlich zur Fabel wurde. Geschichte eines Irrthums, in: IDEM, *Götzen-Dämmerung oder Wie man mit dem Hammer philosophiert*, KSA 6, Berlin $^{2}$1988, 80–81, 81; How the 'True World' Finally Became a Fable: The history of an error, F. Nietzsche, *The Anti-Christ, Ecce Homo, Twilight of the Idols and other Writings*, ed. Aaron Ridley and Judith Norman, transl. by Judith Norman, Cambridge 2005, 171.

the immanence side the distinctions that are derived by means of iteration or developed culturally in the world from the fundamental difference. It is a fallacy to maintain that, by abandoning intra-mundane distinctions such as *sacred/profane, monastic/secular, church/state* and so on, or by secularising them and embedding them in worldly, social contexts, one can eliminate the world's relation of transcendence and live without reference to God in a world which is now purely worldly. A world which results from the eradication of the *sacred/profane* distinction is neither sacred nor profane, but it remains an immanent world as long as the relation of transcendence to God has not been effectively negated; as long, in other words, as it is only a difference *in* the world, not the fundamental difference *between* the world and God that has been eliminated. That, however, is inconceivable, since what would remain – from a theological point of view – would be not a completely natural world, but no world at all: Without the relation of transcendence the world would lose not simply its immanent character, but its very self. Given that this relation of transcendence is not an internal differentiation or structural order of the world, but owes its existence solely to the self-differentiation of the creator from his creation, it is true that on the immanence side the world can be ruined, but its relation of transcendence and createdness cannot be eliminated, negated and erased. Nothing that the world is in itself or of itself makes it a creation, but solely the fact that the creator differentiates himself from it. As long as that is the case, it is and remains a creation, whether or not this is perceived and honoured in the world.

No distinction in the world is a clear sign of the distinction between the world and God, which is why no negation of a distinction in the world can constitute the termination of the distinction between the world and God. The world's dependence upon transcendence cannot be deduced from any of the world's characteristics, since the very fact that it exists even though it need not exist – that it is, in other words, contingent – is not evident from that fact that everything that is (or was or will be) could also not be (or have been or come into being). The fact that each individual phenomenon is contingent does not mean that the existence of phenomena in general is contingent. Husserl drew quite the opposite conclusion: that while it is true that every world situation and factual circumstance can be called in question, the same cannot be said of the overall relationship of consciousness with the world. Heidegger, too, expressed this in his own distinctive way by describing existence as being-in-the-world, which does not first establish a relationship with the world in order to exist and act, but which can and must realise itself only on the basis of its relationship with the world. To state it in theological terms: the creation concept does not delineate a distinction within the world, but a distinction between the world and God. It is not that some things in the world are created and others are not: either everything is created or nothing is. Neither can be proved phenomenologically. Rather, both are determined according to *how* one sees the world and lives in it. To affirm the world as creation is not a theoretical statement, but a practical *difference of orientation* characteristic of those who orient themselves and their relationship with the world by the distinction between God and world. Nothing in the world corroborates the one any more than the other. It is only the practice or non-practice of this orientational difference in the human life that demonstrates whether a particular life is being lived in a Christian (or Jewish or Muslim) manner or not.

### *16. The worldlification of the world in Christianity*

Without this practical relationship the distinction between transcendence and immanence loses its point. That much was clear to Christian thinkers from early on. In his dialogue *Octavius*, the Roman advocate Minucius Felix, who became a Christian shortly before the end of the second century, defended the Christian faith against the criticism of its religious and political opponents.[17] Christians do not participate in any religious cult and

[17] In relation to what follows cf. M. MINUCIUS FELIX, *Octavius*, cap. XXXII, http://www.thelatinlibrary.com/minucius.html (11/12/2012): "Putatis autem nos occultare quod colimus, si delubra et aras non habemus? Quod enim simulacrum deo fingam, cum, si recte existimes, sit dei homo ipse simulacrum? Templum quod ei extruam, cum totus hic mundus eius opere fabricatus eum capere non possit? Et cum homo latius maneam, intra unam aediculam vim tantae maiestatis includam? Nonne melius in nostra dedicandus est mente? in nostro intimo consecrandus est pectore? Hostias et victimas deo offeram, quas in usum mei protulit, ut reiciam ei suum munus? Ingratum est, cum sit litabilis hostia bonus animus et pura mens et sincera sententia. Igitur qui innocentiam colit, deo supplicat; qui iustitiam, deo libat; qui fraudibus abstinet, propitiat deum; qui hominem periculo subripit, optimam victimam caedit. Haec nostra sacrificia, haec dei sacra sunt: sic apud nos religiosior est ille qui iustior.

At enim quem colimus deum, nec ostendimus nec videmus. Immo ex hoc deum credimus, quod eum sentire possumus, videre non possumus. In operibus enim eius et in mundi omnibus motibus virtutem eius semper praesentem aspicimus, cum tonat, fulgurat, fulminat, cum serenat. Nec mireris, si deum non vides: vento et flatibus omnia impelluntur, vibrantur, agitantur, et sub oculis tamen non venit ventus et flatus. In solem adeo, qui videndi omnibus causa est, videre non possumus: radiis acies submovetur, obtutus intuentis hebetatur, et si diutius inspicias, omnis visus extinguitur. Quid? ipsum solis artificem, illum luminis fontem possis sustinere, cum te ab eius fulgoribus avertas, a fulminibus abscondas? Deum oculis carnalibus vis videre, cum ipsam animam tuam, qua vivificaris et loqueris, nec aspicere possis nec tenere?

Sed enim deus actum hominis ignorat et in caelo constitutus non potest aut omnes obire aut singulos nosse. Erras, o homo, et falleris: unde enim deus longe est, cum omnia caelestia terrenaque et quae extra istam orbis provinciam sunt, deo plena sint? Ubique non tantum nobis proximus, sed infusus est. In solem adeo rursus intende: caelo adfixus, sed terris omnibus sparsus est; pariter praesens ubique interest et miscetur omnibus, nusquam eius claritudo violatur. Quanto magis deus auctor omnium ac speculator omnium, a quo nullum potest esse secretum, tenebris interest, interest cogitationibus nostris, quasi alteris tenebris! Non tantum sub illo agimus, sed et cum illo, ut prope dixerim, vivimus."

they recognise neither temple, images of God nor altars. But they have good reasons for this. Indeed, "What image should I devise for God, since the truth of the matter is that the human being is himself God's image? What temple shall I build to Him when this whole world, the work of his hands, cannot comprehend him?" The whole cosmos is God's dwelling, and the human soul is his sanctuary. Where *God* is concerned, one cannot make reference to any kind of worldly structures or religious phenomena in the human life, but solely to the fundamental antithesis between the world as a whole and the One who, through his self-differentiation from the world, unites its Many into a single Whole distinct from himself. And where the *knowledge* of God is concerned, one cannot point to specific worldly phenomena, but must hold to the place where God's presence can be discerned: the human being. In so doing the world becomes disenchanted through its distinction, in its entirety, from God, who distinguishes himself from it. The human being becomes the place where the world is afforded a clarity regarding its dependency on God which can nowhere be deduced from the world itself. And God is the one without whom the world would not exist, but who is wholly and entirely transcendent in relation to it.

That is not to say, however, that God will have nothing to do with the world or that he does not allow himself to be recognised by humans. On the contrary. While it is true that one cannot see God anywhere, one can recognise him everywhere. "In his works, in all the movements of the world, we see the presence of his power, whether in thunder and lightning or when the skies are clear. Do you suppose that this God knows nothing about the doings of the human race? Do you suppose he could not come down to each and every one of us from his throne in heaven, or that he does not know each of us? Then you are deceived and in error. How can God be far away! The whole of heaven and earth and everything beyond the circle of the earth is filled with God. He is near us everywhere. Far more than that: he is in us. Again, look at the sun! It has its place in heaven, yet its light is shed over every land. It is present everywhere alike. It penetrates everywhere. Nowhere is its brightness darkened. How much more is God present, who creates and watches over everything and from whom nothing can remain hidden! He is present in the darkness and present in our thoughts, which encompass a different kind of darkness. All our actions take place beneath his gaze. We live, I would almost like to say: together with him."

There is no phenomenon nor any distinction in the world, from which God's presence can be deduced more readily than any other. The correlate of God's transcendence is his universal presence. God is present, not just sometimes and with some people, but everywhere and with everyone. There is no need of special places, temples and images of God to remember his presence. This is not because it is obvious everywhere, but quite the opposite, because although it can show itself anywhere, it only shows itself incontrovertibly and in specific form where a human being understands himself or herself to be the place of God's presence. The distinction between the world and God has its significance in the fact that it is a distinction *for* the human being and in relationship to the human being. We can orient our lives by this when we recognise that we are God's creatures and neighbours, that the world in which we live is God's creation and that all other humans with whom we live in this world are God's neighbours. Although nothing can be explained where God is concerned, it is certainly possible to recognise that everything that exists does so only in God's presence.

### *17. The sacramental presence of transcendence within immanence*

That is not the only position adopted by early Christianity. Without calling into question the worldliness gained by the world through creation theology, others have emphasised the special significance of certain events in the world for the perception of the presence of God, pointing to the incarnation and the sacraments as examples. Augustine, too, underlines the fundamental dissimilarity of creator and creation, and thus the essential worldliness of the world: all the world's phenomena are signs (*res significantes [signifying things]*) which point to things (*res*), which, as *res significatae [things signified]*, are themselves always simultaneously res significantes to which one should not cling (*frui*), but which one ought to utilise (*uti*) as pointers towards God's transcendent truth, the only place where one can and should find rest. But this world-transcending truth has become present in the world in Jesus Christ; as such it has articulated itself in a way that can be understood, so that one can believe in it. And it does so even in the absence of Jesus, inasmuch as by Word and sacrament the Christological presence of the transcendence which has revealed itself in the world throughout the ages, is made present afresh to different people over and over again. So the sacraments are distinct from all other signs, in the sense that they make present that to which they point, even as they point to it, so that the correct use (*usus*) of them is in fact their enjoyment (*fruitio*). A distinction is therefore drawn *in* the world between what is merely worldly (profane) and what is holy (sacramental), and this appears to negate the strict distinction between the created world and the creator of the world: the fully transcendent God is himself present in the immanent world in Jesus Christ, in Word and sacrament.

However, even here the crucial point is that it is not the material, natural phenomenon which is the decisive factor, but the Word which is added, making water, bread or wine to be the medium and locus in which God makes himself present in the world. It is only the *Word*, that is its sacramental *use*, which turns the worldly phenomenon into a sign which mediates and reveals God's presence. In the immanence of the world there are thus specific places of transcendence – practices in which the transcendence of the *There* is revealed in the immanence of the *Here*, as the liturgical use of language adds value to the meaning of material, natural phenomena which they do not possess in themselves.

However, it has to be said that, even here, it is only *through someone* and *for someone* that they acquire this added value. It is only *for the human being* that the world becomes the place where, through the Word of God, transcendence and the immanent character of the world are revealed. And this is only the case when the differentiation between transcendence and immanence takes place *through God himself* – in his making himself present as Word and in the Word, and in the self-interpretation of his self-presentation through the Spirit in faith: Transcendence itself reveals its presence to the human within immanence; as humans we do not achieve transcendence through self-transcendence. Without the self-communication of transcendence, no self-transcending on the immanence side could ever attain this transcendence or orient itself by it. There is nothing in the world that represents the distinction between the world and God unambiguously. It only becomes unambiguously clear when the transcendent God himself makes himself comprehensible to humans in his transcendence by revealing to them that the place where they exist is the immanent correlate of his transcendence. This can come about in and with everything and in all contexts. But it only takes place when God's self-transcendence is enacted in the immanence of the world (which God is able to do because it is he, as creator, who establishes the distinction) and not as a self-transcendence of human beings into the divine transcendence (which human beings cannot do, because, as creatures, they can only transcend themselves and others within immanence). It is only as self-giving that God's transcendence reveals itself for human beings within immanence. But this self-giving underlines the distinction between God and all that is worldly, rather than establishing a distinction between the holy and the profane in the world. The world is the world and God is God, even where – indeed, precisely where – God effectuates himself as God in the world.

### *18. The Christian understanding of transcendence and its consequences*

From then on, three insights became normative for the Christian understanding of transcendence:

1) God is God and the world is the world. Where the world is concerned, God is wholly and entirely transcendent. Where God is concerned the world is wholly and entirely immanent (God / world distinction).

2) God's transcendence towards the world makes possible his unbounded and universal presence in the world. God's transcendence is not to be understood as an inaccessible remoteness, but as the condition upon which his still greater nearness to the world depends (God / God distinction).

3) The place where this can be recognised in the world is the human being. Not everyone recognises this, but anyone can. This does not take place automatically, but when God makes himself present to a human in such a way that it becomes possible to believe in his presence since it reveals itself as the presence of his love, meaning that, oriented to this love, one lives – not just factually, but consciously – in God's presence (God / human, or God / faith distinction).

Two things are particularly noteworthy here. Firstly, a double movement is being described: as God's divinity becomes wholly transcendent, the worldliness of the world becomes wholly immanent, with the human being as the place where the presence of divine transcendence is perceived within the immanence of the world. Secondly, while it is true that human beings can perceive God's presence everywhere, they are not compelled to do so.

With the elimination of every religious distinction within the world, not only does it become possible to find God's presence everywhere; it is also possible to cease to expect it. "With the disappearance of the enchanted world, an important obstacle to non-faith disappears."[18] As God becomes transcendent and the world becomes immanent this not only sets up the possibility of faith, but also advances the possibility of non-faith.

From then on, the history of Western thought and religion is defined by two lines: the line of faith and the line of non-faith, both of which have given encouragement, not only to clear, but also to less-clear thinking. Thus, for instance, in order to differentiate faith from non-faith and to strengthen the confidence of faith, the distinctions of the old disenchanted world, such as *sacred/profane, church/state* and *religious/secular*, were dusted down, thus setting up the preconditions for what became in modern times, from a scientific point of view, the critique of sacramental thinking and, from a societal point of view, secularisation. The cosmos idea of the old world was similarly reinvigorated, and attempts were made to enshrine it within the experiential processes of the world as the divine world order. Even the Reform movements of the 16th century, "which dispelled the ancient world of the spirits, and the new world order instituted by them, were animated by a Christian faith – or later by a deistic vision. This order followed the divine plan and made God present in another way. If he was no longer essential as a power in the sphere of spiritual powers, he became even more unavoidable as the architect, guarantor and spiritus rector [guiding spirit] of the cosmic as much as the social order."[19] This influenced even the founding documents of the USA, which were understood as the realisation of this divine order in the ordering of a human society: "The famous words of the Declaration of Independence bear

---

[18] TAYLOR, Ein Ort für Transzendenz?, 2.

[19] Ibid.

testimony to this: 'We hold these truths to be self-evident, that all men are created equal, that they are endowed by their Creator with certain unalienable Rights.' It was a matter of building a society that would put this into practice – and for the first time."[20]

In the French Revolution the tone was quite different, which shows that the other line was always present as well. The motto is no longer "one nation under God"; rather, the social and political order is founded on nature and reason, while expressly factoring out any reference to transcendence. This is precisely why we cannot characterise it as the basis for a life, existence and society that are purely immanent. Where transcendence is excluded, what remains is not an immanent world, but one that is still merely worldly. Reason, sympathy, altruism, morality – all these are now constructed without the relation of transcendence and are set up as a transcendence-free humanism in opposition to the traditional faith system.

Where the idea of transcendence is still picked up at all, it is construed strictly horizontally – as an epistemic, ethical, alteriological transcendence. This is expressly uncoupled from the earlier function of symbolising in the world the distinctions between transcendence and immanence, the divine and the worldly. The horizontal transcendencies of human life do not point to anything beyond themselves. Where once the issue was one's identity before God and others, today's focus is on – as Taylor puts it – "an expressivist culture steeped in an ethic of authenticity".[21] We are each, first and foremost, ourselves. That does not rule out the relation of transcendence. But it is no longer packaged with a way of life which may place obligations on others.

Admittedly it would short-change this position to describe it in purely negative terms. Charles Taylor gives specific examples

[20] Ibid.

[21] Loc. cit., 5.

of phenomena which he considers ought to be treated as places of transcendence by a current hermeneutic of transcendence: Humanitarian involvement is one such example: "I believe it is not an exaggeration to say that no previous culture has placed such high importance on the obligation of rendering assistance to other human beings, wherever it may be required and in the face of all adversity."[22] Another is "the search for meaning: For two hundred years our culture has confronted a problem of meaning. We are searching for the meaning of life. This means that human beings have the feeling that it is possible for life to be meaningless. This is new. In an era in which one is afraid of damnation, there cannot be any question of meaning. Everything has its own established meaning; the key question is, on which side one finds oneself, now and ultimately. Concern about meaning is a phenomenon confined to the world of the eclipse of God."[23] Or the artistic movements engaged in search processes, whether in poetry, music or painting, which establish entirely different symbolic systems that follow their own logic and neither have nor claim to have any further representational function for the worldly or the divine. Or the spiritual productivity associated with modern subjectivity, which is perpetually seeking new forms of inwardness and self-discovery.

If we just open our eyes we will find such phenomena of transcending everywhere. But what do they achieve? Such phenomena are not intra-mundane indicators of something extramundane, nor are they immanence phenomena of a transcendent world, but are ways of dealing with life occurrences that are new and different, unexpected and incomprehensible. This immanent transcending is no longer integrated into the fundamental creation-theological difference of vertical transcendence, which is why it cannot be re-established or reintroduced

[22] Loc. cit., 6.

[23] Ibid.

increasingly into discussion. No anthropological, religious or spiritual self-transcending, can ever, of itself, become a reliable indicator of the transcendence of God. People are interested in the process of transcending, but not in faith and religion, and when it comes down to it, they prefer to have spiritual interests rather than religious ones.

The fundamental creation-theological distinction with which faith is concerned can only be asserted in contrast to the intra-mundane process of transcending, not as its continuation and deepening. No such continuation and deepening can point beyond the immanence of the creation unless the transcendence of the creator himself is communicated and revealed in it. Yet recognition of the creation-theological *God/world* transcendence does not increase with the growth of spiritual interest – the churches have been aware of this for a long time. It hinges rather on two processes which have become very unlikely today: the *cosmological unification* of the world *into a whole by the One* who neither belongs to the world nor is a part of it; and the *anthropological positioning of the individual in relation to the One* through whom the world becomes whole for him or her, even though it can in no way be grasped or easily comprehended. Only when one is able to speak of the world in its *unity* (not just in its multiformity) and of oneself as an *exclusive individual* (not just as a particular instance of a universal), does the meaning of vertical transcendence in its fundamental distinction from immanence begin to enter one's field of vision: the process by which creation takes place through the *self-differentiation of God from the world*, leading, as *God makes himself present to the individual in the creation*, to the perception of God in the world.

Today the question of transcendence is no longer about the return of the gods or a fresh enchantment of the world, but about the recovery of the clear differentiation between the divinity of God and the worldliness of the world as a benefit for human beings and the world. In a secular world without orientation to

God or a post-secular world without any memory of God there is a constant risk, just as there is in an enchanted world, of the worldly replacing God (the idolisation of the worldly) and demanding unconditional allegiance without free insight (placing the humanity of the human being in jeopardy).

Nor indeed is human self-transcending exempt from such risks, since it is itself constantly ambivalent. It can be a *secular substitute* for orientation to divine self-transcending. Or a *post-secular form* of human self-transcending as one of numerous modes of transcending. Or indeed the enactment of faith, which attains an understanding of its own passivity as the ground of its creativity (gift-character), thus, within immanence, referring back to divine self-transcending.

The criterion for this is orientation to God's self-transcending which takes place in his *self-differentiation from the* creation and as *his making himself present to the individual in the creation*. This divine self-transcending is not an intensifying continuation, deepening or surpassing of human transcending, but is rather its critical clarification in the light of the *manner* in which God makes and has made himself present: as Father (Son, Spirit) in creation; as Son (Father, Spirit) in redemption; as Spirit (Son, Father) in consummation. So it is not the fact *that* human beings transcend themselves, but *how* they do it that matters: It becomes apparent from the *mode* of human self-transcending whether it is enacted from within the divine self-transcending or not. This is because the conduct of one's life will then draw upon something one can never set up for oneself: a distinction between immanence and transcendence that is not merely relative, but absolute. And to orient oneself thereby – that is, to allow the world to be the world, and God to be God – will mean that one expects to encounter God's presence everywhere, rather than nowhere.

## D. Faith or reason? Critique of a confusion

### *1. A false antithesis*

The distinction between faith and reason is repeatedly perceived as a conflict between faith and reason, in which either faith is criticised from the perspective of reason as unreason or as a fideistic hostility to reason, or reason is criticised from the perspective of faith as unfaith or rationalistic superficiality. This can take various forms, based on differing perceptions of 'faith' and 'reason', but it is always a fallacy. The negations occurring on both sides of the distinction demonstrate that the distinction between faith and reason must be understood another way. The opposite of faith is unfaith (or non-faith), not reason. And the opposite of reason is unreason (or non-reason), not faith. From a theological point of view, *faith* is a gift of God which makes it possible for human beings who are unaware of God's presence to trust in God's promise and to live lives that are good and right within the fellowship offered by the creator to his creatures. *Unfaith* on the other hand consists in actually ignoring or actively rejecting this gift of life. *Reason*, for its part, is the ability to determine, by means of correct differentiation, that one wishes to live one's life in a manner considered good for others and ourselves. And it is *unreason* not to do that, and to fail to perceive the opportunities open to one. *Unreason*, in other words, is not to make use of the abilities one has, to not value the uniqueness of the others with whom one lives, to ignore God's gifts even though one ought not to, or to reject them decisively and to live as if God did not exist. It is thus important to treat the comparison between faith and reason more carefully than is normally the case. What follows will take a closer look at this. I will begin with by supplying a clearer understanding of faith and belief[1].

## *2. The many sides of belief*

Is it human to believe? The question is not as strange as it seems. It certainly has many meanings. Are we talking about belief, and if so, in what sense? Or are we talking about human beings, and if so, from which perspective? Does the question suggest a thesis that is being advocated or one that is to be challenged? What would the counter-thesis be? 'Belief is inhuman'? Or 'non-belief is human'? Are we trying to say that humans believe but other living beings do not? Or that human beings only live in a human way when they believe? Or that while it is true that humans beings believe many things, they cannot know anything? Or that belief is the form in which humans know, whereas there are all sorts of other kinds of knowledge – in books, libraries, stock exchanges, public authorities, academies, publishing houses, business enterprises or on the internet?

Or perhaps it has nothing at all to do with *believing* (assuming factual probability: 'I believe that this or that is so'), but rather to do with *faith* (placing one's trust in a person: 'I believe you'; 'I have faith in you') or even to do with *faith in God*? Where *faith in God* is concerned, ought we not rather to say, *unfaith is human*, whereas faith is anything but, since faith can only ever be a divine gift, not a human ability, an attitude of which humans are

[1] Translator's Note: The German terms '(der) Glaube', '(das) Glauben' and ‚glauben' can mean either 'faith', 'belief' or 'believe' in English. The correct translation depends on the context. I have tried to use 'faith' for '(der) Glaube' and 'belief / believe' for '(das) Glauben / glauben' but this has not been possible throughout.

capable or a human asset? Ought we not to say, when it comes to *faith as trust*, that *it is by no means solely human to believe*, but is an ancient type of behaviour common to all gregarious animals; after all, cows follow the leader cow and a dog follows its master no less trustfully than some people follow some other people? And ought we not to state precisely, when speaking of *factual belief*, whether we are dealing with an *epistemological problem*: 'Belief is human, since all human beings strive for knowledge, and striving for knowledge is precisely what we mean by "believing" or "having faith"? Or whether the thesis under debate stems from the *sociology of knowledge*: 'To believe is human, since there can only be belief in the sense of human belief, whereas knowledge, as "the sum total of all organised information and its interdependent contexts, upon which a rational system must be based",[2] no longer has anything to do with human beings, but is merely a system-related concept?' Consequently, anyone who speaks of belief always implies that there is someone who believes. Anyone who speaks of knowledge, on the other hand, is not implying that there is someone who knows, but only that the knowledge alluded to exists somewhere and is represented somehow.

Belief is human, not to believe is human, believing is not just human, it is not only belief that is human – our thinking needs to take all that and more into consideration. Even the most generous thinker will not argue that the word 'believe' is used and understood in a similar way in all these instances. 'Belief' can have many meanings. What it actually means hinges on the context in which the word is being used, and these various concrete usages cannot be integrated into a single concept by means of unbridled oversimplification.

---

[2] Art. Wissen, *Wikipedia*, http://de.wikipedia.org/wiki/Wissen#Formen_des_Wissens (10/10/2011).

This plethora of meanings is one of the chief sources of the many misunderstandings associated with the subject of faith. So if we hope to have a tolerably sensible discussion on the subject, we will need to bear in mind a series of distinctions triggered by the use of the word 'believe' in everyday speech.

People believe that it is raining or that the government is getting things wrong; they trust in friends and in themselves; they put their faith in God or in wind power; they believe, trust or have faith in far more things in heaven and earth than one sometimes dares to dream of. All these manifold ways of speaking of 'believing' draw on differentiations which mark off what is meant from other meanings, thereby defining it. These differentiations can be summed up in four key distinctions, each of which provides a separate precise definition of the word 'believe': the *grammatical distinction between belief in a fact and trust in a person*; the *epistemological distinction between faith and knowledge*; the *anthropological distinction between faith and non-faith*; and the *theological distinction between faith and unfaith*. These key distinctions can be combined in various ways, but cannot be reduced to each other or to a common alternative. They provide the answer to different questions. For this reason they cannot be integrated into a univocal understanding of faith without diminishing and distorting them. In other words, there is not just *one concept* of faith, nor is there just *one problem at issue*: there are at least four different sets of issues. I shall explain this in more detail, albeit with appropriate brevity, under four headings.

### *3. The grammatical distinction: belief in a fact vs. trust in a person*

In German (and not only in German) the term 'believe' is used in three ways: firstly, in the sense of *holding a circumstance to be true* ('I believe something to be the case'); secondly, in the sense of *trusting a person* ('I trust someone'); and thirdly, in the sense of *reliance on someone* ('I have faith in someone').[3]

The first is a *theoretical attitude* rooted in the fact that what is believed does not come about because it is believed. A person who believes that it is raining does not believe that the rain comes about because of his belief; rather, when he notices the fact that it is raining, he believes it. He could, of course, be mistaken, in which case his belief is incorrect and he need not have taken an umbrella with him. But he does not have to *want* to believe what he believes; he cannot help but believe that it is raining once he notices it. Belief as holding something to be true does not originate with the will to believe; it is not the result of a decision, it is (not only, though in an important respect) the consequence of recognising a fact. A person who becomes aware that it is raining cannot decide not to believe it, however much he wishes it were not true, since that would be simply to close his eyes to reality. Holding something to be true is not the result of a decision to believe, nor can it be abandoned or overriden by means of a decision. If someone tries to do so, we are justified in considering him or her to be blind to reality, or perhaps ill.

But the same does not apply to the second and third use of 'belief'. Trust and reliance are *practical attitudes* which cannot exist unless one makes them the subject of a decision or upholds them through a resolution of the will. I do not have to trust anyone, but I can do so. I can follow the rule, "Do not trust anyone who has not proved trustworthy," or I can trust someone in order to give him or her the opportunity to prove trustworthy. If I ask someone on the street what time it is, I do not assume that she will lie to me; instead I trust the information she gives me, unless there is good reason not to do so. The maxim of trust, 'Trust everyone, as long as there is no reason (or no sufficient reason)

[3] Cf. I. U. DALFERTH, *Malum. Theologische Hermeneutik des Bösen*, Tübingen 2008/2010, 308–329.

not to,' is sensible and appropriate in one's dealings with fellow humans, friends or family members. However, when dealing with banks, public authorities or officials we would do better to observe the maxim of mistrust: 'Trust no one unless there is a reason (preferably a good reason) to do so'. Of course, both of the above maxims underline the fact that we can, but do not have to, trust other human beings. It follows that belief as trust can only exist as the result of a resolution of the will.[4]

Thus we use the word 'belief' to mean either theoretically *holding a circumstance to be true* (factual belief) or a practical *trust in* or *reliance on a person.* This can be given further substance.

### 4. *The epistemological distinction: belief vs. knowledge*

"All humans," wrote Aristotle in the opening sentence of his *Metaphysics*, "strive for knowledge by nature."[5] Knowledge is the knowledge of what is true, and if it transpires that what one thought one knew is not true, then one did not know it, one was in fact mistaken.

Aristotle contends that all humans strive for the knowledge of what is true. Did he not know human beings? Or was he not familiar with the distinctions between a particular sentence and a general sentence ('Some humans strive for knowledge') or between an assertion that something is the case and a wish that something is the case ('It would be lovely if at least a few humans were to strive for knowledge')?

[4] Cf. I. U. Dalferth, In God We Trust: Trust, Mistrust and Distrust as Modes of Orientation, in: A. Grøn / C. Welz (eds.), *Trust, Sociality, Selfhood*, Tübingen 2010, 135–152.

[5] Aristotle, *Metaphysics*, 980a 21: "πάντες ἄνθρωποι τοῦ εἰδέναι ὀρέγονται φύσει".

Aristotle was thoroughly familiar with all these distinctions, and was perfectly precise in his formulation of the opening sentence of the work later to be entitled the Metaphysics. Anyone who strives for something does not have it yet. If one had it, one would no longer be striving for it. But how can one strive for something if one does not know of it? Surely one must, at the very least, know that one does not know it in order to be able to strive for it?

It this were true, Aristotle's sentence would necessarily be incorrect. It would certainly not apply to every human being, but only, at best, to a handful of philosophers. In ancient Athens it was only Socrates who once applied it to himself. Aristotle put it more cautiously: We strive for knowledge, not because we know that we do not know, but 'by nature'. Humans are beings who strive for knowledge because as humans we cannot help but do so. It is not the knowledge that we do not know that makes us human beings; rather, it is because we are human that we strive for knowledge – without knowing what we are doing thereby and what it is that we lack. It is not knowledge but the striving for knowledge that is human.[6]

Our striving for knowledge already brings us fairly close to what would later be termed 'belief'. It is not part of this striving for knowledge to know that one is striving for it. It is belief that is human, not knowing that one believes. It is not necessary to know that striving for knowledge is human in order to be human. This was the way Joseph Simon understood it: "If the human being is perceived as the living being which *possesses* the logos, and the essence of something (τὸ τί ἦν εἶναι) is perceived as that *of which* the logos determines the nature (ὅσων ὁ λόγος

[6] So philosophers are merely a special instance of what we all do. They too are not those who know (σοφοί), but lovers of knowledge (φιλόσοφοι), so they strive for what we all wish for but do not have. It is just that they are aficionados of knowledge: they love to do what we all do, one way or another.

ἐστὶν ὁρισμός),[7] then we may *assume* that the human being possesses, in and of himself, the true definition of his nature, accordingly he determines the logos in which the essence of *all things* is expressed."[8] The human being knows who and what he truly is: the logos-being. If, however, the human being knows himself, he knows the logos, in and through which he knows everything that can be known. ΓΝΩΘΙ ΣΑΥΤΟΝ (know yourself) thus means, 'Know what you are (that is, logos): then you will know everything you are capable of knowing.' However this is rather more of a transcendental philosophical figure of thought[9] than the one expressed by that keen observer of humanity, Aristotle. Humans strive for knowledge *by nature*, but it is not the recognition that that is what they are doing that makes them human. Birth, not the first day of school, is the entry ticket to the human race.

To strive for knowledge *by nature* means that one is human to the extent that one strives for knowledge, because one *cannot help but do so* (and not because one *knows* that one is doing so or ought to do so). Philosophers differ from other human beings, not in that they strive for knowledge, but in that they know that they know nothing. But whether or not we know that: we are beings who strive for knowledge – that, according to Aristotle, is what marks us out as humans. But from whom and in what way does that mark us out?

Firstly, from those who *know* and are not just *striving* for knowledge. And secondly from those who *neither* know *nor*

---

[7] ARISTOTELES, *Metaphysik*, 1030a 6–7.

[8] J. SIMON, Horizonte der Wahrheit bei Kant, in: I. U. DALFERTH / PH. STOELLGER (eds.), *Wahrheit in Perspektiven. Probleme einer offenen Konstellation*, Tübingen 2004, 119–140, here 119.

[9] Cf. B. LONERGAN, *Insight: A Study in Human Understanding*, New York / London 1958, xxviii (in italics in the original): "Thoroughly understand what it is to understand, and not only will you understand the broad lines of all there is to be understood but you will also possess a fixed base, an invariant pattern, opening upon all further developments of understanding."

strive for knowledge. The first can be said of the gods or of God, whereas it can only be said of humans occasionally, in certain respects and imprecisely. Humans are not gods, and in most cases they do not know the truth, but must grapple with opinions. The other applies to animals: Admittedly they strive as well, although not for knowledge of the truth, but rather to secure what is necessary for their survival. Striving for knowledge is what differentiates human beings from animals and makes them like the gods. It is the gods who possess the truth. We strive to know it. Animals live without striving for it. Or, to put it another way: The gods know the truth. We strive for it. Animals have no interest in it.

According to Aristotle, the knowledge for which we strive is truth-related. This makes his metaphysical thesis interesting from a theological point of view. For if God is the truth, then to strive after knowledge, and hence after truth, is to strive after God. 'Belief is human' because it is not animals, but only human beings who strive after knowledge, and thus after the truth that is God.

The truth-relation thus becomes the central criterion for distinguishing between *knowledge*, *belief* and *opinion* as different ways of relating to truth. Here we have an unusual development: initially belief and knowledge focus on the same goal (truth), but knowledge is independent of belief (one who knows does not need – any longer – to believe). At this point belief becomes concentrated on what we do not know, but can only believe: divine truth. In contrast, modernity secularises belief and integrates knowledge into belief (knowledge is the limit value of a belief that is highly likely to be true). And today, either we speak only of *belief*, dispensing with the concept of knowledge, or else knowledge and belief are uncoupled so that knowledge functions as a system-related concept which no longer has anything to do with belief as a subjective assumption of probability. Here I will give a concise recapitulation of the key stages in our development of the problem.

## 5. From knowledge to belief

(1.) *Either knowing or believing*: Ancient thought – and here I am following Augustine's text *De mendacio*[10] – distinguished between *thinking* (*opinari*), *knowing* (*scire*) and *believing* (*credere*). *Thinking* in the sense of *opining* or *holding an opinion* is always associated with an error (*vitium*). A person who thinks in this sense believes he knows something that he does not know. As a result he stops seeking and therefore, in a state of false certainty, fails to examine his opinion and to move it forward into the realm of knowledge. One who believes, on the other hand, knows that he does not know what he believes, even though he is in no doubt as to its truth. For this very reason he endeavours to convert his belief into knowledge. After all, the one who has knowledge knows that what he knows is true, and that he cannot be in error.[11] This is because *knowing* (*scire*) is *semper sine vitio*, in other words always true. If something we thought we knew turns out to be incorrect, it becomes clear that what we possessed was not knowledge, but merely an opinion. Someone who knows no longer needs to believe, and someone who believes does not yet know and thus strives for knowledge.

(2.) *Both knowing and believing*: The essential features of this analysis of the relationship between *scientia*, *fides* and *opinio* was adopted by mediaeval thinking[12] and handed down in numerous different variations. Thomas Aquinas, for instance, gives the following definition: "fides est media inter scientiam et opinionem".[13] While it is true that belief does not have the certainty of verifiable knowledge, it goes beyond mere opinion, to the extent

---

[10] Cf. Dalferth, *Malum*, 309 f.

[11] K. Flasch, *Augustin. Einführung in sein Denken*, Stuttgart 1980, 314–326.

[12] Thomas von Aquin, *Summa Theologica* (STh.), IIa IIae q.1 a.1 und a.2.

[13] *STh.* IIa IIae q.1 a.2.

that "fides importat assensum intellectus ad id quod creditur."[14] On the one hand, *fides* is "movetur ab ipso objecto" (i.e. from that towards which it is oriented and in which it believes) to this *assensus*, while on the other hand it is also "per quamdam electionem voluntarie declinans in unam partem magis quam in aliam" (i.e. capable of a decision of choice which inclines deliberately towards one side rather than the other). If this decision is taken in a state of doubt and anxiety as to whether perhaps the other side might after all be the correct one, the result is an *opinio*, but if it is taken without any such anxiety, it is *fides*. Hence, whereas it is impossible that someone can simultaneously know and believe the same thing, it is by no means impossible that what one person knows, another merely believes.[15]

(3.) *Holding something to be true*: At the end the Age of Enlightenment this traditional analysis of belief was classically taken up by Kant in his *Critique of Pure Reason* and formulated as a distinction between three modes of holding circumstances or propositions to be true.[16] Someone who *thinks* something considers it possible, but is not convinced, either in respect of the fact (i.e. objectively) or in respect of himself (i.e. subjectively) that it is really so. Thinking, or holding an opinion, is a 'problematic' or 'provisional' judgement, which may turn out to be correct or incorrect. Someone who *believes* something, on the other hand, while subjectively convinced that it is not only possible but actual, has no objective grounds on which to defend the truth of his conviction as universally accepted knowledge. Belief is therefore an assertoric judgement concerning a fact that I hold to be true without being able to substantiate it. Someone who *knows* something is, after all, not merely subjectively convinced that it

[14] *STh*. IIa IIae q.1 a.4.

[15] *STh*. I q.1 a.5. "impossibile est quod ab eodem idem sit scitum et creditum. Potest tamen contingere ut id quod est visum vel scitum ab uno, sit creditum ab alio".

[16] I. Kant, *Kritik der reinen Vernunft*, B 851/A 823, AA III, 533–534.

is true (possible and actual), but has objective grounds for this which can be demonstrated to others. Knowledge is an apodictic judgement which articulates the substantiated certainty that the fact under discussion is true.

(4.) *Everything is belief*: Kant's attempt to place opinion (thinking), belief and knowledge in a sequence of increasingly stronger modes of holding something to be true was developed further in more recent approaches of doxastic belief within the framework of a logic of *belief*.[17] To believe that something is the case means to believe that it is more probable than its opposite.[18] Someone who believes that today is Friday believes that it is more probable that today is Friday than that it is some other day of the week. Knowledge and opinion thus become limit cases of belief. If we assign a circumstance a subjective probability between 0 and 1, depending on how we are inclined to treat it, then opinion, as a belief which subjectively considers the circumstance to be fairly improbable, offers a poor basis for rational action, whereas knowledge, as a belief that the circumstance is (almost) certain offers an excellent basis, while belief represents a more rational basis for action than opinion, but a less rational basis than knowledge. It follows that it is always advisable to convert opinion into belief and belief into knowledge in order to be able to live and act more rationally. But this conversion is not a transition to something categorially different from belief, but a heightening of the belief probability which guides our actions.

Knowledge thereby becomes a limit case of *belief*, while belief becomes the weak form of knowledge. Where with Aristotle we had 'Striving for knowledge is human', we now have 'Belief is human', where 'belief' is understood as a subject-based form of the probability-led holding-to-be-true.

---

[17] W. LENZEN, *Glauben, Wissen und Wahrscheinlichkeit*, Wien 1980.
[18] R. SWINBURNE, *Faith and Reason*, Oxford 1981.

However, this elegant solution comes at a price: on the one hand the concept of knowledge becomes systematically superfluous, while on the other hand the concept of belief is epistemologically short-changed.

### 6. *Of knowledge without belief*

First of all knowledge is defined, within the framework of the development outlined above, as *justified true belief*. A subject S knows p if, and only if, (1) S believes p (conviction condition), if (2) p is true (truth condition) and if (3) S has good reason to believe that p (justification condition). The conviction condition implies: *one can only know what one also believes*; the truth condition: *one can only know what is true*; the justification condition: *one must be able to give reasons for one's conviction*. Each of these conditions poses problems. But as Edmund Gettier has shown, the third condition is particularly inadequate, since one can easily construct examples which satisfy it without necessarily being able to state that knowledge exists.[19] For instance, I may have good reason to believe that the euro rescue mechanism will be effective because the government has declared it to be binding. In reality, however, the government has merely made this assertion because it wanted to remain in power, and did not in fact believe it itself. If the euro rescue mechanism is effective even so, I was right to believe that it would be, *but I did not know that it would be*, since my reasons were not good and correct but incorrect.

Much ingenuity has been expended to remedy these inadequacies and put forward a tenable definition of knowledge. But it appears virtually impossible to clear up the difficulties

[19] Cf. E. GETTIER, Is Justified True Belief Knowledge?, *Analysis 23* (1963) 121–123.

completely. Given this state of affairs, the following options exist:[20]

(1) *Not a concept, but a network.* One can argue, with Wittgenstein, that the everyday term 'knowledge' has no sharp boundaries, but that its various uses show, at most, family resemblances that one can describe more or less exactly, but cannot reduce to a conceptual core of necessary and sufficient conditions.

(2) *Not one, but various concepts.* One can attempt to understand 'knowledge' as a diffuse or complex concept and specify typical characteristics for what qualifies as knowledge in certain contexts without adhering to a unified concept of knowledge.[21]

(3) *Uncoupling of knowledge and belief.* One can reduce the concept of knowledge entirely to its information content aspect and concur with Robert Solso's definition of knowledge as "storage, integration and organisation of information in the memory".[22] Or adopt a still more general definition without reference to the memory: "Knowledge is organised information; it forms part of a system or network of structured items of information"[23] which is implemented in different media and institutions, by no means only or even primarily in human thought and recall. Belief may therefore be human, but knowledge is not.

(4) *Dispensing with the concept of knowledge.* Finally, as Ansgar Beckermann suggests, one can "dispense with the concept of knowledge entirely. There is no interesting epistemological question or proposition that could not be formulated equally well

---

[20] Cf. Art. Wissen, http://de.wikipedia.org/wiki/Wissen#Formen_des_Wissens (10/10/2011).

[21] N. Gottschalk-Mazouz, Was ist Wissen? Überlegungen zu einem Komplexbegriff an der Schnittstelle von Philosophie und Sozialwissenschaften, in: S. Ammon et al. (eds.), *Wissen in Bewegung. Dominanz, Synergien und Emanzipation in den Praxen der 'Wissensgesellschaft'*, Weilerswist 2007, 21–24.

[22] R. Solso, *Kognitive Psychologie*, Heidelberg 2005, 242.

[23] G. Reinmann-Rothmeier /H. Mandl, Art. Wissen, *Lexikon der Neurowissenschaften*, Band 3, Heidelberg 2001, 466.

without this concept. What is the goal of our cognitive efforts? Truth."[24] And everything we want to say on the subject, we can say with the concept of *belief*.

The outcome of this development is paradoxical. It appears that on the one hand it is only the concept of belief that is important, while on the other hand it is only the concept of knowledge.

*Epistemologically*, the concept of knowledge is dismissed: it can be used in everyday language, but not in the scientific sphere, since it cannot be defined with precision and everything important can be said without it. 'Belief is human' since all knowledge can be traced back to belief.

From the point of view of *cultural and scientific theory*, in contrast, the concept of belief is no longer important, but only the concept of knowledge: In our society *knowledge systems* are information stores which far exceed everything an individual human being could know. Human belief as a striving for knowledge no longer offers any useful starting point from which to explain or comprehend this. By *belief* we mean the assumption of probability with which we respond to specific possibilities in specific situations. And it is against this background that we say 'belief is human': Belief as an assumption of probability is a preliminary, shrunken form of knowledge. In an information society one should not foster belief but strive for knowledge.

This understanding of knowledge of course disposes of any reference to the human being along with any reference to belief. Knowledge is explicated in terms of system theory, and belief only plays a role to the extent that it too is understood in terms of system theory.

In view of this development, the proposition 'belief is human' can be heard as a protest against the attempt to reduce belief to

---

[24] A. Beckermann, Zur Inkohärenz und Irrelevanz des Wissensbegriffs. Plädoyer für eine neue Agenda in der Erkenntnistheorie, *Zeitschrift für Philosophische Forschung* 55 (2001) 571–593.

the operation of a system which can be explained on the basis of probability theory. This is because trust in a person no longer plays a part, but only belief in a fact. Or worse still: Trust in a person is understood in accordance with belief in a fact, which is developed along the lines of an objective system knowledge, not those of human life. Where once there was a human being, only a system remains. Concentration on knowledge has displaced not only belief, but even the human being. Consequently, we have lost the horizon within which it was important to enquire about belief and knowledge at all. In order to understand belief, we must therefore now turn to understanding humans and what is human, and examine the other two key distinctions from our list.

### *7. The anthropological distinction: belief vs. non-belief*

If human beings are considered in their capacity as believers – and this is certainly one particular way of looking at them – then their belief can be described anthropologically, not only in a theoretical sense as a holding something to be true ('Belief is human', since human beings can only survive if they behave in a manner appropriate to the situation), but also in a practical sense as trust in and reliance on others.

In a theoretical sense, we typically define 'belief' by contrasting it with *knowledge* or *action* or *both*. Thus belief is understood *cognitively* as being different from knowledge. This could be as a mutually exclusive contraposition (belief is not knowledge, knowledge is not belief: 'Someone who believes something does not know it, and someone who knows something does not need to believe it.') Or it could be as an inclusive contraposition (belief is a weak form of knowledge, while knowledge is a strong form of belief: 'Someone who believes considers something to be more or less probable; someone who knows has reasons for considering the existence or occurrence of something to be highly probable.') Or belief is described *pragmat(ist)ically* (in an action-oriented way) in the sense of a subjective assumption of the probability of acting in a specific way or of doing or not doing something specific: ('What someone believes is apparent from what he is prepared to do.') Or belief is defined in an *emotion-oriented* way as a mode of experiencing something or indeed oneself: ('The experience of someone who believes is aligned with his or her life.') Or it is defined anthropologically as a basic existential feeling: ('Belief is the basic prereflexive trust, without which one can neither live nor ask questions about life.')

In all these instances belief is described as an operation that creates, cognitively or emotionally, a mental representation of something that is given independently (thus 'holding it to be true'), bringing it to consciousness more or less clearly. 'Belief is human,' since human beings can only live and survive by gathering information from their environment and processing it mentally in such a way that they can behave in a manner appropriate to a given situation and act with a prospect of success. Someone who – in this sense – does not believe, is not only failing to live in a human way, but will very shortly not be alive at all.

From a practical point of view, on the other hand, belief is an *attitude of trust* in other people, which, under differing sets of conditions or circumstances, can be variously understandable or sensible, wrong or right. Admittedly, one can argue over each individual instance as to whether it is reasonable or unreasonable to place one's trust in a certain person or to rely on them. But human beings are not solitary predators who rely solely and exclusively on themselves, but are socially gregarious animals who do not live alone, but with others. Thus an instance in which a human at no point relies on or places his or her trust in another must be inconceivable, or at any rate extremely rare. In any concrete instance the confidence may be misguided or the decision to trust may be wrong, but the fact that human beings take a decision to trust at all is part of their humanness: belief – in this sense – is human, since human beings are fellow human beings, that is, they live in fellowship with each other. It is true that human beings are animals, but these particular animals can live in a human or an inhuman way. As members of the human race, they have shaped their coexistence with others so that it is possible for them to believe that they can place their trust in each other and rely on each other.

The thesis 'belief is human' is thus to be understood not only against the background of the *biological human/animal distinction*, but also (and primarily) against the background of the *anthropological human/human distinction.* Belief is not something that distinguishes human beings from animals in a fundamental way (after all, cows, dogs and birds are also aware of changes in their environment and place trust in others and, indeed, in each other). But the way in which human beings live out their belief is a decisive factor in whether they are living a human or an inhuman life, a life of human dignity or not. Where the circumstances are such that everyone must be distrusted and one cannot rely on anyone, it is just as difficult or even impossible to lead a human life as it is in a situation where the basic requirements for sustaining life are not present.

The real challenge of the thesis 'belief is human' lies, not in the fact that one spends one's entire life avoiding holding anything to be true, but rather that one cannot live a truly *human* life without being able to trust and rely on others. Belief as a mode of *biological survival* is one thing, belief as a mode of *human coexistence* is another and faith as a mode of *human life together before God* a third. What is at issue is not the biological *question as to what is human*, but the anthropological *question as to the humanness of the human*, and the theological answer to this question is that, where human life before God is concerned, the distinction is between whether one orients oneself thereby (faith) or not (unfaith).

### *8. The theological distinction: faith vs. unfaith*

In theological terms this is expressed as the distinction between *faith* and *unfaith*. I shall limit myself to four comments.

(1.) *The modal understanding of belief.* So far we have been discussing forms in which 'believe' is understood grammatically either as a noun (faith, belief) or as a verb (to believe = *cum assensione cogitare*). As a noun, belief is differentiated from knowledge and action, while as a verb it is differentiated from to know and to think. Here in contrast, 'to believe' is construed neither as a noun nor as a verb, but modally, adverbially or (in a metaphorical sense) locally – in other words not as 'Peter believes', but as 'Peter lives *believingly*' or '*in a believing manner*' or '*in faith*'.

Now it is possible to consider each living human being and to distinguish between the fact *that* he is (existence), *what* he is (definition) and *how* it comes about that he is, and that he is what he is (mode). The first raises the existence question (Does Peter exist?), the second the definition question (Who or what is Peter?) and the third the question of mode (How does Peter live or exist?). The question of mode can be asked from two standpoints: with regard to how humans conduct their lives (their mode of life), and with regard to how humans exist as they conduct their lives (their mode of existence). Both of these questions can be asked in a descriptive sense (How do humans actually live or exist?) or in a normative sense (How should humans live or exist in order to live well or aright?). The descriptive questions can be answered historically or empirically by the appropriate humanities disciplines. In the normative sense, however, the first instance relates to the moral question of the difference between a good life and a bad life, while the second instance relates to the existential question of the difference between a right life and a wrong life. The subject of ethical reflection is the nature of a good life (How *should* we live – as humans amongst humans, as human beings amongst other living beings?), whereas the subject of theological reflection is the nature of a life that is right and true (How *can* we exist – before God, with God, through God?).

While there can be various different ethical answers to the moral question, the existential question can have only one answer from a theological point of view, namely that human beings exist before God in one of two modes: *faith* or *unfaith*. Both are possible modes of existence for every human being and, where God's presence is concerned, they are the only two.

Thus the theological distinction answers the question as to the How of human life, not in terms of how a human being lives out what he is (the question of the mode of life), but in terms of how, in living, he fulfils his existence *before God* (the question of the mode of existence). The question 'How does Peter live?' and the answer: 'rationally or irrationally, trustfully or hopelessly, religiously or irreligiously' is one thing. The question 'How does Peter exist *before God*?' and the answer: 'in faith or not in faith' is quite another. Just as saying that Peter exists contributes nothing to the definition of who and what Peter is, neither does saying that he believes (or does not believe). One provides much more information about *how* he exists, and indeed much more exact information as to how he exists *before God* and how his life is to be judged, if one considers that and how it is conducted in the light of God's presence.

This is not a perspective which is immediately obvious. In fact, the How-question can be answered on various levels [and in ways that build upon each other], by defining, in a process of increasing concretisation, the How of what it is to be human biologically as *humanness* (*human / non-human*), the How of humanness ethically as *humanity* (*human / inhuman*) and the How of humanity theologically as *love of God and neighbour* (human / divine) which is lived out in faith but not in unfaith.

(2.) *The religious vs. the theological understanding of faith*. The theological distinction does not describe a religious life phenomenon, but highlights a practical orientational differentiation. It does not serve as a way of sorting phenomena or classifying people, but is based on the human attitude to the presence of God as a fundamental alternative. But this cannot be described in phenomenological terms any more than can the modes of existence of belief and unbelief. As an orientational differentiation of a theological kind they are just as little independent of those who orient their lives by God's presence as the distinction between *left* and *right* is independent of those who orient themselves thereby in space.

But this means that it is necessary to distinguish between the *religious description of faith* and the *theological judgement about faith*. From the point of view of practical religious life, 'faith' is seen as a way in which humans conduct their lives, and is understood as *trust and reliance on God*, or on what one takes to be God, whether one calls it 'God' or not. Someone who has faith places his trust in his 'God', i.e. in that to which one looks for help when one is in need. This practical approach to life can occur at all levels of conviction – confident, sceptical, questioning, doubting – and in all hybrid forms of faith and superstitious belief. Someone who has faith places his trust in 'his God' (whether or not he calls it 'God'), but what 'God' means, and whether the term 'God' actually identifies anything, whether the true God or an idol or false god, cannot be clarified beyond doubt in phenomenological terms. Faith and superstitious belief cannot be distinguished descriptively with the aid of anthropological or religious phenomena, but only in orientation towards God. God's presence, however, is not a life phenomenon, but that which qualifies the phenomena of life in their entirety as the realm of his operation and thus as his creation. It is the operator which makes the world the creation, which stands in front of the brackets which enclose all worldly phenomena, which is precisely why it does not itself appear phenomenologically within the created world. Hence it is not natural for us to be mindful of God's presence (i.e. to live in faith); on the contrary, it is natural that we are not mindful of it (i.e. to live in unfaith).

In theological terms, accordingly, 'faith' is understood as a mode of human existence before God and is defined as the *overcoming or negation of unfaith* ('One who believes has undergone a life-changing transition from unfaith or non-faith to faith'), from a view and practice of life which knows only what is worldly to a view of the world as creation. In this sense, faith only exists as a turning away from unfaith – whether 'faith' as the actual ignoring of God's presence, or superstitious belief in an idol which is erroneously held to be God or the active denial of belief in God as error, fantasy or malicious deception on the part of human beings. One way or the other, believers *are no different* from non-believers, but they *live differently* insofar as their lives are characterised by thanksgiving and petition, praise and lament to God.

Neither the characterisation of religious belief (trust in God) nor the theological understanding of belief (the overcoming of unbelief) are to be understood as contributing to the definition of the humanness of humans as distinct from animals. If they are understood in this way, they are misunderstood. The question to which they provide the answer is not: 'What is a human as distinct from an animal?' Rather, it is the other question of importance – for the most part greater importance – for the way we live our lives: 'What does it mean to live together with others in a human, not an inhuman, way?' This question cannot be answered within the biological context of life, but only in the anthropological context of human coexistence with others. Where theology is concerned, this takes place by working out the answer provided by the Christian faith within the context of the relationships between God and humanity. This leads to the understanding of faith and unfaith as possible modes of existence of every human being – indeed as the only ones possible where God's presence is concerned: Anyone who lives believes or does not believe (i.e. lives in faith or not in faith). This is precisely why they are not options which allow for a neutral choice. Someone who believes always has unbelief behind him, so that he cannot be perceived as believing without this being understood negatively, as a turning away from an unbelieving life, and positively, as a turning towards a believing life in the presence of God. Unfaith is thus the universal mode of the old life (which applies to every human being), whereas faith is the universal mode of the new life (which can apply to every human being).

(3.) *Existential interruption and reorientation of life.* However, no one makes the transition from unbelief to belief of themselves – it is only *in faith* that one is able decide for or against unfaith, whereas one never decides *in favour of faith*, since in unfaith the decision is impossible and in faith it is unnecessary. Thus a life of faith includes the acknowledgement that one has come to faith, not through one's own reasoning and powers, but through God himself, and that it is through him that one has been brought to change one's mode of existence.

This may happen slowly and gradually or suddenly and unexpectedly. One way or another the key theological distinction marks a fundamental change of mode of one's human existence before God, which can be encoded negatively as an existential interruption of one's life hitherto (dislocation and disorientation) and positively as a new orientation to God in the light of this interruption (reorientation). This reorientation does not merely add an extra aspect, hitherto overlooked, to one's life up to that point. God is not one Something amongst others, not even an *ens necessarium et realissimum*, a wholly necessary and fully defined Something, but with God everything is involved, and indeed in a new and different way. When one relates to God in a life-orienting way, it is not only God whom one understands differently (as one's creator), but also oneself (as a creature) and the world (as God's creation). Such people live in a different world of meaning with its own semantic – no longer merely in the *world*, but in the *creation*, no longer merely as *human beings*, but as *creatures*, no longer merely as *members or non-members of a religious community*, but as *believers* or *non-believers*.

(4.) *New orientation of life by the presence of God*. In this world of meaning the ethical question as to the meaning of shared humanity is answered in a new way through the practice of love of God and neighbour. '*To believe* is human' now means that believers live *differently*, in that they recognise, not simply fellow humans, but neighbours – humans to whom God is just as close as he is to them, whose dignity thus consists, not in what humans attribute to them, but in what God sees in them. However, human beings have no control over this, meaning that human dignity is something over which humans have no authority.

This does not mean that a morally good life must of necessity be a life of faith. On the contrary: one can lead a morally good life both in faith *and* in unfaith, but a life that is *right* before God can be lived *only in faith*. Faith and unfaith are not modes of living a moral life (the distinction between a good and bad life), but modes of existence before God (the distinction between a right or wrong life). Someone who leads a life that is wrong before God is not necessarily therefore a morally bad human being, nor does moral failure exist only in those who do *not* orient themselves by God's presence.

Conversely, a morally good life is not the same as a life that is right in faith: One can live either more or less morally, but no increase in the morality of one's life will lead one from unfaith to faith, or from a life that is wrong before God to one that is right before him. Between unfaith and faith there is an existential chasm which cannot be crossed from a position of unfaith, and which can in fact only be perceived retrospectively from a position of faith. The life of faith thus includes the acknowledgement that one owes the change, not to oneself, but to God alone – and the metaphors of the new life, of birth and new birth, of death and resurrection and of the gifts of life and of faith emphasise this.

### *9. The possibility of having faith*

The theological understanding of belief as faith cannot be reduced to one of the other understandings nor can it be adequately unfolded with their aid. It is an understanding of belief *sui generis*, which cannot be understood correctly within either the context of the epistemological differentiation between belief and knowledge, or that of the anthropological differentiation between belief and non-belief. In other words, it cannot be adequately grasped either as the holding of a circumstance to be true or as a trust in or reliance on a person. All this exists in the life of faith no less than in the life of unfaith. The difference between faith and unfaith, however, is not a distinction between particular ways of conducting one's life, but a distinction relating to the mode in which a life is lived before God, so that it concerns and qualifies everything one is, does and experiences: people live (where God is concerned) either believingly or unbelievingly. *Tertium non datur.*

Hence *both are human*: to have faith, since there are people who live believingly; and not to have faith, since no one lives believingly of their own accord.

The only conclusion to be drawn (but a satisfactory one, nonetheless) is: it is *possible* for humans to have faith. But this possibility is not an ability; it is not dependent on whether one is "religiously musical or unmusical" (Habermas); rather it depends upon a realisation that the source of one's existence is a mystery that is neither created by faith nor nullified by unfaith, but which is the prerequisite for both: for a life in faith *and* for a life in unfaith. The fact that every human being *can* believe does not mean that every human being *must* believe or indeed *will* believe. But it certainly does mean that without God one cannot even *not* believe in God.

### *10. Reason and faith*

If one takes this theological understanding of belief as one's starting point, there are consequences for the rational critique criticism of belief. This can have various meanings, since the genitive always conceals ambivalence and ambiguity. Undoubtedly well-known criticisms have been voiced from time immemorial, in the name of reason, of belief and its zealous aberrations: there is no need for me to call these to mind. But there is an equally well-known kind of criticism by faith of reason, which – ostensibly – dissects life with a cold gaze and reduces its diverse aspects to pale abstractions: this criticism is just as familiar. If it were clear what is meant by 'reason' and 'faith', it might be possible to know what the issues really are. But it is not clear. Not because it is impossible to define the two terms, but because there are too many mutually irreconcilable definitions – of 'reason' as well as of 'faith'. Both are systematically ambiguous, and this ambiguity cannot be remedied semantically without it breaking out pragmatically somewhere else.

It is no accident, as we have seen, that, in philosophical and theological discourse, both terms function, not as clear and distinct concepts, but rather as formulae and indications, complex in their definitions, which point to various problematic areas, and rarely both to the same area at the same time. *Reason* and *faith* can be related to each other and distinguished from each other in many different ways, and the formula 'reason and faith', when used to define a problem, has had very different meanings in the 12th, 16th, 18th, and 21st centuries.

Misunderstandings were and are therefore guaranteed, and the game of criticism and counter-criticism can be opened up at any time by either side. After all, which of the sets of problems represented by these formulae should one pick up? Which understanding of 'reason' or 'faith' is normative? Where are the boundary lines between faith and reason? How and where are they crossed, if at all? Who determines whether what faith believes and reason criticises is valid? Is it reason that decides, as some maintain, or is it faith, as others argue? And how do we measure the validity of what faith criticises and what reason believes? By faith, as some would assert? Or by reason, as others state with equal conviction?

The answer is not immediately obvious. Familiar distinctions in our understanding of reason (*per, contra, supra rationem*) or in our understanding of faith (*fides qua, fides quae*) do not suggest a clear verdict. Nor does it help to attribute the distinctions to philosophers or theologians, labelling the first (positively) as people of reason or (negatively) as rationalists, and the second (positively) as defenders of faith or (negatively) as fideists: As if faith could or should be defended by being safeguarded or immunized against the objections raised by reason, or as if reason's strength lies in putting belief in its place or, like a rational Baron Munchausen, in asserting its own rationality over the irrationality of faith.[25] Philosophers have not arrogated reason to themselves, any more than theologians have with faith. Both of them can be confused about either, as indeed they usually are.

So if we wish to avoid the endless loop of hackneyed debates, it is worth defining the problem at issue. This cannot be done in a neutral manner, since not everyone has the problem with reason

---

[25] This misguided thought form still dominates debates in Catholic fundamental theology. Cf. M. Breul, *Religion in der politischen Öffentlichkeit. Zum Verhältnis von religiöser Überzeugung und öffentlicher Rechtfertigung*, Diss. Phil., Catholic Theology, University of Cologne, 2014, esp. Chs. 2 and 5.

and faith. The definition of a problem is driven by one's particular interests, and one is inevitably interested in making an issue of those questions which are important to one, for whatever reason. Scepticism and atheism, both old and new, attest to this, no less than religious fundamentalism and theological dogmatism of all eras.

## *11. Reason of faith or reasonable faith?*

But even when one manages to avoid these extremes, the question is still driven by particular interests. Someone who seeks to clarify how faith comes to offer a reasonable insight, verifiable by others, into one's own ground and substance will conceive of the problem as a question of the *reason of faith*. Studies of variations on this question can start from Augustine and take in Anselm, Nicholas of Cusa and Calvin, right through to Schleiermacher, Kierkegaard and Barth, and it is no accident that again and again we find an understanding of reason that encompasses a faith's critique of an understanding of reason that disregards faith: The reason of faith takes the form of a critique of reason by faith in the *subjective genitive*.

Conversely, anyone who seeks to show how one can safeguard oneself against the exaggerated claims of uncritical enthusiasm without completely rejecting faith as unreasonable, will define the problem, along with Locke, Hume, Kant, Hegel and Hartshorne, as a question of *reasonable faith*. As the rational critique of faith, this takes the *objective genitive* form, since such a critique limits reasonable faith to that which satisfies the universal criteria of rationality – criteria which are applicable, not just here, but in other considerations of what deserves to be called reasonable. This leads in turn to the dispute over what can and should be a valid criterion – reality or epistemic demonstrability? Certainty or formal universalizability? Persuasiveness or integrability? The answers demonstrate that it is at this point that the contrast between the two routes of reason of faith or faith of reason is repeated.

But their actual point of divergence lies elsewhere. While on the first route faith is not affected in any crucial way if its reasonableness cannot be verified, on the second route, no faith remains unless its reasonableness can be demonstrated. In the first instance (the question of the *reason of faith*) faith comes first and reason comes second, whereas in the second instance (the question of *reasonable faith*) reason comes first and faith comes second. The maxims by which one orients oneself vary accordingly: '*If the reason of faith cannot be demonstrated (in one way), then try another way of demonstrating it*' or '*If faith cannot be shown to be reasonable (in the established way), then stop believing*'.

If one follows the first maxim and enquires into the *reason of faith*, one is starting from a position of faith and using a variation of the *fides quaerens intellectum* method. If one follows the second maxim and enquires into *reasonable faith*, one is starting from a position of reason and using a variation of the rational critique of faith method. The two methods only give comparable results if one assumes that reason and faith have the same, or a comparable, meaning in each instance. But this is precisely not the case. If one starts from faith, one bases one's understanding of faith and reason *within the context of faith*, whereas if one starts from reason, one defines reason and faith *within the context of reason* in order that reason can at least relate to faith.

John Locke, for instance, allows reason the last word, rather than faith, so that although reason cannot pass judgement on the revealed truths believed by faith, it must presumably judge whether those truths have been revealed at all. He can only do this because he sets *faith* and *reason* in opposition to each other in such a way that, although he assigns them each *distinct provinces*, in that they arrive at their insights via different routes (*revelation* and *sensation or reflection*), he nonetheless relates them to each other so that they are measured by a shared principle: *the truth of propositions*. Thus *reason* is defined as "the discovery of the certainty or probability of such propositions or truths"[26] as we can arrive at using our natural faculties (*sensation* and *reflection*), whereas faith is the assent to propositions which are believed, not on the basis of our own deductions of reason, but of external authority as God's revelation. While it is true that reason may not be in a position to prove the truth of these faith propositions, yet "it still belongs to reason to judge of the truth of its being a revelation, and of the signification of the words wherein it is delivered".[27] Faith truths, admittedly, go beyond reason, but it is for reason to decide whether they really are faith truths and how they are to be understood.

This solution is only possible because, alongside the truth of propositions, Locke introduces a third element, with respect to which reason and faith can be compared in the context of reason. Without this third element the comparison would be impossible, since every comparison compares something with something else *in relation to something*. This applies in the context of reason no less than in that of faith. But such problems are guaranteed if, as in the case of Locke, this third element (truth) is conceived from the start within the context of one of the two problem formulations, given that the truth of propositions is in fact reason's specialism. This means that curtailments are inevitable, since faith is reduced to one aspect in the perspective of reason, and is therefore measured by it.

However it is not just on the reason route that this is a problem. The same is true the other way round, if reason is curtailed in the light of a third element resulting from the prerequisite of

---

[26] J. Locke, *An Essay Concerning Human Understanding*, Book IV, Chapter XVIII: Of Faith and Reason, and their Distinct Provinces, *The Works of John Locke in Nine Volumes*, Vol. 2, London 1824, 263.

[27] Loc. cit., 269.

faith. If either of these third elements appears, whether in the sphere of reason or that of faith, or even in both, then reason needs to be conceived of according to faith prerequisites or faith according to reason prerequisites so as to be able to relate them to each other. However this means that the relationship between them is being construed in accordance with a positionally determined third element and therefore at the cost of a fundamental curtailment. If the relationship between faith and reason can only be conceived of by curtailing either faith or reason or both, then the construal of their relationship poses more problems than it solves.

### *12. In the context of the third element*

However, that is not the only option. If we take as our starting point, not an underlying similarity, but an essential difference between reason and faith, then neither can they be differentiated from each other on a similar basis, nor can they be said to be arguing over the same territory of meaning or truth. In that case, they are not on the same level semantically, so that there is no objectively relevant opposition between reason and faith. As Schleiermacher and Barth saw, each in his own way, the two do not share a common scale which would allow them to be compared and distinguished: reason is not "more" than faith any more than faith is "less" than reason. Nor is reason "other" than faith any more than faith is "other" than reason. Faith's "other" is unfaith, not reason. And reason's "other" is unreason, not faith. So the two do not rule each other out, nor do they complement each other so that the one is in some way restricted or extended by the other.

This is made clear by Kant's critical understanding of reason. Reason differs intrinsically from other practices in that it is able to treat itself as a subject of consideration and to determine its own boundaries – and in view of its tendency to unfounded metaphysical "ramblings", it is essential that it does so. It is fundamentally in need of a critique for which it is in itself the only source. If it remains critical of its own self-criticism and does not misunderstand it uncritically as an inexorable dogma of an absolutist reason, it will be compelled to recognise that the "greatest, and perhaps the only, use of all philosophy of pure reason is [...] of a purely negative character. It is not an organon for the extension, but a discipline for the determination, of the limits of its exercise; and without laying claim to the discovery of new truth, it has the modest merit of guarding against error."[28] Briefly stated, a self-critical reason knows that it is *not an instrument for the discovery of truth, but at best for the prevention of error*.

Thus one must not restrict *reason* in order to make space for faith, even if one shares Kant's questionable view that knowledge must be restricted in order to make room for faith. Nor must one defend faith in the forum of reason, as if reason were an independent forum for anything and everything just because it can function as a critical forum for itself, even if one believes that faith must be defended. For one can only defend faith *with* reason, not from reason. Precisely because it is its own critic, reason is not the court which passes judgement on faith, but the organ through which faith presents itself for judgement.

If we follow this line of thought, a way out of this dilemma appears. The third element we are looking for is, crucially, to be located neither in the sphere of faith nor that of reason (although it can sometimes and in some ways be construed as being there); rather, as the field which combines both perspectives, it is itself the context in which both reason and faith are construed, each in its own way. The abstract contraposition of a *reason of faith*

[28] *KrV* B 823. English translation: *The Critique of Pure Reason*. Translated by J. M. D. Meiklejohn (http://www.gutenberg.org/files/4280/4280-h/4280-h.htm)

and a *reasonable faith* can be overcome if the two are defined by a third element, in terms of which they can be understood as different elements of different views of a problem. Reason is thus not mapped onto faith, nor faith onto reason; rather, they are both defined as different elements of that without which they would not exist: of *life*. For just as reason is an form of enactment of human life, so faith is a mode of human life.[29] The two are not to be confused, but nor must they be separated – at any rate not from a theological perspective.

## *13. Reason*

Taking this as our starting point, *reason* can be understood as a particular *enactment form of human life*, one in which life can thematize itself and its concrete acts and can, as human life, consciously take decisions and actions in relation to, and as distinct from, what is other than it. Since this can happen in different ways, reason exists only in diverse modes of enactment, both in relation to what is other than itself (practical reason) and also in relation to itself (self-thematized reason). As practical reason,

[29] Life, as the third element, is not a neutral or single-perspective item, but can itself be defined in a whole range of ways. Here this means that reason and faith are defined within the context of life, not life within the context of either reason or faith. Thus life is not understood within the horizon of reason as a context for the explanation or justification of theoretical insights or practical objectives (although it can also be understood in this way), nor within the horizon of faith as the place in which God's presence and absence are experienced (although it can also be understood in this way). Rather, it is understood phenomenologically as the field of human experience and suffering, activity and understanding, in which the aspects of reason (the life that is *reasonable* or *reason-governed* or indeed the life that is *unreasonable* or *not governed by reason*) and of faith (the life that is lived *believingly* or *unbelievingly*) are differentiated and considered.

it is directed *towards life* in its enactments (including itself), so that it is enacted as a self-thematization of human life, given its self-definition as human life in changing environments (situations), social worlds (others) and self-worlds (self-relationships). As thematized reason, on the other hand, it is directed *towards itself* in this enactment, taking the form of the self-thematization of reason as it thematizes and defines human life. The practice (enactment) of reason thus always encompasses a theory of reason (a view of this enactment), which means that reason can also be defined as both the *theory of its practice* and the *practice of its theory* simultaneously: Reason understands itself as it enacts itself, and it enacts itself in the way in which it understands itself. It defines life in its enactments, and it defines itself as the definition of life.

In other words, "Reason is a human *organ*. As an organ, it is a *means* which serves *ends* prescribed by the whole to which it belongs".[30] The whole to which reason belongs is human life as life with what is other (environment) and with others (social world), and reason is the one specific enactment form of human life which allows the latter to have a critical view and understanding of itself. It does this by using symbols to create and recognise contexts (as theoretical reason), by exploring and testing possibilities (using its powers of imagination and judgement), by judging itself, its achievements and enactments (as critical reason), by setting itself goals, selecting methods for realising them and directing those methods by means of guiding moral distinctions (as pragmatic or practical reason), and by justifying and answering for itself before the forum of others (as responsible reason).[31]

---

[30] V. GERHARDT, *Selbstbestimmung. Das Prinzip der Individualität*, Stuttgart 1999, 342; cf 420.

[31] After all, as Kant rightly emphasised, human beings are to be considered and understood, not solely in relation to their animality (life) and rationality (reasoning life), but also to their personality (responsibly lived

In this sense reason is one – excellent – human capacity amongst others, a capacity which, in distinction from other living beings, allows humans to describe themselves in a specific way: As rational beings, we humans are free to explore, know and define ourselves. All these are enactments which essentially place us in community with others and what is other. No human lives alone, which is why every human must (as Kierkegaard said) first *become*, by distinguishing himself and allowing himself to be distinguished from other life (environment) and other reasoning life (social world) in such a way that he is enabled to live a self-determined life as a human amongst humans (self-world). Everyone begins a life as a human, but not every human becomes what he can and should become: a self, living his life responsibly.

## *14. Situated reason*

As an enactment of human life, reason is therefore always *situated reason*. It is embedded in the physical (physiological, emotional, appetitive, volitional, cognitive etc.) enactments of human life (physically situated), and is bound together with these in concrete situations and changing life situations, in interaction with changing environments, social worlds and self-worlds and their chronological setting in pre-worlds, now-worlds and

---

life). And just as life presupposes its relation to other life and its distinction from the non-living, and reasoning life presupposes its relation to other human beings as constituting the social world of one's own life, it follows that personality keeps in view its relation to a forum of others, before which every human who lives as a person among persons can and must answer for themselves again and again. In each of these respects, human life stands in a relationship of exchange and communication with something other, apart from which it would not be what it is: human life. Cf. I. Kant, *Die Religion innerhalb der Grenzen der blossen Vernunft*, B 15, AA VI, 25–26.

after-worlds, which acquire it in experience and activity (naturally, socially, culturally and historically situated). Human beings live their lives in specific situations which can be thematized as belonging to their environmental, social or self-worlds. These are distinguished respectively, in the context of their lives, as pre-world, now-world and after-world. Human enactments of reason are also situated in the real world and can be similarly distinguished. As practical reason, it thematizes life in its concrete situatedness as environment, social world and self-world in their respective chronological settings of pre-, now- and after-world; as thematized reason it is directed towards itself as being situatively determined and conditioned. It is enacted concretely and understands itself concretely. It is enacted concretely, in that it relates what is real to what is possible and determines the reality of life within the context of its possibilities, and it understands itself concretely, in that it understands the reality of its enactments within the context of the possibilities it has for thematizing and determining life. Reason is concrete, in the sense that it relates what is real to what is possible and determines it within that context, and it understands itself concretely in the sense that it understands and determines its reality from the perspective of the possible.

The situatedness of reason is plain to it, both in what it does and in how it does it: it brings about correlations and uncovers correlations by making distinctions; indeed it is the capacity to make controlled distinctions by deciding, on the basis of its self-imposed rules, how such distinctions are to be made in specific contexts and in relation to specific questions. This is clear, for one thing, from the way in which reason discerns the reality of the life it thematizes, recognising its own reality as contingent, with the result that it relates this reality to what is possible, distinguishing it from the impossible and the necessary. It is, but it could also not be, which is why it faces the challenge of taking its own contingency and finiteness into account in its practical and theoretical enactments. It is also clear from the fact that situated reason is always practised *in a specific way* and thus *in modal specificity*: as a form of contingent life acting through controlled distinction, its practice is determined by the mode in which this life is lived. The mode of life in which reason is situated determines its own enactments as well. Just like life itself, reason is enacted in one way or another, and from a theological perspective first and foremost: *in faith* or *in unfaith.*

### *15. Faith and unfaith*

Unlike reason, faith is not an enactment form of life, but a specific *mode of existence*, that is, a particular way of existing as a human being. This mode of existence does not arise automatically from life; it enters our field of vision only once we consider and appraise our life as a whole (that is, in all its actual and potential enactments) in the light of the fundamental distinction between *faith* and *unfaith* which positions it in relation to a third element and understands it from the perspective of this relationship. Once human life, in all its forms of enactment, is related to a third element which is not an aspect or element of life, but is designated as *God*, to whom all life owes its existence, then that life is assessed theologically as regards its relation to God and can be identified as life *in faith* or *in unfaith.* This depends on whether life is lived in this relationship with God or not, that is, on whether the presence of God is taken into account in the practices of life (a believing life) or is ignored (a non-believing life). One who believes, lives and experiences his life as an unmerited gift of God, whereas one who does not live and experience his life in this way, does not believe.

Both of these ways of living, in faith (believingly) and in unfaith (non-believingly), manifest a particular attitude and approach to life, but neither manifests itself as a special life phenomenon among or alongside others. Faith and unfaith are not emotional, cognitive or voluntative ways of conducting one's life; they are the existential modality in which life is enacted from a theological perspective. A modality is *existential* if it qualifies, not the What and How of life, but its *That*; thus it affects *the overall way in which human life is enacted in this world*, so that it characterises and defines what human beings experience, perceive and do in their environment, social world and self-world. *That* we live, however, is not the result of our own decision, and nor is *how* this That is qualified. Anyone who lives always necessarily lives in a specific mode, which affects both the That of his life (existential mode) and – as a result – the What and How of the ways in which he conducts his life.

When we consider a life from a theological point of view, assessing its That with regard to its relationship with God, to whom it owes its existence, then *unfaith* is the factual mode of existence of human life, while *faith*, on the other hand, – formulated from the point of view of the actual life – is the counterfactual mode of existence. The life modality defined in the light of the fundamental theological distinction between faith and unfaith, also characterises, as a That mode, its enactments (What and How), thus presupposing that human life is enacted in one or the other determinacy: as a life *before God* it is lived either as a life *in unfaith* or *in faith*. The determinacy of human life as *unfaith* or as *faith in God* cannot be thematized in disregard of its relationship with God (life *coram deo*), but only from the perspective of God's operation on and in the human life, by means of which the latter becomes what it can become: it cannot be deduced or proven phenomenologically from the human life, but can only be *reflected in a theological assessment of this life*. God's relationship to human life is not an aspect or element of this life, but is that without which it would not exist, and is thus also the viewpoint from which this life can be assessed as being open or closed to God, as a life in faith or in unfaith.

Judged from a theological point of view, God is present to all life (otherwise it would not exist), and indeed in more than one way. All human life, in the fullness and diversity of its forms of enactment, therefore takes place, when judged theologically in the light of the fundamental distinction between faith and unfaith, in the mode of existence of unfaith (non-believingly) or of faith (believingly). The grammar of this fundamental distinction states, in essence: each human lives either in unfaith or in faith. No one lives in neither. No one lives at the same time and in the same respect in both. No one lives in faith who did not come from unfaith.

None of these are descriptions produced by the human life itself or generalised from individual life phenomena, but are grammatical statements concerning the human life in the light of the key perspective of faith and unfaith. As theological judgements they go well beyond the describable and observable in life, in that they understand it *coram deo* and thus judge it within the context of a relationship which sheds light on the whole life without being an element or aspect of that life: Formally articulated, faith and unfaith are the theologically determined existential modal operators which qualify the whole range of enactments of a human life, but they are not themselves specific life enactments within this range. They qualify everything but are not part of what they qualify.

That is why it is crucial to keep in mind the specific grammar and usage of these theological modal operators as they apply to human life, and not to try to extract them from the life phenomena themselves: *Faith* and *unfaith* do not denote special experiences of human life, but a modal qualification of all experiences in the light of relationship with God, understood from a Christian perspective. It follows that the use of these modal operators in Christian theology is regulated in a particular way, which needs to be borne in mind. It is only possible to distinguish between unfaith and faith from the perspective of faith, not from that of unfaith. The enactment of human life in unfaith is not discernible to itself: from the point of view of unfaith it is impossible to define the boundary between faith and unfaith, since unfaith cannot see and identify itself as such, but at best as another kind of 'faith'. Conversely, it is characteristic of life in faith that it can be intelligible to itself in principle. For faith is always and only *faith in God*. It believes in God as the distinct and separate ground to whom it owes its existence, and in this way it differentiates itself from unfaith and superstition, which do not believe in God, or believe in him differently, or believe in something other than God, so that life under those conditions is lived from a fundamentally different standpoint.

### *16. Faith and reason*

The consequence of this modal understanding of belief is that we must exchange the customary way of setting the orientation coordinates of the relationship between faith and reason for a different one. I will restrict myself to six points.

1. Faith's "other" is unfaith, not reason. And reason's "other" is not faith, but the other ways of conducting one's life. In other words, *reason* is not an alternative to faith, but a form of reflection, a way of exploring possibilities and a way in which human life defines itself, whether *in unfaith* or *in faith*.

2. But between unfaith and faith there are no differences of degree which can be bridged through ongoing advances in knowledge or insight. It is possible to have more or less knowledge *in faith* and more or less knowledge *in unfaith*, but there is no such thing as *faith which equals unfaith with an increase in knowledge*, nor is there any such thing as *unfaith that equals faith with a reduction in knowledge*. The difference between faith and unfaith cannot be conveyed by a third element which places the two in a relationship of degree. Rather, it is a chasm that is

as deep as the chasm between Jesus' death on the cross and his raising by God. Neither chasm can be bridged by anyone or anything other than God.

3. Since human life, judged from a theological point of view, is always lived either in unfaith or in faith, in practice reason can only exist either as a *reason of unfaith* or a *reason of faith*. The *reason of faith* is a *reason which takes God into account*, the *reason of unfaith* is a *reason which does not*. Every type of reason does one or the other, albeit in quite different ways, and includes the whole of life, from the highest degree of certainty about God to the deepest doubt, or from an unfaith that is as sure as possible of oneself to a sceptical 'Maybe, but then again, maybe not'. When we consider the situation of life as it is judged *coram deo*, there is therefore, as regards the differentiation of faith and unfaith, no neutral reason, but only a reason defined respectively in specific terms. Just as *unfaith* precedes *faith*, it follows that the *reason of faith* is preceded by the *reason of unfaith*, not by a neutral reason whose imperfect wisdom will be perfected in faith: The *reason of faith* is *not a perfecting of the reason of unfaith*, but the enactment of reason in the life of faith, which has put behind it the transition from unfaith to faith for which God alone is responsible.

4. Unlike reason, *faith* is therefore not one anthropological attribute amongst others (reason, understanding, will, feeling, experience etc.), but the *qualification of the human being with all his attributes from the perspective of what God is doing in him and for him*. The crucial thing that God does in and for those who ignore him is that he opens the path from unfaith to faith: faith only exists as the *transition from unfaith to faith through God*. This transition cannot be made by the non-believer (otherwise he would not be a non-believer), nor can it be made by the believer (since it is always the *result*, not the *subject* of the transition). No intensification of a life in unfaith leads to a life in faith, and no modifications to one's ways of living one's life in themselves accomplish the change of mode from unfaith to faith.

No life practice can change one's life in such a way that it becomes, not merely *other*, but – in the modal sense – *new*. Such a change of mode is attributed by believers, not to themselves, but unreservedly and exclusively to *God*: "I believe, that God created me … I believe that it is not I, by my own reason and strength …, but the Holy Spirit who has called me through the gospel …" (Luther). There is no good reason why we should refuse to take this seriously as their own description of their own experience.

5. The Christian understanding is that faith is therefore essentially faith *in God*, that is to say faith in the one who transplants human beings from unfaith into faith by being so present to them, even in their unfaith, that they can believe, and by being so present to them in Word and Spirit that they do not remain in unfaith. A necessary condition of the transition from unfaith to faith brought about by God is that that one is living the life of unfaith in the place where God makes himself present in a life-giving and life-sustaining way, even though one is ignoring and disputing this: God is present to *every* life – only thus can it be *life*. And it is a condition of the reality of this transition that God makes himself present *in* the life of the one who is living in unfaith; God thus comes back to his own presence with the non-believer in such a way that the latter perceives God's good presence, recognises his unfaith and is transplanted by God into a life in faith: God becomes present *in* his life – and only thereby does it become *new* life. Both need to be stated. From a formal standpoint, the possibility and reality of faith go hand in hand with God's effective presence; they cannot be shown to be determinative of human life in independence of that presence. And in its content faith is always faith in God the creator, redeemer and consummator, who not only transplants human beings into faith, but is present to them in their unfaith in such a way that they come from unfaith to faith, from a way of life that ignores God's presence to a life which takes God's presence into account and places its confidence in it.

Hence, no intensification of a life in unfaith leads to a life in faith, and no modifications to one's ways of living one's life in themselves accomplish the change of mode from unfaith to faith. Rather, faith is essentially *faith in God*, since a life in faith is due definitively to the transition from unfaith to faith, which in turn is attributable solely to God. As a process, life is permanent change. But no life process can change one's life so greatly that it causes one's modal determination to make the transition from unfaith to faith. To become different is one thing, to become new is quite another.

Faith and unfaith are thus not anthropological abilities, but *existential modal designations (modes of existence) of human life* which characterise its enactment *coram deo*. From a theological point of view, 'I believe' is not to be understood and analysed as 'I think' or 'I hold to be true' or 'I feel' or 'I trust'; rather, it denotes the existential mode in which I exist and live my life *coram deo*, including all that I think, hold to be true, feel and trust. Confessions of faith do not articulate what we are or do or what happens to us, but *how we exist and live our lives before God*: open to God's presence or closed to it.

6. Since the change in existential modal designation of a life does not result from its own acts, but is determined by God, the life in faith is a life defined by God's presence. And since, according to the Christian faith, God makes himself present in the precise manner articulated in its credal confession of Christ and made specific in its confessions of the various aspects of God, including his love, mercy, righteousness, sovereignty, friendship, liberation etc., life *in faith* is described using theological equivalents as life *in Christ, in the Spirit, in the body of Christ, in God's love* and so on. Each of these metaphors brings a different aspect of life *in faith* to the fore, but one thing they all have in common is that they do not allude to separate aspects or dimensions of the life of faith. Rather, each in its own specific way describes the place where the life of the believer, in all its

aspects and dimensions, is lived and where every human life can be lived *coram deo*.

## *17. Reason of faith*

From this it follows that the *reason of unfaith* is a reason which ignores God in the conduct of its life because his presence has no consequences for its way of living: The mode of existence of unfaith manifests itself in practice in the modality of the conduct of life, both when it is thinking about God and when it is not. This applies to theologians and philosophers alike: thinking about God or trying to do so (positive theology) or deliberately to refrain from doing so (negative theology), are in themselves no evidence of faith. It is not only one who denies God who could be living in unfaith, but also one who does not. The *reason of faith* in contrast is a reason which counts on God as the one who transplants humans from unfaith into faith, and the fact that it does this is apparent from the way one lives.

Similarly, the *intellectus fidei* consists, on the one hand, of the insight that faith is always and everywhere essentially *faith in God* (namely, in the one to whom the transition from unfaith to faith is owed), but also, on the other hand, of the differentiation between *faith* (the God-engendered change in one's mode of existence from unfaith to faith) and the *life of faith* (the conduct of one's life in the awareness of God's presence, in the realm of faith). One who believes lives, as a human with all his abilities and inabilities, *in the realm of faith*, as one who is counting on God's presence and is seeking to live his life in thankfulness to God in the light of this presence. For everyone faces the alternative of a life of gratitude or ingratitude to God. But that can only be rationally understood in faith and not in unfaith.

The *fact that* human beings live *in faith* is thus not due to their decision or choice, but to God's effective presence; however, the *manner* in which they *live in faith* most certainly is. On the one hand, unfaith is the factual mode of existence of every human being: *One only ever comes to a life of faith from unfaith.* On the other hand *there is no one who could not lead a life in faith*, since God is present to and at work in every life. Since there is no one who does not live either in unfaith or in faith, then every human being is distinguished, both by the *fact that he lives in unfaith*, and by the fact that he *is destined to live in faith.*

One can either fulfil or fail to fulfil this destiny, and each of these can be done with either more or less reason. But one cannot make it possible or realise it using reason, and it is not necessary that one can understand, appreciate or explain it with one's reason before one can realise it. One who believes can understand and justify what he does, as can one who does not believe, although he will not have to or need to understand or describe his situation in such a way. But the step from unfaith to faith cannot be taken *sola ratione*, since every step taken *sola ratione*, is taken either in unfaith or in faith, but cannot lead from one to the other.

### *18. Reason of faith or faith of reason?*

The preceding reflections were not an attempt to prove the reason of faith. Rather, they outlined, with the aid of a phenomenological difference (enactment /mode of life), a theological view of human life in which the difference between reason and faith is explained as the distinction between a (self-determined) *conduct of life* and a (factual or counterfactual) *mode of existence.* From a theological point of view the question of the reason of faith and the faith of reason does *not* concern a decision for or against faith, but for a *life* in faith or a *life* in unfaith: Faith or unfaith are not options between which one can decide. They are modal determinations of the *That* of life, not of the *What* and

*How* of life's enactments. Where determination of the *That* of life is concerned, however, one is always factually located in unfaith, even though one is not aware of this until one finds oneself in faith. But it is neither *faith* nor the *transition to faith* which are the result of human choice and decision; rather, it is the way one lives in faith or in unfaith. Here reason has its part to play. In faith it sees a sound basis for living, not in unfaith but in faith. In unfaith, conversely, it cannot come up with any good grounds for considering a life in faith as a serious option: there is insufficient evidence to support it, even if in principle there is nothing to be said against it.

That all human beings live in unfaith and only come to faith from unfaith is a judgement of faith. That all human beings only live in unfaith because they are destined to live in faith, is similarly a judgement of faith. Neither of these faith judgements can be demonstrated to be reasonable by reflecting on ultimate validity criteria, but only by the practical conduct of one's life in their light, although not for the arbitrary onlooker or observer, but only for those involved. *Unfaith* is able to recognise life in faith as a religious phenomenon, but not as superstitious belief, since its criteria do not enable it to differentiate between *faith* and *superstitious belief.* For *faith,* conversely, the fact that one can *live* in unfaith is an indication that God *is near to those who do not believe, as well.* From a theological point of view, every human being is destined for *life in faith*, and is therefore not bound to a life in unfaith. This can be explained and substantiated with theological arguments. But these explanations and substantiations are no substitute for the practical consequences of our lives, which reveal – not to all of us, but to those of us who have eyes to see as God sees – whether we are living in faith or in unfaith.[32] Which is why reason cannot be first on the scene here either, but always arrives too late.

---

[32] It is not the practical enactments of life as such which manifest faith

Here too, reason acts in a similar way. It makes distinctions, works thoughtfully through their consequences, compares different distinctions, examines the arguments for and against them and explores the contexts of meaning disclosed thereby. This applies to the reason of faith just as much as to the reason of unfaith. Both explore how life can be oriented in a reflective and reflecting manner by (a) establishing distinctions (deciding to distinguish in a particular way), thereby (b) creating a determinacy by which one can orient the conduct of one's life (a determinacy generated by process of elimination), and thus (c) opening up horizons of possibility which surpass the actual reality, without becoming lost in the infinite, but instead finding its boundary in the impossible (and thus allowing impossibility to be revealed as the boundary horizon of all distinctions and orientations). These three aspects of reason-directed differentiation will be the subject of the following three chapters.

---

or unfaith; rather, they are manifested *in* these enactments, a conclusion which finds expression in the theological judgement of these enactments: that, considered in the light of God's judgement of them, they are enactments of a life in faith or in unfaith.

# E. On the one hand / On the other hand. Decision-making as orientation through the making of distinctions

## *1. Deciding as distinguishing*

One who distinguishes establishes a difference, and to establish a difference is to make a decision one could also refrain from making. However, once a difference has been established, then, in the light of this difference, one can make further distinctions by deciding what further distinctions one will make on one side or the other. How this happens in practice can depend on many things: on interests one is pursuing, on questions to be answered or on challenges to which one is attempting to respond. By making such distinctions one develops schemes of orientation with the aid of which one can orient one's life and thought processes. All distinction takes place between an initial decision (the establishment of a difference) and subsequent decisions which build upon it. Through the establishment of further differences on both sides of the initial distinction, these subsequent decisions give tangible form to what had been distinguished by means of the initial differentiation. The meaning of a distinction only becomes clear from its actual and potential consequences, but each distinction presupposes a position from which it is made and which is hidden from the distinction itself (a blind spot).[1]

---

[1] When one distinguishes between left and right, one does so from a position which is neither left nor right, even though it may be left or right to others. But it is different when one is distinguishing between faith and unfaith. One who makes this self-referential distinction localises himself

On the one hand, each distinction makes other distinctions possible and refers back to other potential or actual distinctions: A decision does not open up a new series of decisions unless it is itself (or could be) located in a prior series of decisions. On the other hand, each decision can become the starting point for further decisions and points forward to other decisions which it renders possible. It is only these subsequent decisions that it has made possible that clarify the significance and relevance of the initial decision and what lies at its heart.

Each time a difference is established therefore, three questions arise: What is the difference that has been established and what further distinctions are thereby made possible or necessary? This is the systematic question in decision-making. From which position was this difference established? This is the anaphoric question in decision-making. And from which position within the established distinction will the subsequent decisions be taken? This is the cataphoric question in decision-making. Both questions are asking about the *marked space* from which a decision is made and in which, therefore, the decider himself is located. In the anaphoric case it is an indeterminate Whence, which has not yet been determined as such in the light of the established decision, but is employed as an indeterminate determinacy. In the cataphoric case, conversely, in those instances when the distinction is total, leaving no alternatives open (i.e. everything is either A or ¬A or neither or both), the Whence is, in principle, always restricted to one or the other side of the established difference; to which side becomes apparent from subsequent distinctions. Each decision has thus an indeterminate, but factually effective *Whence* (From whence is the distinction being made?); it takes place in an actual but not yet clearly defined *Where* (Where is

either in faith or in unfaith, not in a third position distinct from either. Only someone who is alive can differentiate, and only someone who lives either believingly or unbelievingly is able to differentiate between faith and unfaith.

the distinction being made and how?); and it has, in principle, a *Whither*, albeit one with as yet no concrete specificity, but which will become specific in the further decisions which will follow the first decision (From which side of the distinction will further differences be established?).

To differentiate thus necessarily involves tiered decision-making processes and decision-making involves interleaved consequences of differentiation. How can we understand this more precisely, and what does it mean for our endeavour to orient ourselves rationally and reliably, by means of controlled differentiation, to ultimate presence in our lives?

## *2. Choosing between alternatives*

Behaviour is enacted through decision-making,[2] and decision-making can be described as choosing between alternatives. But what do we mean by 'choosing' and 'alternative'? The behaviour of something may also be governed by *circumstances*, and the mode of behaviour will change with time, as one circumstance is replaced by another. Can this type of behaviour be described as 'decision-making'? Or should we reserve this description for cases in which it is not *something*, but *someone who is behaving – towards something, towards others, towards him or herself* or *towards God*, even though he or she need not have behaved in that way? Is 'behaviour' a shorthand term for the possibility that *something is thus-and-not-otherwise,* which

[2] This is just one way of addressing the subject of *decision-making*. One could also develop it in terms of a logic of self-determination from the perspective of *distinction* or in terms of existential ontology from the perspective of the question as to the fundamental decisions which shape every life. However, when examining decision-making as a *phenomenon*, i.e. how it appears to someone as something, one is led to focus primarily on behaviour.

can change over time, or for *thus-and-not-otherwise behaviour towards something or someone on the part of someone* who could in fact behave differently towards others or another, meaning that one needs to distinguish more precisely between *behaviour towards something or someone* (practical life issues), *behaviour towards oneself* (a practical existential issue) and *behaviour towards God* (a theological issue)? Could and should all the above be understood as 'choosing between alternatives' and hence as 'decision-making'? Or is there a problematic blurring of the difference between the actualisation of potential circumstances in time and the choice between alternative behaviours by the protagonists?

### *3. Theoretical approaches*

These uncertainties are reflected in the literature on decision-making. The (socio)scientific debate is dominated by three approaches.

The first takes a broadly defined *system theory* standpoint to describe all decision-making as the reaction of a system to stimuli from its environment, leading to a before/after distinction between system states.[3] Distinctions such as regulated or unregulated, conscious or unconscious, rational or intuitive decision-making are, in contrast, introduced at a secondary stage as more precise definitions of specific types of system.

In the tightly controlled *action theory approach*, on the other hand, human decision-making is taken into account and is reconstructed as a complex action sequence which distinguishes, from a *neuropsychological perspective*, phases or stages of the

---

[3] Cf. N. LUHMANN, Soziologische Aspekte des Entscheidungsverhaltens, in: IDEM, *Die Wirtschaft der Gesellschaft*, Frankfurt am Main 1988, 272–301; IDEM, *Organisation und Entscheidung*, Opladen 2000.

decision process, such as *consideration, planning, execution* and *evaluation.*[4] Alternatively, it adopts an economic perspective, from which it paints a picture of a *rational decision-maker*, who, conscious of his preferences and of the possibilities, opportunities and risks of the available options, takes the decision that maximises his benefits, or at any rate minimises potential harm.[5]

The third approach is the *process-analytical approach*, which analyses decisions as processes that can be reconstructed as *decision trees,*[6] that is, as hierarchically organised decision algorithms, or – by taking various such processes into consideration – as *decision forests*, the branching consequences of which can barely be grasped by human beings. Rather, they can only be represented using computer technology, as sequences of complex majority decisions which have a reciprocal influence on each other and do not lead individually to predictable results, but have a purely statistical outcome.

The first approach takes insufficient account of the distinguishing qualities and specific complexity of human decision-making. The second, conversely, underestimates the number of human decisions that are pre-reflective, habitual

---

[4] Cf. W. SEIDEL, *Das ethische Gehirn. Der determinierte Wille und die eigene Verantwortung*, Heidelberg 2009; W. BRAUN, *Die (Psycho-)Logik des Entscheidens: Fallstricke, Strategien und Techniken im Umgang mit schwierigen Situationen*, Bern 2010.

[5] Cf. W. STEGMÜLLER, *Entscheidungslogik (rationale Entscheidungstheorie)*, Berlin et al. 1973. The basic model of the rational decision-maker is only marginally modified if, in addition to his preferences and risk considerations, he also takes into account the incompleteness of his knowledge and the influence of his emotions and values (altruism) on the decision-making process.

[6] Cf. J. R. QUINLAN, Induction of Decision Trees, *Machine Learning 1*, Boston 1986, 81–106; P. DÖRSAM, *Entscheidungstheorie anschaulich dargestellt*, Heidenau [5]2007.

or instinct-led.[7] The third considers the phenomenon of decision-making so abstractly that the medium in which the process is actually implemented appears to be of no significance. Systems, people and machines are so closely intertwined that the difference between them becomes irrelevant to the decision-making process.

How can such deficiencies be avoided without ignoring the indisputable insights of these various approaches or being compelled to choose between them?

### *4. Phenomenological description*

One option is to view the phenomenon of decision-making phenomenologically. I understand 'phenomenologically' to refer to a mode of description that is mindful of how a phenomenon represents itself when it appears, in distinction from other phenomena and from its prevalent scientific thematization, as something specific for someone. As such, *something always appears as something*, and this is invariably a process of interpretation, in that an *interpretandum* (*something* in the first thematization) is defined, by means of an *interpretament* (*something* in the second thematization), as something for an *interpreter*, and is thus further defined in terms of its first thematization. Phenomena are thus not 'objects', but *interpretation processes* in which the meaning of something is disclosed to someone in such a way that it is articulated and intelligible *as something*.[8]

[7] Cf. G. Gigerenzer, *Bauchentscheidungen. Die Intelligenz des Unbewussten und die Macht der Intuition*, München 2007.

[8] It goes without saying that complex cultural and social frames of reference are always inevitably involved in this process.

## *5. Decision as explanans or as explanandum*

If we attempt to unfold this interpretation process in the case of decision-making, however, we need to differentiate methodologically between two sets of questions. The first seeks to understand decision-making *as something*, whereas the second conceives of something *as decision-making*. In the first, decision-making is the *explanandum*, the understanding of which is at issue; in the second, decision-making is the *explanans*, with the aid of which something else is explained and thereby rendered intelligible.

In the phenomenological approach the first set of questions is given prominence, but decision-making, which functions thereby as *explanandum*, is in fact what scientific explanations refer to as the *explanans* of a process of change, which cannot be satisfactorily explained without reference to that which is called 'decision-making'. If all change consists of the *transformation of an initial position into a new position* replacing the first, then the phenomena of decision-making can be defined as *the processes of change or transformation of an initial position into a new position* (before / after distinction), which *would not exist without the act of decision-making* (the establishment of the before / after distinction through the actualisation of one of the possible alternatives). It is not changes in general, but changes *through decision-making*, together with the distinctions established thereby, that need to be illuminated phenomenologically and understood hermeneutically.

For that to take place, it is of course necessary to clarify the meaning of 'to decide', so that we are able to understand the phenomenon of decision-making; and if 'to decide' is defined as 'to choose between alternatives', then we must explain what we mean by 'choose' and 'alternative'. In what follows, I shall seek to do this by describing the phenomenon of decision-making, first as *choosing* between alternatives, and then as choosing *between alternatives*; in other words, I shall consider the same phenomenon from two different angles.

## *6. Either / or: the weak concept of decision*

As I have said, decision-making can be described as choosing between alternatives. This sounds straightforward if we understand 'choose' in a very broad sense to mean simply an either / or stance within a single possibility space. This type of decision-making behaviour can be found not only in human beings, but also in unicellular organisms such as amoebae, in plants like sunflowers or in systems such as heating installations. When the heating starts up because the thermostat registers a fall in temperature and switches the burner on, in cybernetic terms this is just as much a decision as when sunflowers turn towards the sun because they are reacting to the light.

Every reaction by a system to an environmental intervention can be coded as a decision. This simply means that the state of a system is converted, causally or stochastically, to a new state that is one of various possible alternatives. The multiplicity of possibilities is reduced to a Yes / No alternative, so that the system state changes when there is a "Yes" decision in respect of a defined continuation possibility (*a pro decision*), or does not change when there is a "No" decision (*a contra decision*).

Since this kind of process is constantly taking place, the state of a system is one of constant change or rejection of change. The system state changes in a more or less regulated way within an either / or possibility space, without there being any need for a distinct decider who takes the decision to convert the initial system state to a new one.

## *7. On the one hand / on the other hand: the strong form of decision*

The situation is quite different with the *strong form of decision.* Here decision-making is not merely a systemic reaction to environmental stimuli, but an interruption to this regulatory context in the form of a *choice.* This choice constitutes a third element in relation to the initial and the new states of the system, a choice without which this change would not have existed. In contrast to a mere before / after sequence of events, here a *sphere of alternative possibilities* is inserted between the stimulus and the system reaction. None of these possibilities is realised, either by chance or by unregulated probability or by regulated causality, with the result that, despite available decision alternatives, no decision (in the weak sense) is reached and no change occurs. This non-change is not the consequence of there being no alternatives to the now-state. On the contrary, although there are possible alternatives, viewed from the system perspective and on the basis of the system information, none of these possibilities is to be preferred, either to one of the others or to the now-state. This results in an impasse, and the factor that resolves the impasse and enables a change to a new state is what I term '*choice*' or '*decision in the strong sense*'.

It is not sufficiently precise to define such a choice as a decision between alternatives that change the state of a system. A system can persist in its state because there is no trigger for change (in other words no intervention presents itself), or because there is no possibility of reacting to an existing stimulus by actualising one of the possible alternatives, since, under the rules of the system, none of them is to be preferred to the now-state. A choice can put an end to either – it can bring about a change without there being any trigger for change, or it can lift a blockade. In the strictest sense it is the second and not the first, since it is a decision that not only brings about a change for which there is no trigger, but ends a state of non-decision resulting from a systemic inability to decide and thus makes possible a change where the system cannot. It is only in a situation that allows, not just the possibility of an alternative not available for decision within the system (that is, the possibility of being able to choose), but also the necessity of deciding for one of these alternatives (that is the necessity to choose), that choosing becomes not only possible but necessary. To *be able to* choose then means to *have to* choose, since it is only through choice that the stasis of non-decision or undecidability can be overcome.

### *8. Another way to make a decision*

In order to reach a decision even when it is impossible to decide between the system alternatives, one must introduce, alongside the existing system state and the potential continuationstates, a third variable, *a decider*, which is not part of the system, but which changes the system state through the choice of an alternative based not on system-dependent reasons, but on its own: if the heating does not come on automatically because the temperature is not high enough to activate the thermostat regulator, I will switch it on manually if I'm cold. I feel cold, so I decide on an action that ends the non-decision state of the heating system and brings about a change.

The choice of a decider can thus be based on criteria quite outside the system, with the result that the decider can bring about a decision when the system is not in a position to do so. There is no doubt that the change which occurs results from a decision, but *not* from the *either / or of a systemic decision*, which did not in fact take place, but from the *on the one hand / on the other hand choice-decision of a decider* whose only relevance for the system was that it resulted in an action which intervened in the system's operation. This choice-decision must orient itself by the system alternatives, but not by the system criteria. Thus it can be enacted in an entirely different way: as a weighing up of the one hand / other hand alternatives in accordance with *subjective preferences* (predilections, aversions, experiences, memories, feelings, values) or on the basis of *rational considerations* (reasons). And just as for each decision-maker subjective preferences can be different, and indeed highly individual, so also the rationale put forward or the grounds that are actually critical to the relevant decision and action can differ greatly, taken on a case by case basis. In other words, they will include, not just elements which must be binding upon everyone, whatever their location or circumstances, but also special situations which may, in one specific case but not in every comparable case, lead to a particular decision.

This does not exclude choice-decisions from being simplified into either / or decisions. As the *explanans* for the change in a system, however, reference to such decisions is valid only if they do not (either wholly or partly) fit in with its systemic either / or-decision structure: after all, they are intended to make it clear how a change can be brought about when the rules of the system itself result in *no* decision and do *not* bring about a change. The decision-maker's choice will therefore have to orient itself by criteria outside those of the system, since there would otherwise be no change.

When weighing up the one hand / other hand alternatives, choice-decisions are complex processes; they can diverge from the system operation at many different points: in respect of alternative decisions, alternative types of action, alternative objectives for those decisions and actions, consequences anticipated or feared, the means and methods of the decision-making and action processes, and so on. They can be *decisions taken with certainty* (the consequences are known) or *with uncertainty* (the probable consequences can be gauged) or *in ignorance* (the probable consequences are unknown). They can be oriented by the decision-maker's own interests, by the well-being of others or by the well-being of all, even if that were to run counter to the decision-maker's own interests in the relevant decision situation: even though I feel cold, I do not switch the heating on because I want to save energy and reduce greenhouse gas emissions.

## *9. Staged decisions*

The problem addressed above is an old and familiar one. Our decision-making, according to the philosophical tradition, can be guided by reason or desire. *Reason* is understood as that which has *the Whole* in mind – cosmologically and anthropologically just as much as socially or politically. It is directed towards what is universal and common, the well-being of all, the best for each individual, the inner harmony of each individual and his harmony with the social and natural environment that surrounds him. *Desire*, in contrast has solely its *own interest* in view, consisting of what is particular, not shared, not common. Thus, if one wants what is good, one may not allow oneself to be determined by one's desires, but must be guided by reason.

Given the same conditions and the same problem areas, opposing choice-decisions can arise – not simply because one can make a well-founded decision for various options, but because one can decide on different grounds for one's decision. Not only can we choose between different alternatives (*first-order decisions:* freedom of action), we can also choose the motives and grounds (form) or manner (mode), on the basis of which we intend to choose between different alternatives (*second-order decisions:* freedom of will), and we can orient this decision as to the form and mode of our decision-making by means of rules we ourselves establish, free and independently of the circumstances and demands of this or any other actual situation (*third-order decisions:* free self-determination, that is, autonomy).

Neurophysiological challenges to the concept of freedom of decision typically relate to the first level. But what was traditionally meant by the simplifying abbreviated formula 'free will'[9] does not appear until the second level, and what Kant called 'autonomy' not until the third level. The interdependence of the levels does not mean that freedom of action presupposes freedom of will, which in turn presupposes autonomy, but quite the opposite, that autonomy enables freedom of will and freedom of will enables freedom of action. We do not *possess* free will, rather we *become those who are exercising free will*, when we decide upon a specific form and a specific mode of will by setting ourselves a rule of will. And we do not *possess* freedom of action, rather we *act freely*, when we choose between the different alternatives of a given situation in such a way that we act according to the promptings of our wishes, interests or inclinations only if this action is in accordance with the rule we have set for our will. We are free to the extent that we *make concrete use of our freedom*, (on the one hand) as we *distinguish our selves in our will from our actions*, thereby as self (i. e. as willing self, or as will) distancing ourselves from our actions (the will / action distinction); and (on the other hand) as we *distinguish our selves from our will* (i. e. from ourselves as will) *by means of the self-establishment of our will*, thereby distancing ourselves from our selves (the self / self distinction); and indeed in such a way, that we *open ourselves towards others* (the self / others distinction), by determining our will (in other words ourselves) in accordance with the rule that directs us to want only what anyone can want who wants only

---

[9] Neither 'free will' nor 'will' are terms designating something to be sought in the human brain or nervous system, nor are they descriptions of an aspect or capability of the human soul. Rather, they are abbreviated formulae for a complex of problems which one must unpack if one wants to articulate the meaning of 'will' or 'free will' or 'unfree will'. Cf. *I. U. Dalferth*, Glaubensfreiheit: Über Freiheit als Fiktion und Glaube als Einbildung, *ThLZ 143* (2018) 163–180.

what anyone can want (in other words, to want to become only such a self as anyone else could and should want to become). What does this mean?

## *10. The place of freedom*

My explanation draws on Augustine.[10] I can be compelled to do evil. But no one can compel me to will evil. There can always be a reason which compels me to do the evil that I do, even if it is my brain that induced my behaviour. The same is not true when it comes to the evil that I will. I and I alone, reasoned Augustine, am in control of my will. So it follows that I alone am responsible for my will to evil and need look no further for a cause. I am in control of my will, because my will or non-will have no ground and no other cause than that I will something or do not will it. It makes no difference whether I include *my will in me* or *me in my will*: The decisive point is that it is not possible to draw a meaningful distinction between me and my will, since it is not something I possess or might not possess – it is what I *am*. I do not *have* a will that wills, rather I *am* my will, which is why I am also in control of my will, i.e. of myself – insofar as I control anything at all.

However, I am not in control of what I do in the same way, since not everything that I do or do not do is done or not done because I will it or do not will it. It is far from being the case that I do everything that I will and do not do everything that I do not will. It is far more likely to be the case that I do something without willing it, or that I will something but do not do it. I may will to do good and yet I do evil, or I may will to do evil but achieve what is good. I am not in control of either. Whilst there is thus no

[10] A. Augustinus, *De civitate dei*, CChr.SL 47–48, Turnhout 1955, XII.

distinction between me and my will (*I am my will*), between my will and my action there is a gaping chasm (*I am not my action*) which constantly brings me into a conflict situation in which I, the willer, will to do something other than what I, the doer, do.

It is therefore not my actions (first-order decisions), but my will (second-order decisions) that is the locus of the freedom problem. But this freedom does not manifest itself in the fact that I will what I will and therefore am who I am (that is, as a quasi natural phenomenon of my will, with which I am identical: that would be a downright invitation to naturalise the will and ignore freedom). Quite the contrary, it finds expression in the fact that I *can and must make a distinction between me and myself, in order not to remain who I am, but to become who I can be*. My freedom becomes apparent, *not* in my identity with my will (*I am my will*), but in the fact that (put negatively) I am capable of *non-identity with myself* (in other words, I do *not* have to will what I will, or that I do not have to will it in the way that I will it, but can will it differently, or can indeed will something different) and thus (put positively) am capable of *identification with others*, i. e. the interests of others: that is, I can make third-order decisions. I do not have to will what I will; rather, I can direct my will (that is, myself) so that I do not orient myself by my own interests and by what seems good for me, but by what others need and what is good for them; or – in Kantian radicality – that, in my willing, I orient myself solely by what all humans would orient themselves by, if they oriented their willing solely by what all humans would orient themselves by, if they oriented their willing solely by what all humans would …

## *11. Situation and self*

This is more than an empty iteration. In fact, it becomes apparent from the mere possibility of orienting oneself by such an open rule that it is not the alternatives with which we are presented, and thus the stimulus locations of the actual life situations in which we decide, that determine our decision. Rather, at every level of decision-making – between alternative actions: first-order decisions; between forms and modes of willing: second-order decisions; between ways of committing oneself to certain forms and modes of willing: third-order decisions – it is *we ourselves* who are the ones to decide what are to be regarded as relevant alternatives. We are selves in *situations* which are changed by decisions we take in establishing a concrete before/after distinction, which are, in other words, transformed from an initial state into a new state, and we are *selves* who are becoming selves, which change themselves, even as they *become selves.*

*Situation* is what I call a state of the world with reference to a choice. Situations are not restricted to the actual scenario; they include the totality of possibilities which are accessible to them, and into which the current state of the world could be transformed (including the possibility of remaining as it is). There are no situations *per se*; they exist only *for decision-makers.* Decision-makers for whom a state of the world, a situation and the potential continuations to this state are the decision alternatives of this situation, I call *selves.* Just as there are no situations *per se,* so equally there are no selves *per se. Self* and *situation* are instead two poles of the same constellation: Only a self has a situation, situations only exist for a self.

Situations are *decision situations* insofar as the transformation of or change to a state of the world does not take place causally or stochastically, but when a self brings about the given possibility by taking a decision: if it did not take a decision, everything would remain just as it is.

However, not all possibilities that are accessible from a given state of the world are relevant to the decisions of a self, but only those which represent serious decision alternatives for this self in this situation: not everything is possible all the time. Not everything that is possible is a serious alternative for us, i. e. something we have occasion or reason to choose. And not everything that is possible in a given situation for one person is also possible for another. Not only do we live in situations with possibilities specific to each of us, we each have specific inclinations, wishes, interests and maxims (if indeed we have any), and we live together in situations encompassing different alternatives for each of us, between which we can and must choose.

What this means becomes clear when we consider decision-making not purely as *choice*, but as a choice between *alternatives.*

### *12. Possibilities vs. alternatives*

*Alternatives* are possibilities between which a choice can be made. They are not merely possibilities as such, that is, something which *per se* is not impossible. Rather, they are possibilities which are subject to three conditions:

Firstly, they must be *accessible*: Not everything which is possible is accessible to everyone at any time, i.e. a possibility that would actually be open to everyone: Not everyone can become pope. However, it is not impossible to become pope, even though it is only actually possible for cardinals.

Secondly, they must be accessible *to the relevant decision-maker*: Not every possibility that is in principle accessible to us is also an *option which can in fact be chosen* by us. I could have bought the Bugatti I saw in Berlin. It was for sale. But I could not buy it, since I didn't have the money. The possibility was there, but *for me* it was not an affordable alternative and was not within reach. For me the only alternative within reach was the opposite one: not to buy the Bugatti. And now it is no longer for sale. That is often the way it is: "When the time comes in which one could, the time has passed in which one can."[11]

Thirdly, possibilities are only alternatives if they are not just accessible in practical terms and within someone's reach, but offer, in a given place or at a given time or for a given actor in a situation or a given state of the world, *alternative continuation possibilities*. In order for possibilities to be alternatives, two things must be true of them: They may not be compossible with each other (otherwise they are merely partial aspects of the same alternative), but there must be a shared third element with which each of them is compossible. To be pregnant and not to be pregnant are possibilities which are not compossible with each other. For a woman, however, but not for a man (currently at any rate), they are alternatives, since both possibilities are compossible with her state, although not with his current state.

To put it another way: In order to be alternatives, possibilities must, on the one hand, be *incompatible* with each other, that is, they cannot be true together. But on the other hand, they must be able to connect to the existing state of the world without conflict, in other words, they must be *compatible* with it. Only where there are at least two possibilities that can be connected compatibly to an existing state of the world without being compatible with each other, do we have a decision alternative. This is formally always a given when a compatible possibility is contradictorily negated. I could fill up the almost empty petrol tank of my car, but I also have the option of not doing so. The consequences will be different, but both are alternatives between which I must decide. However, where there is no 'on the other hand' which cannot be true simultaneously with an 'on the one hand', there is nothing to decide.

---

[11] Marie von Ebner-Eschenbach, *Aphorismen*, Stuttgart 2002, 21.

### *13. Decisions for us vs. decisions by us*

There is also nothing to decide where, although it is true that incompatible alternatives exist, *no decision is necessary* because there is *no decision trigger*, so that a change to the state of the world is neither sensible nor desirable (with the result that the state of the world remains just as it is in respect of this alternative). This may be because *no decision possibility* exists, so that a change to the state of the world occurs merely on a *random principle* basis, which now and again, for no (discernible) reason, allows one of a host of possible continuation states to become a reality; or it may be because there is *no decision necessity,* inasmuch as a *causally regulated* change occurs, so that the existing state of the world causes one of the alternative possibilities to put this cause into effect: the fact that the world is as it is makes A more likely to happen than B or C or …, since, given that the world is as it is, it is more probable that A will occur than any alternative.

Where there is no change trigger in this sense, or where chance rules or the nexus of cause and effect relationships is the driver of the change, then nothing is decided, or at any rate not *by us,* if one of various possibilities is realised de facto. The world has then indeed changed *for us*, but not *by us*.

*Strictly speaking,* a state is only changed *by a decision* when, not only is a new possibility realised, it is realised *by us*, i.e. it would not have come about if we had not decided in favour of it and made the decision effective as change by our action. The fact that a glass shattered because if fell off the table is only attributable to a decision (and not merely to an event such as an earthquake), if it would not have fallen from the table, if I had not (deliberately) pushed it.

If, on the other hand, one wants to attribute every change in the state of the world to a decision, thus understanding the idea of decision-making in the broadest sense, so that each realisation of an as yet unrealised possibility is perceived as a decision between alternatives, then the sphere of human decision-making does not begin until chance and causality have done their work, so that any change can no longer be adequately explained by reference to them. As Heinz von Foerster has said: "It is only *those* questions that are in principle undecidable that can be decided by *us*."[12] Most changes to our life situations take place by the stochastic and / or causally describable development or reshaping of an initial situation (a before) into another situation (an after) which can be understood, in the strict sense, without recourse to decisions. They happen *for us*, but are not brought about *by us*. If a decision between the continuation alternatives of a situation were only ever made fortuitously or causally, meaning that things would only happen if a third or additional element were to occur between the initial state and the target state, then there would be nothing for us to decide.

Only if not all that happens in a sequence of events occurs by unregulated chance or regulated causal sequence can we say that there are *decisions* in the strict sense of the word, since reference to targeted choice as the explanation for the change is then inescapable. However, where this is so, there is a choice between alternatives which are, for us, *really possible* (capable of continuation), *irreconcilable with each other* (incapable of being realised simultaneously) and *undecidable per se*, between which there would be no decision *unless a decision is made by us*. Decision-making in this sense consists not only of the choice between possibilities that are alternatives *for us*, but in the decision between such alternatives *by us*. This means that something which does not represent an actual possibility *for us* – one that we could choose – is not an alternative for us. But only alternatives which can be chosen *by us*, are not just either / or system alternatives , but on the one hand / on the other hand decision alternatives.

[12] H. von Foerster, *KybernEthik*, Berlin 1993, 153.

### *14. Decision-making: impossibility, reluctance and inability*

This does not mean that in every such case we take, or ought to take, a decision. Sometimes situations are such that the few possibilities open to us do not consolidate into alternatives between which we can decide. For instance, a decision may be impossible because it is not open to me at all, so that it is not a decision that can be taken *by me*; (I cannot make myself an heir, although of course I can accept or reject an inheritance that is left to me); or because the now-state (I have no income because I am unemployed) offers no serious alternatives (because there are no jobs available). Sometimes, however, there are alternatives between which one could decide (to work as a thief or as a banker or as both), but between which (for whatever reason) one does not want to decide (reluctance to decide) or is unable to decide (inability to decide): One could live *in this or some other way* (none of it is impossible or self-contradictory *per se*), but *I* cannot live *either in this or the other way*, since none of it is consistent with what I want to do or refrain from doing. So the alternatives certainly exist, and in fact they exist for me because I could choose between them, but I do not want to decide in favour of any of them because I am the way I am.

### *15. The impossibility of not deciding*

Ultimately, there are alternatives between which we not only can, but must, decide – decisions which are *made by us* because we cannot *not* decide between them. They are not simply decisions in the strict sense of the word; they are *unavoidable decisions*. Two examples in particular are worth mentioning here.

Firstly, there are decisions which are made unavoidably on my behalf by the decisions of others. One who is addressed by another cannot fail to communicate, since even ignoring the address will be understood as a response from the perspective of the one addressing him. Many of our everyday decisions are thus contingent upon the prior decisions of others. These bring about a situation in which it becomes impossible for us to make no decision. Someone who is appointed heir by an unknown uncle can – depending on the legacy – be pleased or annoyed about it, but he cannot choose whether or not to be the heir, but only to take up the inheritance or not.

Besides these decisions, which are contingent upon and provoked by the decisions of others, and from which one cannot extricate oneself once they have taken place, there is a second group of *fundamental decisions* which we do not make ourselves, but which arise nonetheless, and which do not remain undecided even if we abstain from making a decision, since our abstinence is in itself a decision. Shall I go on living or put an end to my life? I cannot decide to begin life. But once I am alive I can decide whether I will continue my life or end it. This alternative arises, not just once in a lifetime, but for as long as one lives and is capable of decision-making. Fundamental decisions can be never permanently dealt with, but arise over and over again; one cannot evade them, since in evading them one makes a decision by not deciding.

Briefly stated, only what is possible *for us*, is an alternative for us. Only alternatives between which a decision can be made *by us* are decision alternatives for us. Not all decision alternatives are ones between which we can decide or want to decide. But many decisions are ones from which we cannot extricate ourselves, no matter what we do. Not only can they be made by us, they are made by us, and because they are invariably decided in one way or another, they are fundamental alternatives which no one can evade.

## 16. Fundamental decisions

Everyone living is faced with these questions which are answered by means of fundamental decisions, and we are faced with them precisely because we are alive. But they arise in various ways in relation to the *That* of our Being-There ('Ought we to go on living?': the existence question), the *What* of our Being ('What are we as humans?': the essence question) and the *How* of our Living ('How do we want to, or how should we, live as human beings?': the mode of being question).

The *existence question* can only be asked by us because and to the extent that it has a positive answer: only because it *is already decided*, and not indeed by us, but for us, can we ask whether we intend to accept this decision or rescind it by means of another decision. Only one who is there (i.e. is alive) can question his or her Being-There, but if one decides that one does not want to be there any longer (i.e. does not want to live any longer), one cannot reverse this decision by means of another decision. Just as we do not enter life through our own decision, so also we cannot, through our own decision, reverse the decision not to live any longer. The existence decision is not simply asymmetrical in its presupposition of a non-retractable passivity before all activity: *that* we are alive is not our decision, but it is only on account of this positive prior decision that we are able to decide against continuing to live. It is also asymmetrical in that, if we want to make a further decision, we can only decide in favour of one of its alternatives: one who decides against continuing to live, has, in so doing, decided to relinquish the ability to make any further decisions. And this decision is irreversible.

The *essence question* is a decision question, since the answer to the question as to the What of our humanness is never merely descriptive, but encompasses a normative decision as to what we want to be as humans: 'What is a human?' is not a question to which a biological answer will suffice, since humans are beings who make their own decisions about their humanness, in that they live their lives in a specific way, either humanly or inhumanly. Since it is possible for humans to live inhumanly, they are compelled to decide what they want to be as humans and how they want to live as humans.

Precisely this is the *mode of being question* which none of us can evade: How do I live my life as a human? How can I live it? And how should I live it? Each of these questions has more than one possible answer, which is why one can and must make a decision. It has to be said that, as with the existence and essence questions, we can only ask the mode of being question because and insofar as we already live our lives in a particular way. Here too, the purpose of the question is not the making of a decision, but to examine, in the light of a decision already made, whether we could, or whether we want to or ought to, decide to live differently.

In contrast to the existence question and the essence question, there can, as we have seen, be two ways of posing the mode of being question:[13] (1) How do we live our lives (the How of our Being-What)? (2) How do we exist, as we conduct our lives (the How of our Being-There)? The first question regarding our *mode of life* focuses on the manner in which we conduct our lives and thus, treated normatively, on the *moral question of the good life* (as distinct from the bad life): how should a human live, so as to live in a truly human way? The second question regarding our *mode of existence* focuses on the manner of our being or existence, and thus on the *existential question as to the right life* (as distinct from the wrong life). Both questions presuppose that one can live (be) in one way other another, and can exist (be there) in one way or another. Just as ethical reflection has as its theme the question of the good life (How *should* we live – as humans amongst humans, as human beings amongst other living beings?), so in the same

[13] Cf. above Chapter D.

way, theological reflection has as its theme the question of living aright (How *can* we exist – before God, with God, through God?).

The theological answer is: human beings exist before God in one of two modes: *faith* or *unfaith*. Both are possible modes of existence for every human being and, where God's presence is concerned, they are the only two. Where God is concerned there is no neutral position. Anyone who lives, lives either in faith or not; the only one who lives in faith is one who comes from a position of unfaith; and, since no one comes from unfaith into faith of their own accord, the one to whom one owes this is the one whom, from the perspective of faith, one calls 'God'. Just as we did not decide of our own accord to come from Nonbeing into Being, i. e. to be there (to live), so in the same way we did not decide to come from unfaith into faith, i. e. to live in faith. Just as *Being-There* locates us, within the sphere of the world, amongst the real, so in the same way *Being-There-in-faith* locates us, within the sphere of the presence of God, amongst those who are only there (i. e. real) because God is really present to them. Being-There and having faith (being there in faith) are *determinations of existence* which are experienced as gifts, not ways of conducting one's life which one can ascribe to one's own decisions and activities. Rather, they are ascribed to him whom one calls 'God', and just as he is encoded, from the first perspective, as the *creator*, to whom one owes the gift of life, so from the second perspective, he is described as the *new creator*, to whom one owes one's ability to be thankful for the gift of life.

The theological reference to faith, Being-There and God is not a contribution to the determination of who and what we are or how we should live in order to live well. Rather, it clarifies *how* we exist, if we are alive, and indeed more precisely, how we exist *before God*, and as what our life proves to be when one considers it from the perspective of living it in the light of the presence of God: as a gift from God, which one ignores or for which one gives thanks. Both are clear from the way in which one actually lives. Nevertheless, the theological reference to God as the giver of the gift of life answers and decides, not the moral question as to how a good life is to be lived (it is we ourselves who are to decide that), but the fundamental existential question as to how we are to live aright before God (this is decided in accordance with the decision God has made).

However the mode of being question is by no means limited to this. As we have seen, it arises at all levels of human life, calling for a different answer at different points. Thus the *How of what it is to be human* is determined biologically as *humanness* (key antithesis *human / non-human*), the *How of humanness* ethically as *humanity* (key antithesis *human / inhuman*) and the *How of humanity* theologically as *love of God and neighbour* (key antithesis: *human / divine*), which in faith is lived out and in unfaith is not lived out. But these various answers are by no means answers to the same question, but to different ones. Confusion invariably arises if one seeks to give a theological answer to ethical or biological questions, or an ethical answer to biological or theological questions, or a biological answer to ethical and theological questions. Decisions that are correct in relation to one question will miss the point of others completely. Moralism when dealing with biological or theological questions is just as misguided as is naturalism in relation to ethical and theological matters or theism in the context of biological and ethical issues. Each of these fundamental questions calls for its own type of decision-making and thus opens up the horizon for a fundamental decision that is normative for it. But each of these fundamental decisions also acquires its profile by bringing to mind and remaining aware of the 'on the one hand' and 'on the other hand' of the others. For where 'on the other hand' is no longer said and thought, the questions become unclear and the answers uncritical (generalised) and dogmatic (indiscriminate) – whether they arise scientifically in the form of naturalism, ethically as moralism or theologically as theism.

### *17. From choosing to determining*

In summary: if behaviour is understood as decision-making and decision-making as choosing between alternatives, then decision-making in the strong sense is to be more fully expressed, not simply as systemic deciding between an either / or, but as a choice-decision between an on the one hand / on the other hand. This means that

1. we have here *firstly*, not merely different possibilities, but possibilities that are incompatible with each other, both of which can be continued to the now-state; *secondly*, we have possibilities between which one not only can, but must, choose in order that something changes; and *thirdly*, we have a decision which, in the case of the systemic non-decision, brings about a decision on the basis of criteria other than those of the relevant system.

2. That such strong decisions are possible is settled, not at the level of alternative possibilities for action (freedom of action), but at the level of alternative ways in which the will can determine actions (freedom of will) and, beyond that, of alternative possibilities for establishing the mode of determining one's own will (i. e. oneself).

3. The fact that such determinations can be directed by rules or regulations which are focussed, not purely on one's own interest, but on the well-being of the whole, which can indeed go against one's own interests for the sake of the good of the whole, reveals two things. From a negative point of view it shows that our self-determination (autonomy) consists in our being able to distinguish our selves from our own will (i. e. ourselves). From a positive point of view it shows that, when it comes to our decisions regarding the mode (the How) of our will, we can allow our selves to be governed, not by the actual circumstances of our concrete life situation, but by our orientation to the other as it coalesces into our self-determination.

4. The phenomenon of decision-making thus focusses, not on the solitary decision-maker after the model of the *rational agent*, but quite the contrary on the fact that humans live and can live humanly as human beings because, at the heart of their capacity to decide in the strong sense, they are not self-referential and self-limited, but open towards others. We live in the light of prior decisions taken by others *for us*, and there is no way we can decide to appropriate these as our own decisions.

5. It follows that, in all decisions made *by us*, we must pay attention, not only to whatever makes it possible for us to live a good life amongst our fellow humans (the moral question as to the good life), but also to whatever enables us to live a life that is right before God, together with our fellow humans (the existential question as to the right life). In both cases our decision options are contingent upon decisions that have been taken for us by others or by God, and in both cases we remain so dependent on these pre-existing decisions made by others that we can neither replace them with our own decisions nor dispense with them. Our very autonomy is testimony to our passive dependency on decisions made by others for us. Without such decisions we would not exist (be there), and without them we would not, as human beings (among other living beings), be who we could be (as humans among our fellow humans) and should therefore become (persons among persons).[14]

[14] Cf. I. U. Dalferth, *Creatures of Possibility: The Theological Basis of Human Freedom*, Grand Rapids 2016.

## F. Wholly other. Negativity as a possibility condition for differentiation

### *1. The impossibility of radical negativity*

God, so it is said, is wholly other. But can there in fact be something other that is not merely other *than* something, but is simply, exclusively and purely other; can one even speak meaningfully of such a thing? From our point of view, such a 'something' would have to be defined in exclusively negative terms. Yet nothing which is defined purely *negatively* is even rudimentarily *defined*. It is not clear whether one is speaking of Something, or, more likely, of Nothing. Something which is wholly differentiated from everything can no longer be spoken of as Other. Likewise, the wholly Other, if it is to be differentiated from the Nothing, need not be characterised purely negatively. Nothing can be radically negative, since radical negativity is impossible.

The reason for this is simple, but has significant implications: "All possibility presupposes something actual in which and through which all that can be thought is given," as Kant rightly emphasised.[1] If radical negativity is to be possible, then either it or something else, must be actual. If something else is actual, which is what it is without radical negativity while radical negativity could not be possible without it, then radical negativity is not radical, but impossible. For negativity is *radical* precisely when, in order to be actual, it has to take itself into consideration, when it thus has nothing to which it can make reference without

[1] I. Kant, *Der einzig mögliche Beweisgrund zu einer Demonstration des Daseins Gottes* (1763), A 29–31, AA II, 83.

*also* relating itself to itself and assuming its own actuality; and it is *absolute,* when, in order to be actual, it does not and need not refer to any actuality other than itself, so that it takes *only* itself and its own actuality into consideration. If it is only a contingent actuality, in that it could also not exist, then there would have to be something actual that is absolutely necessary, the removal or repudiation of which would make negativity impossible as well; and consequently negativity would indeed be possible, but not radical. If, on the other hand, it is itself absolutely necessary, then it would be something which can never be thought of as non-existent. It would then be necessary to itself, but would not be something which could be only possible, but something which must be actual. If radical negativity can exist, then it must exist. But can it exist? And is it in fact anything?

## *2. Negation as operation*

Negativity, as we know, is something other than negation. But what is it, if it is something? Even that could be the wrong question. Not everything for which we have a sign can be defined semantically (that is, by contrasts of meaning alone) as something ('What is ...'). Signs can describe something when they are applied to it in a conventional way within the context of a code ('table', 'Tisch', 'la mesa'). They can point in any direction when they are used thus (as a signpost). They can qualify something by distinguishing it from something else in a specific way ('... is red'). But they can also have a primarily pragmatic function rather than a semantic one (time and place indicators, personal pronouns). They can function as a medium which uses what they say (describe) in order to show (reveal) something else, so that their communicative point lies, not in what they show or say (directly), but in what is revealed (indirectly) in and by means of them (illocutionary force; symbols). Or they can indicate an operation which is or is to be carried out with or by other signs.

This last group includes logical operators for *comparisons* (greater, smaller, equal, unequal), for *quantifications* (all, some, many, at least one), for *modalities* (possible, impossible, necessary, contingent), for *logical or semantic inferences* (imply, deduce, conclude) or for *connectors* such as the *conjunction* (and), the *disjunction* (or) or indeed the *negation* (not). These logical signs do not describe or represent anything.[2] They do not stand for anything that could be discussed or examined independently of themselves. They are not descriptions, but *operators*, or, more precisely, they are signs which indicate that a specific operation is to be performed on something – a negation operation, for instance. In so doing, however, they presuppose more than one thing without which the performance of an operation would not be possible: It is necessary that (1) there be something to be operated on (something *negatable*), (2) something which performs the operation (a *negator*), and (3) something with the aid of which the operation is performed (a *negation device*). The necessary condition for this kind of sign operation is invariably not only logical, but also pragmatic. Only where there are two (possible) clauses can they be connected by 'and'. And only where there is a (possible) clause p, a clause which negates it and something by means of which it is negated, can it be negated as non-p. In itself, the *negation* operator has no meaning. One cannot simply negate. One always negates *something* – either in certain respects (determinate or partial negation) or completely (total negation). If there is nothing negatable, then there is no negation. However, only where there is someone or something that can and does perform it, is there a negation. As an operator, negation

[2] L. Wittgenstein, *Tractatus logico-philosophicus. Logisch-philosophische Abhandlung*, Frankfurt a. M. 2003, 4.0312: "My fundamental idea is that the 'logical constants' do not represent anything."

is not just dependent on there being something on which it is performed (p), but also on there being someone or something by whom or which it is performed. If there is no negator, then there is no negation. And finally, there is only negation insofar as there is something with the aid of which it is performed, i.e. a device without which the sign operation of negating cannot be performed. If there is no negation device, there is no negation. Thus, negation is always *negation of* … (the negatable), *negation by* … (the negator) and *negation with the aid of* … (the negation device), and all three elements indicate prerequisites without which negation is not possible.

### *3. Negativity as an attribute of negation*

Is this also true of *negativity*? That depends on how we understand the term. The form of the word suggests that the term does not denote an operation, but an *attribute* – that which renders the negative negative. The *negative*, however, stands in contrast to the *positive* and is thus determined by its antithesis to the positive just as the positive is by its antithesis to the negative. If negative and positive always stand in relationship to each other, then not only is the negative characterised, in relation to the positive, by the structural attribute of negativity, but the same is true of the positive in relation to the negative: without negativity there is neither negative nor positive. Negativity is that which not only makes the negative to be negative, but also the positive to be positive. This does not mean that negativity is a structural attribute of *both* the negative *and* the positive (it determines neither the negative nor the positive); rather, by expressing its reciprocal otherness, it marks the *distinction* between the two (thus determining their difference) which the process of negating articulates: negativity characterises neither the positive nor the negative, but the relationship of contrast between them.

Is that all? Surely not. If it characterises this relationship of contrast, then it characterises every such relationship. Nothing can be other than something else without the involvement of negativity, which expresses itself variously in specific distinctions, differentiations, or negations. That applies not only to the *factual* (nothing is factual without something else being non-factual), but also to the *possible* (nothing is possible without being distinguished from other possibilities), not only to *signs* (every sign is what it is because it is different from all other signs belonging to its particular system), but also to what is *signified* (everything is determined by being distinguished from what is other: *Omnis determinatio est negatio*[3]). As a necessary attribute of distinctions or relationships of contrast, negativity is that which makes possible the differentness of the different, which negates its non-differentness (or identity) and reinforces its reciprocal otherness (or non-identity). Without negativity there is no differentness. *Negativity is the necessary condition which enables all differentness.*

### 4. *The aporia of radical negativity*

But what is the necessary condition for negativity? Only if it were possible or necessary to answer negativity by pointing to negativity itself, would radical negativity be possible or actual in the sense envisaged here.[4] Negativity would be radical if it were

---

[3] B. DE SPINOZA, Letter to Jarigh Jelles on 2 June 1674, in: Benedictus de Spinoza, *Spinozas Briefwechsel.* Verdeutscht und mit einer Einleitung und Anmerkungen versehen von J. STERN, Leipzig 1904, Nr. 50. Cf. W. RÖD, Omnis determinatio est negatio, in: W. HOGREBE (ed.), *Grenzen und Grenzüberschreitungen. XIX. Deutscher Kongress für Philosophie. Bonn, 23.-27.9.2002*, Berlin 2004, 478–489.

[4] This need not be an *absolute* negativity, i. e. such a radicalisation of radical negativity that negativity is made possible, not just through itself, but through itself *alone*.

not only the necessary condition for differentness, but also, in reference to itself, the necessary condition for its own differentness from itself. Only thus would it be, not only the necessary condition for differentness, but the necessary condition for its self-differentness as the enabling of the necessary condition of differentness. Its self-reference would indicate, not a different identity, but, on the contrary, such a non-identity or reciprocal otherness between it and its self, that not only does it itself become possible thereby, but also the differentiation between what is different. Differentiation between what is different would, accordingly, be made possible, not only through negativity, but through the differentness of negativity from itself.

Not only does this allow the concept of radical negativity to be more clearly formulated, but at the same time shows that it is impossible, and why. If negativity is the necessary condition for differentness, then radical negativity is the enablement of this condition through its differentness from itself – whether it be through structural *self-differentness* (negativity stands in a relationship of reciprocal otherness to itself) or as active *self-differentiation* (negativity differentiates itself from itself through itself in the process of differentiation). In the first instance negativity would be characterised by a fundamental differentness from itself, a differentness which cannot be subdued, but can only ever put it into effect, since it realises itself as differentness from the differentness which realises itself as differentness from the differentness which … This means that negativity would not only be something negatable (p), but would differentiate itself permanently into the distinction between the negatable and the negated (p = p / non-p), that is, it would appear as something which, on account of its intrinsic structure of self-annulment, cannot appear at all. In the second instance, on the other hand, this differentness would be the result of a distinction which would be attributed to negativity itself, which, as the distinguishing of itself from itself, distinguishes itself from that which, as the distinguishing of itself from itself, distinguishes itself from that which, as the distinguishing of itself from itself, distinguishes itself from that which … This means that negativity would be not only something negatable, but simultaneously its own negator.

Both are aporetic. In the first instance, negativity would be *in itself* (and not merely in contrast to the other) the Other of itself, which seems a contradiction in terms. In the second instance, it would be *through itself* (and not through what is other) the Other of itself, which seems just as much a contradiction in terms. One way or the other, it would be negativity, not in the antithetical relationship of the reciprocal otherness of the different (*this/that*), but in the antithetical relationship of the differentness of its relationship to itself (*this/this*). It would enable differentness by entering into a relationship of differentness (i. e. of reciprocal otherness) to itself, so that not only would it negate the identity of the different, but would in turn negate this negation, and indeed would negate this negation of its negation, and so on. There would be no end to this negation, which would continue its self-referencing by negating that which is thereby established as reciprocal otherness – *ad infinitum*.

### *5. Negativity as the enactment of reality in time*

It is clear that negativity, viewed thus as the formal necessary condition for differentness, is transmuted into a process of positing and annulling differentness which requires one thing above all: time. While it is possible to distinguish between *this* and *that* by reference to attributes which characterise their relationship of contrast, it is not possible to distinguish between *this* and *this* through recourse to attributes, but only through recourse to the sequence of references to *this* in time. In itself, the dependence of the enablement of reciprocal otherness on the distinction of that which enables this distinction, does not have recourse to any ultimate identity, but to a difference which exists only in repeating itself, and can only repeat itself in annulling, over and over again, what it posits. Negativity is enacted as the negation of negation and thus as a process in time.

In this process, as pre-eminently Hegel reasoned, there is no pure being and no pure nothing, but only a becoming which, in the dismantling and reconstruction of the different by means of negation, converts it into something else different. Absolute nothing is a void (*ex nihilo nihil fit*); it is a purely abstract contrasting concept which cannot be distinguished from its antithesis, pure being, but rather coincides with it: "This pure being is […] *pure abstraction*, as is the *absolute-negative*, which, likewise taken directly, is *nothing*."[5] Only non-being, considered retrospectively from the perspective of being, directed as it is towards being, carried within itself the dynamic to become: It is the *possibile* of a *not-yet-being*, which presses on towards realisation. But this applies to each stage of finite becoming. The realisation process is accomplished through the negation of each position which, in the light of the not-yet, further develops that which has come about thus far, driving it forward into the deepening, unfolding and actualisation of its truth.

Negation thus takes the form, not merely of an operation for the determination of truth, but of a means for the construction and unfolding of a reality determined by reason and truth. It can and must be iterated time and again, establishing thereby, as the process of determining signs, a truth process of reality. But this means that, for the negativity process, the operation of negating needs *time* to be able to move from p to non-p. It presupposes something *actual*, on which it operates by extending it against the background of its possibilities into its not-yet-ness or otherness. It requires a (sign) *medium*, with the aid of which it can be

---

[5] G. W. F. Hegel, *Enzyklopädie der philosophischen Wissenschaften, Werke 8*, Frankfurt a. M. 1986, § 87, 186.

accomplished. And because of the time and media expended, the iteration of the negation can never return to the formal starting point of the negation process (p): to negate non-p (non-non-p) results, not in the starting position p, but in a new state q, which can, in its turn, be further extended by negation. Despite the elementary and inexorable nature of the process of negativity, there is little that is elementary about the negation operation as the enactment form of this process. It invariably presupposes a complex signifying practice in time, which is taken into account in every act of negation. Without time, mediation (actuality), possibility (extensibility) and signifying practice there is no negating and no negation.

Without the enactment form of negating, however, there is also no negativity process. Negativity cannot therefore be radical: it cannot originate entirely from the positing of differentness in a self-relationship. To be possible, radical negativity would have to presuppose itself – and in fact, as absolute negativity, itself alone. But it cannot do this without enacting itself in a concrete manner, thus referring back to something which does not owe its existence to its self-differentiation, but which actually makes it possible in the first place. This can be elucidated as follows.

As I have said, negativity would be radical if the *negatable*, the *negator*, the *negation device* and the *enactment of the negation* were coincidental. In that case it would not be determined by its antithetical relationship to something else, but solely by itself, in negating its own negation – which is negated in its turn, and so on. Thus it never concludes or completes the negating process, but continues it self-referentially in negating what it posits thereby – *ad infinitum*. This very process, however, presupposes more than merely its own enactment. A negativity that, in the process of negating, posits itself over and over again, would consequently be the ground of time and of all being in time. For, in repeatedly negating itself, and thus positing itself as negation in the negating process, it gives itself again and again, time to negate itself. In this succession of negations it posits permanent differences which subsequently and self-referentially nullify themselves, thus constituting time as the sequence of negation by negations successively negated: nothing is that is not becoming; nothing is becoming that does not negate something else; and nothing negates something else that does not negate itself and thereby cease to be. In order that this negativity process can begin at all, something must be presupposed that can be negated, and that something cannot be a negation itself, since such a negation would in its turn have to make the same presupposition. This, however, is paradoxical and must mean that radical negativity is only possible when it is impossible: To be possible, it must presuppose itself, but this it cannot do without making itself impossible. That which would have to be true to make it possible is simultaneously that which would make it impossible if it were true. To paraphrase Derrida: *The necessary condition for radical negativity is simultaneously the condition for its impossibility.*

## *6. Versions of negativity*

It is not the possibility of negativity that is thereby called into question, but that of radical negativity, and indeed in a fundamental way. It is true that negativity can be understood, not just semiotically as a structural attribute of distinctions which for their part require something different from mere signs, or, as Hegel does, ontologically as the self-referential dynamic of permanently self-negating negation in the reality process which cannot start with itself, but must begin from and with something entirely other. But nor can it be radical other interpretations and versions, either, since each must posit something other than mere negativity in order to make negativity possible. Just to take a few examples:

In the *practical sense*, negativity is a shorthand term for experiences such as pain, loss, fear, suffering, failure and permanent breakdown or the depressing discovery that all one's endeavours end in the opposite of what one had intended, hoped or expected. But only one who lives can experience this, and no life is determined solely by such experiences and events. One can only experience pain, fear or breakdown against the background possibility of a successful life. Both as the reality (of actual life) and as the possibility (of a successful life), more must be present than merely the negativity of failure.

In the *ontological sense*, a reference to negativity functions as an allusion to the origin (the whence) or the future (the whither) of being, i.e. the about-turn from non-being to being, or the converse turn from being to non-being. Since this presupposes a position *in being*, from which or towards which the change from non-being to being or from being to non-being can be considered, being has priority, both methodologically and ontologically. The negativity of non-being cannot be conceived of radically, either as the origin or as the future of being. Rather, the change can only ever be described modally as a change from being possible to being actual, or from being actual to being possible. In either case, the being-possible is considered from the perspective of the actual, whether it be retrospectively as a not-yet-being or prospectively as a no-longer-being. Each can be understood either as a change to being (a coming-into-being) or from being (a ceasing-to-be), or as a change in being (a becoming-other). Thus *coming-into-being* is a change from non-being to being-there and *ceasing-to-be* is a change from being-there to non-being, while *becoming-other* represents a change from being-thus to being-other, which can be more precisely defined in various specific ways (as a quantitative, qualitative, locational or temporal change etc.).

In the *epistemological sense*, negativity can mean that which, from the perspective of the positive, can be considered and acknowledged as that which precedes it, accompanies it or follows it without ever being able to be sublated into the positive. Of course, this too cannot be defined in a radical and positive way, but only ever in terms of boundary concepts. The negative, against which the positive is set in contrast, can be described from the perspective of, and within the horizon of, the positive, but not within its own horizon (to the extent that it has one at all): As Hegel emphasised, it cannot be viewed as nothing, but at most as non-being. Epistemically it is thus only ever a negativity which is "grenzbegrifflich" i.e. a boundary concept beyond precise description, to be found under the sign of positivity. Such "boundary concepts", as Kant emphasised, do not have a descriptive or determinative function. Rather, they serve to limit claims to validity and to mark out the sphere available for the meaningful use of descriptive concepts of meaning. They do not describe something negative, but state where and how the positive has its boundaries and under what conditions it can be recognised as positive. However, necessary conditions are only available *with* what is conditioned, not without it and in their own right. They flag up a relative difference from that which they conditionally enable, but they are not in themselves assumed and accessible. Thus they never appear alone and unattached, but only ever with and in relation to something else.

That applies equally when one construes negativity *in its semiotic sense.* The meaning of a sign is the totality of its differences from all other signs. Unless this totality is limited, its meaning would be indeterminable or only ever a relative, hypothetical construal. In order that the negativity of differentiation can operate in a determinative way, it must be circumscribed by a boundary. Limitless differentiation is the dissolution of all meaning. Without the demarcating distinction from all that is senseless, meaningless and nonsensical, there is nothing that is meaningful. But it would be a methodological and material error, from the perspective of the meaningful to attribute meaning to the meaningless (as can be demonstrated when dealing with evil). Without the existence of a *difference* between sense and non-sense there is no sense. However, taken in isolation, that does not allow one to explicate the negativity of non-sense as the sense of the senseless.

Ultimately, that applies also to attempts to understand negativity *hermeneutically*, and to construe it as non-understanding, misunderstanding or incomprehension, as deficiency or lack of meaning or as meaninglessness or nonsense. Even if it were true that all understanding presupposes a background of non- and misunderstanding, it does not follow that some instances of the incomprehensible may be understood, or that everything that is not understood or misunderstood could, in fact, be understood, or that non-understanding is itself a type of understanding. Here too, the negative other to understanding is not to be construed in a descriptively determinative way, but as a demarcating boundary. From the perspective of understanding, the negativity of the incomprehensible can be understood only as a boundary line, not as fundamentally determinative in itself. Without meaning it is impossible even to speak of nonsense and meaninglessness.

### *7. Ramified negativity: contradiction and conflict*

The possible understandings of negativity we have outlined can be split into two lines of thought which have surfaced repeatedly in the history of reflection on negativity and can be formulated as semantic *contradiction* and empirical *conflict*. Kant's analysis was systematically clear. In his treatise, *Attempt to Introduce the Concept of Negative Magnitudes into Philosophy* (1763), he differentiates *logical contraposition* or contradiction from *actual contraposition* without contradiction,[6] and he further subdivides

[6] I. Kant, *Versuch den Begriff der negativen Größen in die Weltweisheit einzuführen*, A3–A6, *AA II*, 171–173.

the latter into *oppositio actualis* and *oppositio potentialis.*[7] In the mathematical sense, the concept of negative magnitude is a mere relative or contrasting concept: "A magnitude is negative in regard to another magnitude inasmuch as it cannot be conjoined with it except by an opposition, that is, inasmuch as the one magnitude makes a magnitude equal to itself disappear from another. It is clear that this is an antithetical relationship, and magnitudes which are mutually opposed in this way offset each other in equal measure, so that one cannot simply call a magnitude negative, but must say that +a and −a are each the negative magnitude of the other: purely because this is always an implied meaning, mathematicians have adopted the practice of using the term negative magnitude for magnitudes in front of which the – sign [negative sign] stands, whereby one must not fail to take into account the fact that this nomenclature does not indicate something which is of a special type according to its inner characteristics, but indicates its antithetical relationship with other things marked with the + sign, which with they are conjoined in opposition."[8]

---

[7] Loc. cit., A47–A49, *AA II*, 192–193: "So far I have merely considered the grounds of real opposition, in so far as they *actually* posit in one and the same thing determinations of which one is the negative of the other. A case in point would be motive forces of the same body acting in exactly opposing directions, so that their reciprocal consequences cancel each other's movements out in real terms. For this reason, for the time being, I shall call this opposition *actual opposition* (oppositio actualis). On the other hand, to take predicates of the following kind: although they belong to different things and although the one predicate does not immediately cancel the consequence of the other predicate, nonetheless, the one may legitimately be called the negative of the other, in so far as each is so constituted that it is either capable of cancelling the consequence of the other, or is capable of cancelling something which is determined like that consequence and which is equal to it. This opposition may be called *possible opposition* (oppositio potentialis). Both are real, that is, distinguished from the logical opposition; both are in constant use in mathematics and both deserve to be employed in philosophy as well."

[8] Loc. cit., A9–A10, *AA II*, 173–174.

In the case of "real opposition" this is different, since "real repugnancy [...] only occurs where there are two things as *positive grounds* and where one of them cancels the consequence of the other. Suppose that motive force is a positive ground: a real conflict can only occur in so far as there is another motive force connected with it, and in so far as each reciprocally cancels the other. The following may serve as a general proof. *Firstly*: the conflicting determinations must exist in the same subject. For, suppose that there is one determination in one thing and another determination, no matter what, in another thing: no actual opposition arises therefrom. *Secondly*, one of the opposed determinations in a real opposition cannot be the contradictory opposite of the other, for if it were, the conflict would be logical and, as proved above, impossible. *Thirdly*, a determination cannot negate anything other than what is posited by the other determination, for otherwise there would be no opposition at all. *Fourthly*, in so far as they conflict with each other, the two determinations cannot both be negative, for if they were, neither of them would posit anything to be cancelled by the other. Accordingly, in every real opposition the predicates must both be positive, but in such a way that, when they are combined, there is a reciprocal cancellation of the consequences in the same subject. In this way, if two things, of which one is regarded as the negative of the other, are viewed in themselves, they are both positive; only if they are combined in one subject is the result of the combination zero. A journey westwards is just as much a positive motion as a journey eastwards; but if we are dealing with one and the same ship, the distances thus covered cancel each other out, either completely or in part."[9]

It follows that, rather than adopting the traditional position, one must describe negative phenomena – or, more precisely: phenomena that are called negative – differently, that is as something

[9] Loc. cit., A13–A14, *AA II*, 175–176.

which lacks something because something else has deprived it of that something (*privatio*), or as something which is not (yet) what it could be (*defectus*). "A negation, in so far as it is the consequence of a real opposition, I will call a *deprivation* (privatio); But any negation, in so far as it does not arise from this type of repugnancy, will be called a *lack* (defectus, absentia). The latter does not require a positive ground, but merely the lack of such a ground; But the former involves a true ground of the position and another ground, of the same magnitude, which is opposed to it. In a body, rest is either merely a lack, that is, a negation of motion, in so far as no motive force is present, or alternatively, rest is a deprivation, in so far as there is indeed a motive force present, though its consequence, namely the motion, is cancelled by an opposed force."[10]

Thus Kant distinguishes, not only between *logical opposition* and *real opposition*, but also between two forms of real negativity, which he defines more precisely as *deprivation* (*privatio*) or as *lack* (*defectus, absentia*). Neither should be confused with formal negation, but are reality phenomena – either something is not what it could and should be (*absentia*), or something cannot be what it is because it is being prevented by a counterforce (*privatio*). For Kant, therefore, *privatio* (conflict as deprivation) and *absentia* (conflict as prevention) are *negativity phenomena* and not *forms of negation*; they are not the results of formal sign operations directed towards the avoidance of *conflict*, but are *negative reality phenomena*, that is, phenomena of *conflict*, which highlight the fact that something is not as it could and should be, because it has not yet developed its potential, or is being prevented from doing so by opposition from something else.[11]

---

[10] Loc. cit., A17–A18, *AA II*, 177–178.

[11] H. Tegtmeyer, *Gott, Geist und Vernunft: Prinzipien und Probleme der Natürlichen Theologie*, Tübingen 2013, 310 has not grasped this point because he is thinking, not critically, but dogmatically. The question at

This has consequences for our understanding of the negation operation. It operates on and with signs (*non*-p), but it can also indicate negativity or conceal it. It is necessary, therefore, to distinguish between the *determinacy* constituted by separating it from what is other (p) and the *negation* of what is thus determined (non-p). Only something which is *something* can be negated. And it only is something if it is *determined*. And it is only determined insofar as it is distinguished from what is other (as something determined), or from everything else (as fully determined).

We must therefore make the assumption that there are *branches* of negativity: Every sign is what it is, only by being distinct from other signs (differentiation), and only something which is distinct from other somethings can by symbolised by a sign (otherness). We must distinguish between them both, since the *determinacy of the sign* and the *determinacy of what it symbolises* are not one and the same. The negation of the sign and the determinacy of what is signified have only one thing in common, namely that they each represent a *separation*: p is something other than q, r, s etc., and the negation of p is an operation on this sign, not on what it signifies. But a separation can be a *boundary* or a *border*. Either it can function purely negatively or critically, marking off an area, without it being possible or necessary that there is anything else behind it (horizon). Or it can function positively like a border, allowing one to move beyond it and look back to what preceded it from the perspective of what comes after it or is different from it. In the first instance we have a (non-determinative) *boundary concept*, in the second we have a (determinative or descriptive) *transcendence concept*.

---

issue in the passage he quotes is not that of the understanding of *privatio* as a "robust ontological concept" or as a "mere expression of 'our attitude to the world'", but the question as to why tradition speaks of a *privatio boni* and of a *privatio mali*. Cf. DALFERTH, *Malum*, 127 f.

### *8. Ontological negativity: from the singular to the whole*

Kant's distinction between *logical* contradiction and *real* conflict has important implications. The logical contradiction can be formally iterated without requiring ontologically extended preconditions. It requires merely the possibility of other possibilities and reaches its limit only where a contradiction leads to the compossibility of different possibilities being impossible. Real conflict on the other hand requires not only something else that is possible, but something else that is real, which is not only distinct from the one reality, but opposes it and conflicts with it. Alongside the otherness of the possible, therefore, we have the conflict of the real, and it is essential to differentiate between them.

This is the point at which Hegel begins his definition of negativity. It is not merely a formal sign operation, but the fundamental principle of reality. Everything real is what it is because it became what it is, and it became what it is through the constant ongoing determination and development of what it currently is, through the realisation of what it has not yet become, and the related overcoming of what, as a result, it no longer is. Viewed in this way, everything real is, over the course of time, a point of passage to something else, and is thus, given that it is and that it is as it is, related to what is other, and thereby to itself as that which is other than the other.[12] Negativity thus appears, not as the primary determination of the single real (limit, border, lack), but as the basic attribute of the becoming-other of the real in the process of reality. It is the fundamental character of the distinction of every real thing from every other real thing, that is from another state of its reality against the background of the possible within the whole of the reality process. As the "negation of

---

[12] Chr. Asmuth, Negativität. Hegels Lösung der Systemfrage in der Vorrede der *Philosophie des Geistes*, *Synthesis Philosophica 43* (2007) 19–32.

otherness", the dynamic negation of negation is not negation of the single real, but the determination mode of the relation of the whole to itself in the diversity of its forms (plurality) and in the progressive change in its states (process): "Moreover, when we speak of negativity or negative nature", states Hegel in his *Science of Logic* in 1812, "we do not mean the first negation, the limit, border or lack, but rather inherently the negation of being other, that is, the *relation to the self*".[13] "Negativity – in contrast to negation – focusses on the whole, which is not simply negation or negation of negation, but is the whole of this movement, *the relation to the self*. This view of the whole and its processual aspect deprives negation of its destructive character. Even in Fichte's and Schelling's thought there are points at which negation has to espouse destructive moments. For Fichte, to think in terms of negationless unity, without even the possibility of diversity, is the very task of thought. For Hegel, on the other hand, negation guarantees the diversity of forms and, qua negation of negation, renders a self-enriching, self-developing and intelligible unity possible."[14]

Hence reality itself is marked by the process of negativity, and this in fact manifests itself at the experiential level in human consciousness as infinite pain in the face of the permanent no-more and not-yet of all becoming: "The human being has this consciousness within himself, that there is in his innermost being this contradiction; there is thus an *infinite pain regarding himself*. Pain is present only in contrast to an ought, an affirmative. That which no longer has an affirmative in itself has no contradiction either, no pain. Pain is in fact negativity in the affirmative, meaning that in itself the affirmative is self-contradictory and wounded."[15]

---

[13] G. W. F. HEGEL, *Logik* (1812), *Werke 5*, Frankfurt a. M. 1986, 77.

[14] ASMUTH, Negativität, 28.

[15] G. W. F. HEGEL, *Vorlesungen über die Philosophie der Religion*, *Werke 17*, Frankfurt a. M. 1986, 263.

Here too, negativity is bound up with an affirmation, and is its reverse side. It is true that, unlike in classical metaphysics, there cannot be a full identity, a quintessence of reality, as there is in the classical concept of God, concerning whom it was wrongly held that the reality "still remained, even when all negation, but also therefore all its determinacy is abolished. It alone is being as a whole; it contains being-for-other, and indeed the limit or determinacy."[16]

This means that as *being as a whole* it cannot deny and overcome negativity, but remains perpetually characterised by it. It is therefore not, as Adorno feared, a mere resting identity, in which everything is interconnected with everything, but neither is it an absolute negativity; rather, as pure repose, it is at the same time constant radical movement: "the Bacchanalian revel at which no member is sober; yet, since each member collapses as soon as he drops out, the revel is equally a scene of transparent and simple repose".[17]

### *9. Negative dialectics: non-identity and redemption*

In contrast to Hegel, Adorno had believed in the necessity of insisting on the non-identity of negativity. The openness and incompleteness of the non-identical must not be allowed to be labelled undialectically as "absolute negativity". To do so would, as an unlimited affirmation of the negation of negativity, be itself a positive proposition, incompatible with the assertion of comprehensive negativity. "Negative philosophy, dissolving everything, dissolves even the dissolvent. But the new form in which it claims to suspend and preserve both, dissolved and

---

[16] HEGEL, *Logik*, 65.

[17] G. W. F. HEGEL, *Phänomenologie des Geistes, Werke* 3, Frankfurt a. M. 1986, 46.

dissolvent, can never emerge in a pure state from an antagonistic society. As long as domination reproduces itself, the old quality reappears unrefined in the dissolving of the dissolvent […]."[18] In the finitude of concrete reality there is no identity which is not suspended by negation and included in the progressive determination and development of negativity. But infinitude is not simply an endless continuation of this process – that would merely be a "bad infinitude", in which the same operation would repeat itself interminably. *True infinitude* is the whole, which is not distinguished from the other by any difference, but contains all differences within itself. In the finite this can never be reflected, since in finitude only the finite can represent both the finite and the infinite. Thus there is, within the finite, no representation (sign) of the whole, that can encompass or represent its complexity: Reality is not just inherently plural and diverse, it is, rather, always more complex than every possible representation of it.

But this is just one direction in which this insight can be developed. If we emphasise, not the factual, but the counterfactual in this process, it points, not to the 'still more', but to the 'wholly other'. With Adorno both are present. Thus, on the one hand, he emphasises the insuperability of the non-identical in the concrete life-process of society: so long as domination keeps reproducing itself, the negativity of reality cannot be transformed into its opposite. It persists, in whatever way it may change. Our struggle with the numerous different negativities of our lives therefore leads to a constant endeavour to live differently in our world, but we never find a way of living in a different world, one not permanently characterised by negativity.

---

[18] Th. W. Adorno, *Minima Moralia. Reflexionen aus dem beschädigten Leben. Gesammelte Schriften*, Band 4, Frankfurt a. M. 1980, 280. Cf. L. Heidbrink, Die Grenzen kritischer Negativität. Perspektiven im Anschluß an Adorno, in: W. Ette et al. (eds.), *Adorno im Widerstreit. Zur Präsenz seines Denkens*, Freiburg i. Br. / München 2004, 98: "The critical negativity underlying the philosophy of Adorno […]".

On the other hand, Adorno is thoroughly familiar with the other, counterfactual site of negativity. The other, new, redeemed world is never present in our experience as a reality, but at best as a dream, a wish or a hope. It emerges as an imaginatively framed complement to what we encounter as negativity in this life. Adorno's much-quoted closing thesis to the *Minima Moralia* is the logical application of this insight: "The only philosophy which can be responsibly practiced in the face of despair is the attempt to contemplate all things from the standpoint of redemption."[19] Yet we cannot really afford to adopt this standpoint. It remains the unattainable beyond of a negativity which can neither revoke itself, nor dream of what might be or could have been if it were overcome.

Hence negativity cannot be apprehended as the antithesis of affirmation and negation. The antithesis it flags up is not that between affirmation and negation, but the otherness of the different, which can be conceived of objectively and imaginatively, in our hopes and in our dreams, at each moment of what is real, as its background and bedrock. It is not the fundamental alternative of being or non-being that is the origin of negativity, but the alterity of the ability to be other than what is currently real.

However, if negativity is located, not in the reality process, but in its relationship of contrast to the sphere, invariably implied, of the conceivable, imaginative, desirable and possible, then it must be construed first and foremost semiotically: it is neither contradiction nor conflict, but is that which renders contradiction and conflict possible. At the level of the possible, this means that it makes contradiction possible by creating semantic determinacy and, in so doing, setting conditions for compossibility: not everything is compossible with everything. And, at the level of the real, this means that negativity makes conflict possible by setting conditions for non-compossibility which render it impossible

---

[19] ADORNO, *Minima Moralia*, 283.

that everything possible is simultaneously and jointly real. Thus, through the establishment of differences, within the realm of the possible signs are distinguished from other signs and are thereby semantically determined (negativity as otherness: p is p and not q, r, s, t, …), and, through the formulation of conditional relationships, it is established which possibilities and which conditions can be combined without contradiction and which cannot (negativity as the necessity to decide: if p, then either q or non-q, but not q and non-q). In the realm of reality the exclusion principle applies: not everything possible can exist in the same place at the same time and under the same conditions: "The world is narrow but the mind is vast. Our thoughts make easy neighbours for each other, but *objects in a space will soon collide.* The place one fills is taken from another".[20] Not only is it true that not everything possible is compossible; in practice, everything real excludes other possibilities and realities. Conversely, there is nothing possible that is not bound to reality – as possible *for* … or as possible *of* … If the possible exists, the real must also exist. And if the real exists, the possible must also exist. The problem of negativity must therefore be stated in terms of the possible and the real. And it is this which calls for semiotic reflection.

### *10. Double negativity: determinating and repudiating*

According to Kant's formal mathematical definition, any magnitude is negative in relation to another "insofar as it can only be combined with the other by means of opposition; in other words, they can only be combined in such a way that the one cancels as much in the other as is equal to itself".[21] Thus the magnitudes determine each other reciprocally. This is precisely why the

---

[20] F. Schiller, *Wallensteins Tod*, Act 2 Scene 2.
[21] Kant, *Versuch*, A9, *AA II*, 173–174.

negativity principle is a *principle of finitude*, as the sign-process demonstrates most clearly.[22] Everything determined is contingent upon the other, upon that which is different from it. This contingency upon the other, and with it a direct link to the establishment of a distinction ('the drawing of a distinction'[23]), applies to the entire field of negativity, and therefore also to negation and to the negation of negation. But to what extent?

*Negation*, as we have seen, is a logical operation (propositional negation: It is *not* the case that it is raining) or a semantic operation (conceptual negation: *in*gratitude, *in*comprehension, *mis*trust, *ir*responsible, reck*less*, thought*less* etc.) which we carry out on signs by means of signs. In the literal sense it concerns the negation of something said, the revocation of something posited, the rejection of something offered, the repudiation of something asserted. Concepts can be negated (semantic negation) as can propositions (logical negation), i.e. the semantic content of words and sentences. But negation and that which is negated can be presented, not just verbally, but in many semiotic ways (by means of gestures, actions, images etc.), each of which follows a different grammar.

This has two noteworthy consequences. On the one hand, negation is invariably the second step, not the first.[24] The first step is always something positive, that is, a proposition: *positive* is the opposite of *negative*, and 'positive' comes from the Latin *positum* = posited, positioned. If this positing is conceived of *objectively*, we understand that SOMETHING has been posited,

---

[22] Since the Christian faith and hope are not directed merely toward what is finite, the Christian hope is grounded, not purely in what is experienced, but in what is not experienced, and it is directed, not towards what is not yet real, but to a counterfactual truth.

[23] G. Spencer Brown, *Laws of Form*, Toronto 1973, 3.

[24] In relation to the following paragraph, cf. I. U. Dalferth, *Selbstlose Leidenschaften. Christlicher Glaube und menschliche Passionen*, Tübingen 2013, 311 f.

and that which is posited becomes a datum, something given or existing. If, on the other hand, it is a semiotic positing, then a DISTINCTION is drawn, and that which is posited becomes a difference that can be interpreted semantically in various ways: p / q (propositional); here / there (spatial); now / then (temporal); being / non-being (ontological) and so on. What is decisive, however, is not the two distinct sides of the differentiation (semantically they can always be determined in various ways), but the establishment of the difference itself. If the difference is the original separation, then there is no third place either on this side or the other side of what has been differentiated, rather, the one establishing the difference must be able to locate himself in that which has been differentiated. The side on which he is located is the affirmed side (p; here; now; being) in contrast to the non-affirmed (q; there; then; non-being). By locating himself on the side of being, however, then on this side there is a *re-entry* of the difference, inasmuch as *in being* (or: here and now and not there and then) a distinction is drawn between being and non-being. To put it another way: being and non-being, affirmation and negation, are not simply equal; rather, being and affirmation take priority over non-being and negation because the *distinction* between being and non-being, that is between affirmation and negation, can only be drawn by someone who is himself located on the side of being (that is affirmation), not of non-being (that is negation). Only one who is can distinguish between being and non-being, and where this is a total distinction, i. e. does not allow any third possibility, the one distinguishing is himself located on the side of being and not of non-being.

On the other hand, a distinction must be drawn between negation as a concept (negation) and negation as the repudiation of a concept (negation of a negation). Both denote a difference, but only the second, not the first, relates to a pre-established difference. Something said, posited, offered or asserted that is negated can only be *contested* insofar as it is something that has been *determined.* If it has not been determined, then it is determined by being negated (the establishment of a difference); if, on the other hand, it is something that has been determined, its determinacy is denied by its negation (negating of a difference). According to Spinoza's rule, "omnis determinatio est negatio",[25] something is determined by the very fact that it is distinguished from something else, and it is fully determined when it is distinguished from everything else (in the relevant scope of the universal qualifier). Determination by delimitation (establishment of a difference) and negation of what has been determined have, however, one thing in common, namely that they are the enactment of signs which, if they are enacted in practice, appear phenomenologically as sign-events.[26]

### *11. Semiotic negativity: possibilities and realities*

Now every phenomenal sign-event has four fundamental semiotic dimensions: the relationship *between sign and sign* (the syntactic dimension), the relationship *between sign and signified* (the semantic dimension), the relationship *between sign and sign-interpreter* (the pragmatic dimension) and the relationship *between sign and sign-bearer* (the material or medial dimension). As a result, each such event is also linked to *four horizons of possibility* and *three dimensions of reality.*

The *four horizons of possibility* for sign-events are the reference to the *sum of possible signs* (the totality of possible signifiers), the *sum of what can be signified* ("the signifiable"), the *sum of all possible sign-interpreters* (the totality of all possible communities of interpretation) and the *sum of what can be experienced* ("the

[25] Spinoza, Letter to Jarigh Jelles, Nr. 50.

[26] In relation to the following Section, cf. I. U. Dalferth, *Die Wirklichkeit des Möglichen. Hermeneutische Religionsphilosophie,* Tübingen 2003, 19–22.

experienceable"). In the syntactic sign-dimension, every sign-event refers to the *sum of possible signs (or sign-codes)*, and thus actualises only one possibility from the totality of the possible sign- and communication-repertoire. In the semantic dimension it refers to *the sum of what can be signified*, and thus actualises – insofar as it follows the laws of logic – a possible world. In the pragmatic dimension it refers to the *sum of all possible interpreters*, but actualises only one among all possible communities of signs, communication and interpretation. Finally, in the material or medial dimension, it refers to the *sum of all that can be experienced*, but makes use of something as a sign-bearer (a medium) that can be appreciated, at least in principle, by a particular community of interpretation.

Every sign-event takes place as a specific combination of these four horizons of possibility. By means of certain signs (or sign-codes), a possible world is actualised for one or more sign-interpreters by using certain resources of the real world. Sign-events continuously transform possibilities into facts or actual states of affairs that are then available as concrete projections of meaning because they can be negated in terms of the difference between truth and falsehood. That is to say, the negation of certain possibilities in the formation of structures of meaning creates an actual distance from reality, thus opening up space for freedom. This is so because in the real world possible worlds of meaning come into existence through sign-events. These worlds of meaning not only semiotically transcend the real world without leaving it behind but also represent it in less complex and thus more comprehensible ways. It is the difference between reality and a complexity-reducing concept or projection of reality that makes a responsible use of freedom possible at all.

The *three dimensions of reality* to which all sign-events constitutively remain bound, in spite of all semiotic transcending or modification of that which is given as given, are sign-interpreters (society), sign-codes (culture) and sign-media (nature); these are always presupposed. We consider *sign-media* to be everything that can be perceived directly or indirectly by our senses. They are always *natural phenomena* that represent the order of *nature* that is given and that we do not constitute ourselves.[27] As beings who construct signs, who influence behaviour with signs, and who produce and communicate knowledge through signs, we remain bound to nature because we are dependent on material sign-bearers that we can use and receive.

*Sign-codes*, the repertoire of sign and rules for the use of signs that we make use of individually or communally, are always *cultural phenomena* because we are social beings. They represent the historical ordering of *culture* which, although always coming to us as something given, are also always (co)constituted by us and thus, in principle, changeable and shapeable. Cultural patterns are products of our communal activity and thus expressions of our freedom, which sets the rules for itself. Natural patterns, in contrast, are the predetermined conditions for all our activity and are thus the expression of those necessities that can be laid down as rules. Insofar as our cognitive acts make use of signs, and thereby of sign-media and sign-codes, they are concrete communications between the regulatory patterns of nature that are established *before* our activity, and the regular patterns of culture that are established *by* our activity. The resulting tension between our *binding attachment to natural patterns* and our *freedom in respect of cultural patterns*, to which we are also attached, albeit rather differently, is a fundamental structural attribute of human life and human freedom which is manifest in every act of our lives. After all, we cannot believe, know, recognise, organise or communicate anything without sign-media, which owe their function, but not their existence to us. But neither can

[27] Nature is thus defined by our bodily senses: to the degree that these are technically altered, what we mean by 'nature' will also be defined differently.

we do these things without sign-codes, which owe us both their function and their existence.

## *12. The relationship of difference between systems of differences*

Against this background, a distinction must be made, not only between (logical-semantic) *contradiction* and (actual) *conflict*, but also between the *determinacy* of p, constituted by its separation from the other as part of the sign-process, and 'non-p', the *negation* of this determinacy: The fact that p is not q, r, or s …, but p is one thing; to negate this p is quite another. Only something that has been determined can be negated, and something is determined only insofar as it is distinguished from what is other – from all that is other, in fact. This distinction is always a sign-process, but this process can be described differently at the level of the sign (the signification) and at the level of the signified (the significate). Thus every sign is what it is only through its distinction from other signs in a code. But the *determinacy of the sign* and the *determinacy of what it symbolises* are not to be confused: different signs can signify the same thing ('that one there', 'Hans'), while the same sign can signify different things ('this' in different situations). The structural negativity of the sign and the determinacy of what is signified thereby derive in each case from the positing of separations or distinctions: p is something other than q, r, s … , and in English the sign 'p' conventionally signifies the sound [p] and no other sound. However, the differential system of the alphabet and the differential system of the sounds commonly in use in English are not homogenous, but have different structures, so that they follow different grammars. The act of signification, therefore, always establishes a relationship of differentiation between two difference coherences, (usually) with different grammars.

This has consequences for our understanding of negation. Formally, negation is an operation on a sign ('p') and not on that which it signifies (p), but this operation normally negates, not the sign, but what it signifies (non-p). Given that in a sign-event a determinacy ('p') determines something (p), two difference coherences with (potentially) different grammars are connected with each other. The determinacy of a sign can be regulated differently from the determinacy of the signified, so that we must distinguish between the negation of the sign (not 'p'), of the signified (non-p) and of what is actually said and done in a sign-event ('In English the sign 'p' signifies the sound [p]'). It is one thing to say "In English it is 'not 'b', but 'p' that signifies the sound [p]", whereas it is quite another to say 'non-p' and yet another to say 'It is not the case that in English the sign 'b' signifies the sound [p]."

The question thus arises as to how the *negativity* (i.e. difference) that underlies what is determined (that it is something determined in distinction from what is other), relates to the *negation* (i.e. the repudiation) of that which is determined. If 'p' is only 'p' on the basis of the differences which distinguish 'p' from all the other letters, what difference is then denoted when 'p' is negated – or for that matter p, or the sign-event p? The answer depends on whether one relates the negation syntactically to the sign (not 'p', but 'q'), semantically to the signified (non-p) or pragmatically to the sign-event ('It is not this sign, but that sign, that signifies [p]'). In each case, however, it is clear that a distinction must be drawn between the negativity that is due to the determinacy of something (whether it be a sign, something signified or a sign-event), and the negation of what is thereby determined (as the negation of a negation).

But the negation operation assumes more by this than is immediately evident. At the level of the sign it is performed on a sign 'p' which is differentiated from other signs, e.g. from the other letters of the alphabet (the determinacy of the sign).

Insofar as the sign 'p' serves to signify p, however, a determinacy is likewise introduced at the level of the signified, one which is developed by means of its differences from what is other (the determinacy of the signified). Both these determinacies can, but do not have to, coincide: the differential system that determines the sign 'p' and the differential system that determines p can be, and in fact usually are, different. In each case the negation acts as a sign operation at the level of the sign, not at the level of the signified. And this means that we need to distinguish between two interrelated processes of determination: the determination of the sign and the determination of the signified. Negation operations can only take place at the level of the sign, so that negation of the signified can only be carried out as a negation operation on the corresponding sign.

This has various consequences. Frege contended that the rule of determination implied that for every thought there must be a contradictory thought, otherwise the thought would not be determined.[28] If, however, a thought is what formulates a conclusion (p), then in Frege's terms it does not make sense to distinguish between affirmative and negative judgements, since separation from what is other is intrinsic to the determination of each and every thought: p is a conclusion which may be true or false; conversely, the repudiation (⊢non-p) or affirmation (⊢p) of p is a speech act (or thought act) which is only possible because p is determined, but is not coincidental with the determinacy of p. But even if one accepts this distinction and does not confuse the *determination of p* (semantic negativity) with the *repudiation of p* (it is not [true]), in both cases their negativity is located at the level of the sign. Where p is concerned (not q, r, s, etc.), we have something that is what it is through its separation from what is other (its determinacy). And if p is negated, then that which

[28] G. FREGE, Die Verneinung: eine logische Untersuchung, in: IDEM, *Logische Untersuchungen*, ed. G. PATZIG, Göttingen [3]1986, 54 (67).

is called 'p' on the basis of its separation from what is other is denied, with the result that a negation operation is carried out at the level of the sign 'p' and not at the level of that which the sign 'p' signifies as p (repudiation). In other words, this means that, while there are indeed negative signs ('It is not raining'), there is no negative reality (non-rain), but only the real that is not something else, whether it no longer is, or is not yet, or is not at all. And this is what is expressed by negation – in the positing of determinacy no less than in the repudiation of such determinacy.

### *13. The reality of negativity and the impossibility of radical negativity*

If one accepts the understanding of sign which has been outlined, then the four horizons of possibility and three dimensions of reality of a sign-event make it necessary, in terms of the possible, to speak of negativity in at least four ways: within the spheres of the complex of possible signs, the complex of the signifiable, the complex of possible sign-interpreters and the complex of the experienceable. In each of these spheres, determinacy is developed by means of distinctions which would not exist without negativity; in each the negativity established by this distinction is admittedly fundamental, but not radical, since in each of them it is integrated with a reality without which it would not exist: the reality of sign-interpreters (society), of sign-codes (culture) and of sign-media (nature). Without recourse to the fourfold determination contexts of the possible (negativity as that which generates determinacy) and the threefold dimensions of determinacy of the real (negation as that which establishes determinacy) it is impossible to give any meaningful consideration to negativity. Without recourse to negativity and negation, on the other hand, these spheres and dimensions of sign-events cannot be considered and developed. Viewed in this way, negativity is a basic structural semiotic concept which is formalised in the differential relationships (the semantics of negative determination) and acts of determination (the pragmatics of negation). As such, it is indispensable, but for this very reason it cannot be heightened into a meaningful concept of radical negativity: Precisely because there is nothing determinate that is not characterised by negativity, negativity is not something that can be characterised by itself. Negativity is not negative: rather, (if one can even speak in such terms) it is positive: It takes concrete semantic form in determinacy and pragmatically it leads, in negation, to determinacy, whether it be as the semantic change from the indeterminate to the determinate, or as the pragmatic repudiation of the determinate. If negativity is possible therefore, then radical negativity is impossible – all the more so, if negativity is actual.

# G. Neither possible nor impossible. Impossibility as a boundary concept and boundary horizon of differentiation

## *1. Theories of Everything*

Is there a *theory of everything?* In the philosophical sense: yes, there most certainly is, and not just one. Ontologically, for instance, it is true that everything either *is*, or *is not*, or *both* (that is, it both is and is not), or *neither* (that is, it neither is nor is not). What *is*, is either possible, or necessary, or contingent. What *is not*, is either impossible (that is, it necessarily is not: *impossibility*), or is not actual (that is, it is possible, but not actual: *non-actuality*), or not necessary (that is, either it is actual, although it could be merely possible: *contingency*, or it is possible, albeit not actual: *possibility*). What *both is and also is not,* is either impossible or possible, that is, it can be differently determined from modal perspectives (it is possible, but not actual), from temporal perspectives (it was not, but now it is), from perspectives of relationship (it is for the one, but not for the other) or of aspect (it is in one respect, but not in the other). This means that the (apparent) contradiction can be resolved in one way or another by drawing on appropriate perspectives of differentiation. On the other hand, that which *neither is nor is not* is so contradictorily determined that nothing can be either asserted or denied about it: it is not merely impossible, but is *absolutely nothing,* and is thus nothing possible, necessary or actual, nor is it the negation of such: that is, it is not impossible, non-necessary or non-actual.

In order to be formulated adequately therefore, an ontological *theory of everything* requires, not just the categories of *being* and *non-being*, but also those of a *something* which can be or can not be, and of a *nothing*, which, as neither-possible-nor-impossible is so absolutely impossible that one cannot meaningfully say either that it is or that it is not.[1]

It would seem therefore that a *theory of everything* cannot be formulated without the use of modal categories. In its modal theoretical version this is expressed as follows: everything is either *possible*, or *impossible*, or *both*, or *neither*. That covers all possible cases, but we need the category of the impossible in order to be able to determine the possible. We can only do this from the position of the actual which is neither *impossible* (that is, it *is*, and, what is more, it *cannot not be*: this excludes the *impossibility of being*), nor *merely possible* (that is, it cannot merely *either be or also not be*: this excludes the mere *possibility of being or non-being*), nor *necessary* (that is, it is such that it could *not* not be: this excludes the *possibility of non-being*). And we can only use the category of the impossible from the position of the actual by referring, not only to the alternatives of being and non-being in their modal determinacies (being possible, being necessary, being actual, or, conversely, being impossible, being non-necessary, being non-actual), but also to what is neither possible nor impossible and is, in that respect, *absolutely nothing*.

But this means that we cannot determine the possible *as* possible unless we do so in actual sign-processes which are neither purely possible (can be) nor impossible (cannot be) nor necessary (cannot not be).[2] We cannot address anything by

---

[1] Just as something necessary is something which is that cannot not be (a something that is such that it is impossible for it not to be), it follows that nothing is a non-being that cannot be (that is, not necessarily merely a something that is such that it cannot be, but a non-something that cannot be a something).

[2] It is not only something that is *neither possible nor impossible* that cannot exist and is therefore *nothing*, but also – for Kierkegaard, for instance – something that is *necessary*, whose existence is therefore not

means of sign-processes without doing so from the perspective of the actual within the horizon of the possible. We cannot have recourse to the possible without distinguishing it from the impossible. And we cannot distinguish the possible from the impossible without separating both from what is neither possible nor impossible, but which is quite simply *nothing*.

In this sense – and this is my thesis – *there is nothing impossible, but neither is there anything without the impossible. Neither anything nor nothing is impossible, yet nothing exists without the impossible.*

## 2. Phenomena as sign-events

This needs elucidation. Phenomena are sign-events and as such – as we have shown – are characterised by the four fundamental semiotic dimensions, that is, the *relationship between sign and sign* (the syntactic dimension), the *relationship between sign and signified* (the semantic dimension), the *relationship between sign and sign-user* or *sign-interpreter* (the pragmatic dimension) and the *relationship between sign and sign-bearer* or *sign-medium* (the material or medial dimension). To put it another way: no phenomenon comes alone (*it has a with-structure*: something is something *with and among what is other*); every phenomenon discloses a meaning (*it has an as-structure*: something appears *as something*); every phenomenon is a phenomenon for someone (it has a *for-structure*: something appears as something *for someone*) and all phenomena communicate their as-structure and their for-structure through natural or artificial (cultural) media (they have a *through-structure*: something appears as something for someone *through something*).

---

the result of a becoming, but is such that it always is and therefore knows neither a having-become nor the possibility of a being-no-more.

All four structural elements arise in connection with every phenomenon, even if not all the four elements hold equal focus of attention in each case. Within the context of sign or phenomenon processes that can be decoded thus, however, the following is true.

1. What is *possible* is not self-contradictory and is therefore *signifiable.*

2. What is *impossible* is *contradictory* – it is contradictory in real terms (that is, under real conditions) or it is self-contradictory as such (that is, in itself) – so that, in a real situation or in principle, it can only be signified in such a way that, in respect of the same thing, one says both the one thing and the (contrary or contradictory) other. This can be differentiated more precisely by means of the four distinct structural dimensions of phenomena. (1) Something is impossible within the scope of its *with-structure* if it cannot be actual together with something else (impossibility on the grounds of *incompossibility*): a parked car overtakes a lorry on the motorway. (2) Something is impossible within the scope of its *as-structure* if it can only be described using incompatible descriptions (*objective* impossibility): a car is, at the same time and in the same place, for the same purpose and in the same respect F (red) and Q (green) or non-F (not red). (3) Something is impossible within the scope of its *for-structure* if it is impossible for someone, even though for others it could be entirely possible (*subjective* impossibility): it is impossible for me to jump a height of two metres twenty. If one reflects upon the time factor and the possibility of changing oneself in positive as well as negative ways, one can distinguish between subjective impossibilities according to whether they are initial or retrospective impossibilities, since what is impossible for someone today may once have been possible, while what is possible today may once have been impossible. (4) Something is impossible within the scope of its *through-structure* if it cannot be realised in our world through any natural or artificial, cultural medium (medial

or *factual* impossibility): None of us can balance on a laser beam to the moon, even though this is not in itself a self-contradictory thought and one can conceive of possible worlds in which this might happen.

3. What is *neither possible nor impossible* for the same person at the same time and in the same place and in the same respect, so that it cannot be signified *either* coherently (as possible) *or* contradictorily (as impossible), is *not signifiable*: one cannot say of what one is speaking when one speaks of it.

4. That which is *both possible and impossible* is either self-contradictory and therefore impossible, or is sometimes possible (i.e. in one place, for certain people, in a certain respect), and sometimes not (i.e. in another place, for others, in another respect).

Briefly stated, *the possible* is *signifiable*, while the *impossible* is only *signifiable in contradiction*. The *neither-possible-nor-impossible* is *not signifiable* and is, in the strict sense of the word, *nothing*: when speaking of it, one cannot even say that it is impossible. And the *both-possible-and-impossible* is either only *signifiable in contradiction*, i.e. impossible, or is *non-contradictorily signifiable*, i.e. possible, by introducing *time*, *place*, *point of reference* or *respect* as difference operators for the avoidance of contradiction.

This whole problem field is thus clustered around *signification*, that is, around what can, using signs, be thematized, signified, described, imagined, conceived of, contemplated, couched, notified, communicated, concealed, inferred, denied, asserted, considered, rejected and so on. It concerns what is *signifiable* (the possible), what is only *signifiable in contradiction* (the impossible), the *non-signifiable* (the neither-possible-nor-impossible, i.e. that which is nothing) and the *sometimes-one-way-and-sometimes-another-way signifiable* (that which is impossible in actual fact).

Now, 'signification' is a basic semiotic concept, which means that the subject of the impossible is a *semiotic problem* – and only as such is it also a problem of speech, thought, and imagination, seeing, representation, communication or concealment. All these sign-processes and sign-functions take place by means of specific media (visual, auditory, tactile, olfactory, etc.), and, depending on these, not only is the impossible expressed in varying medial ways, different medial impossibilities are also portrayed: not everything which is a visual impossibility is also an auditory, tactile, significative or verbal impossibility. Hence something which cannot be communicated in one medium can be communicated meaningfully in another: *it is not impossible to speak meaningfully of the impossible.*

If we follow this thread of verbal communication, we find that anything is *contradictorily signifiable* (i.e. impossible) if we can only speak of it in self-contradictory sentences which, taken in isolation, utter what is possible, i.e. non-contradictory, but do so in reference to the same thing in such a way that they cannot be true when taken together. If, on the other hand, from this kind of self-contradictory sentence it cannot even be understood that one is referring *to something*, let alone *to the same thing*, then it is unclear to what extent they actually contradict themselves, since they speak not merely of the *impossible*, but, in the strict sense of the word, of *nothing.*

Something that can only be signified contradictorily can be either something that can be avoided (*the avoidable impossible*), or something that cannot be avoided when one tries to avoid it (*the unavoidable impossible*). The avoidable impossible is that which results from a contradictory act of signification such as 'square circle', so that by avoiding this act of signification, this impossible too could be avoided. The unavoidable impossible, by contrast, is that impossible which is necessarily posited by being signified, since nothing can be signified except in the sphere of the signifiable, and one cannot move into this sphere without simultaneously referring to the limits of the signifiable. Signification only exists within the sphere of the possible, and nothing possible exists without its reverse side – the impossible. Anyone who uses signs brings the impossible into play, yet the impossible evades us as soon as we attempt to signify it.

To put it another way: *The impossible is not something that can be signified in a non-contradictory way, yet nothing can be signified without it.* It is nothing, yet without it there is nothing. How is this to be understood?

### *3. Impossibility as a modal boundary concept*

By 'impossibility' I mean the character of the impossible, which describes the concept of impossibility. Yet the impossible can be detected everywhere – there is *the necessarily impossible*, which (in its *de re* formulation) *necessarily is not*, since it is not possible that it is (such as a square circle or the largest real number). But there is also *the factually impossible*, which neither is actual, nor can it become actual in terms of factual reality: in other words, it is *factually not possible*, even though it could in principle be possible (such as a living organism without metabolism or a perpetuum mobile).

These and other categories of impossible can be determined not only *de re*, but also *de dicto*, and give rise to issues both of being or non-being, that is of (in-)conceivability and (non-) knowability, and also of the representability of the impossible and the communicability of the (non-)representable impossible. The impossible is as variously determinable as is that which appears as its opposite, other, negation, background or limit: it is the *modal companion to everything necessary, possible and actual* and is therefore also the – typically non-thematic – *boundary phenomenon* of all that appears in the everyday life, in science and in religion as real, possible or necessary.

Now boundary phenomena are not concepts themselves, but if their character is conceptualised, then the result is not a determinative concept, but a *boundary concept*. According to Kant, *boundary concepts* are critical concepts which can only be used in a *negative way*. The concept of the noumenon, for example, in its theoretical usage, he considers to be purely a boundary concept intended to limit the pretensions of sensibility. It may not be understood positively as the signification of a transempirical (intelligible) reality, but only in negative terms as an indication that one "cannot assert of sensibility that it is the only possible kind of intuition",[3] without being also able to assert that "objects have been given to us beyond the field of sensibility" of which we can say or know "something positive".[4] Boundary concepts do not serve to signify or determine anything, but are necessary so that one can orient oneself critically within a problem field in which one is determining the boundaries of that which is expressible, conceivable or knowable in a specific way.

## *4. Not possible or not necessary?*

What does it mean to understand impossibility in this sense as a modal boundary concept? Traditionally, the complete system of modal concepts is described in terms of its three modes: *possibility, necessity* and *actuality* and their negations (*impossibility, non-actuality, non-necessity i. e. contingency*). Impossibility is thus understood as the negation of possibility, which is differentiated from the modes of actuality (contingency) and necessity.

This would be a tolerably clear classification if the tradition which this calls to mind did not distinguish between *two concepts of possibility*. Aristotle, for instance, uses the term 'possible'

---

[3] *KrV* B 310.
[4] *KrV* B 311–312.

(ἐνδεχόμενον) for *what is not impossible*,[5] while on the other hand he defines the possible as *what is not necessary and not impossible*.[6] In the one case, therefore, the 'impossible' is that which is *not possible*, while in the other it is that which *necessarily is not*.

Both these concepts of impossibility agree, to the extent that, in relation to the concept of possibility, they state: *what is not possible is impossible*. And both rule out the idea that what is impossible can be actual: *what is impossible cannot be actual*. However, they differ in the way in which they conceive of the relation to necessity. That *which is not possible*, is also *not necessary*, since only the possible can in fact be necessary, as has consistently been held from Aristotle on.[7] But the opposite is not true, namely that *what is not necessary is not possible*, since the actual is also not necessary.

### *5. Becoming and becoming-other*

Neither of these is self-evident. Kierkegaard explicitly denied that only the possible can also be necessary, since he consistently relates possibility to actuality and rigorously distinguishes necessity from both of them:[8] *necessity* is always unalterable self-rela-

---

[5] Aristotle, *De interpretatione* 13, 22a 14–22b 28.

[6] Aristotle, *Analytica Priora* 13, 32a 18–20.

[7] Aristotle, *Peri hermeneias*, 12 (21a 34ff.) and 13 (esp. 22b 29ff.). Recent modal logic reformulates this for the modal systems T, S4 and S5, so that all propositions which are not impossible are possible, while the sum total of possible propositions includes all true propositions, and therefore *a fortiori* also all necessary true propositions. Cf. G. E. Hughes / M. J. Cresswell, *An Introduction to Modal Logic*, London 1968, 22. For if the *axiom of possibility* $p \supset Mp$ is true, then everything that is true is also possible, as is therefore everything that is necessarily true.

[8] S. Kierkegaard, *Philosophische Brocken, Gesammelte Werke, Zehnte Abteilung*, Düsseldorf / Köln 1952, esp. 68–85.

tionship, whereas *possibility*, as a potentiality, is focused on wanting to become actual, while *actuality* is the having-become-actual of possibility. Everything real is therefore the result of a process of becoming – *non-being* (mere possibility) *becoming being* (actuality), not simply of a *becoming-other* (change), which is always the result of the bringing about of something actual (effect) by something else actual (cause).

The two are not mutually exclusive, rather, everything actual is invariably determined in two ways: it has turned *from possible* into *actual* (development *into* something actual), and it has *been turned by something actual into something actual* (development *as* something actual). The first marks a change from *non-being* to *being*, the second a change from *being-thus* to *being-other*, from *being-one-thing* to *being-another*. Since there can only be such a change where there actually is something (being-actual), every change from being-thus to being-other, from being-one-thing to being-another presupposes the change from non-being to being: only what is can become other, even though not everything that is can also become other (the necessary is what it is, and if it could become other or another it would not be necessary). But only what is not necessary, and is not only possible but has become actual, is such that it could become other. The possible can only become actual, not other. The actual, however, can become other because it is a possible-become-actual.

If something possible becomes actual, there is always a double effect. On the one hand, connections become possible that were not possible before. On the other hand, connections become impossible that were possible before. So, through the actualisation of the possible, some things become possible and others become impossible. But nothing *becomes* necessary by becoming actual, and nothing that *becomes* impossible had been necessary: the necessary does not *become* anything, and nothing becomes something necessary. That which *becomes* impossible – and does not just remain impossible because it is impossible always, everywhere and for everyone in every respect – had once been possible, as had that which becomes possible: only what is possible can become possible – that is to say it can become possible for this or that actual. But it is also true that only what is possible can *become* impossible – otherwise one could not speak of a becoming. Similarly, only the actual can become non-actual, i. e. only the possible which had become actual, but is no longer actual. This means that, while it is still possible, it is not actual: if the non-actual were not possible, then neither could it be non-actual; similarly, the possible which has not become actual always accompanies the actualised possible, as an 'other possibility', even when, because of the existing actuality, it has in actual fact become impossible.

Besides the necessary, which is what it is and cannot become other, the only thing which *cannot become* is nothing: since it is not possible, it cannot *become either impossible or actual*; consequently it cannot become non-actual either. And since it *is* not, but quite specifically is *not*, it stands in direct opposition, not only to the possible and the actual, but also to the necessary.

Whereas it is true of nothing (and only of nothing) that it *neither is nor can become*, one must speak quite differently of the impossible. Something which is impossible in concrete terms can, because of altered circumstances, change *from* the impossible *to the possible* or *from the possible to the impossible*, but *as* impossible *nothing* can become *actual*: there 'is' no impossible. On the other hand, however, there is nothing possible or actual without the impossible. The impossible is *implicit* in everything possible and everything actual: as the limit of the horizon of possibility of the possible, that is, as the specifically excluded negation (which can nonetheless be specifically altered) of the possibility of the actual. Only the possible can be actual; the possible is always distinguished from the impossible, which is why the impossible is not simply nothing. As the negation of the possible it stands on the side of being and not on the side of nothing: the (specifically) impossible can become possible, but *ex nihilo nihil fit*, and nothing becomes something *as* the impossible. Rather, everything actual is the result of a double becoming: the modal becoming-actual of the possible *and* of its effective causation by something else actual. Neither exists without the other, but the two are not the same, and neither renders necessary that which has become.

### *6. Hegel's necessary actuality and Kierkegaard's modal paradox*

Kierkegaard reproaches Hegel with having disregarded this.[9] The point at issue is clear from a proverbial saying from Hegel's native Swabia, one which he quoted during his period in Jena: "In Swabia we say of something that happened in the distant past: it's so long ago that soon it won't be true any more. On this basis, it is so long since Christ died for our sins that soon it will not be true any more."[10] If becoming is understood as a process of change in time, then in the course of time that which has become recedes further and further into the past, and if we understand Christ's saving death in this sense as a past event, then there is a real danger that "It is so long since Christ died for our sins, that soon it will not be true any more."

Kierkegaard objects to this kind of thinking, not simply because the immutability of the past may not be misunderstood as necessity, but because from this viewpoint, Christ's death must be understood only as a *change*, a switch from being-thus to being-other, and not in the strict sense of the word as a *becoming*, as a transition from non-being to being. "[T]hat the God *was*"

[9] Cf. his criticism of Hegel's absolute method, KIERKEGAARD, *Philosophische Broken*, 74–75.

[10] G. F. W. HEGEL, *Jenaer Schriften 1801–1807*, *Werke 2*, Frankfurt a. M. 1970, 545.

is, as a historical fact, not necessary, nor is it purely historical and thus exposed to the vicissitudes of time. Rather, it is the expression of what is, strictly speaking, a *becoming-historical*, a transition from non-being to being, which, if it happened at all, happens always and only in such a way that, at any given point, it is present only as becoming in the strict sense and never merely in the mode of a remembered historical past. It is no closer to the first hand disciple than it is to the later disciple, since it is only a repetition of what originally took place: the fact, "that the God became".[11] No necessity of any kind appertains to this fact, nor does it express "any necessity of becoming, but only the *being-thus of becoming*".[12] But this very being-thus of becoming is, as a historical fact, the actualisation, not of a possibility, but of an impossibility, the "utter paradox" that at a specific moment of history *the eternal actually became* and at each moment will become actual again.[13] It is not necessity, nor is it possibility, but strict impossibility that finds in the fact "that the God became" its wholly paradoxical actuality. That the God became is neither possible nor impossible, yet – if true – neither is it *nothing*, but is in an *utterly paradoxical way actual.*

### *7. Possibility as potentia and possibilitas*

Kierkegaard's argument can be understood in principle. Actuality becomes paradoxical where it is the actualisation, not of the possible, but of the impossible. But can this be? It has nothing to do with the necessary, for that would be a *metabasis eis allo genos*, but solely with the possible and, for this precise reason,

[11] KIERKEGAARD, loc. cit., 84. Here the word 'fact' must be understood as something brought about through an act of God.

[12] Loc. cit., 82.

[13] Cf. loc. cit., 34–50.

also liminally and paradoxically with the impossible. For in becoming actual the possible separates itself from what is merely possible *and* from what is impossible. Everything which can become actual is possible, whereas that which cannot become actual is impossible, whether in fact or in principle. However, since everything possible is separate from the impossible (as that which is other than the possible), nothing possible can become actual without actualising, not the impossible itself, but – non-thematically, yet inevitably – the *separation* from the impossible.

If we conceive of the differential relationship between the possible and the impossible *per impossibile*[14] as a minimum / maximum spectrum, then, at one pole of the spectrum of the possible in its orientation towards actualisation, this can mean that the impossible is at risk of disappearing in the face of the plenitude of the possible and of becoming a purely formal delimitation of the minimum. At the opposite pole of this spectrum, however, it can mean that the impossible far exceeds the possible, with the result that, in the limit case highlighted by Kierkegaard, the relevant actuality is determined, not by the possible in its separation from the impossible, but by the impossible in its separation from the possible. Causally it has resulted from something else actual and is thus the actual effect of an actual cause. Modally, on the other hand, it actualises a minimum of possibility and a maximum of impossibility, so that it is not a contradiction-free but a paradoxical actuality – not because either, taken individually, is impossible, but because they are not compossible and cannot be actual simultaneously without contradiction.

Like Leibniz, Kierkegaard presupposed that everything possible possesses an urge towards being which is actualised when it is not obstructed or impeded by something else possible, actual or necessary. Nothing necessary can come into existence, "nam

[14] Impossible is not a determinative concept, but a boundary concept.

necessarium se ipso prius sit, necesse est" (for it is necessary that necessity precede itself), as Kierkegaard emphasised.[15] Everything possible, on the other hand, will indeed become actual by coming into being. For Kierkegaard, therefore, possibility and necessity have nothing to do with each other. Only when one understands possibility, not classically as *potentia* pressing on towards actualisation, but purely formally as *possibilitas*, i.e. as the non-self-contradictory possible, can it be associated with necessity. For, if possibility is understood as *potentia* pressing on towards actualisation, then the Aristotelian sentence, 'Everything necessary is possible', becomes a self-contradictory statement.[16] The necessary is that which cannot be other than it is, whereas the possible is that which can and will be other than it is, in other words, actual. To call the necessary possible, therefore, would be to ascribe to it a tendency towards actualisation, which is just as unthinkable as the idea of its actuality. This would make it the result of a process of becoming, meaning that it could also not have been – which is self-contradictory. Consequently, Kierkegaard rejects Hegel's understanding of necessity as the unity of possibility and actuality just as firmly as he does the Aristotelian linkage of necessity with possibility.[17]

However, his argument is only convincing when the concept of possibility is firmly linked with the concept of actuality. It reduces possibility to that which is not yet actual or which perpetually accompanies the actual that has always come into being out of the possible.[18] If, on the other hand, one conceives of possibility purely formally as non-contradictoriness, then it is implicit both in the necessary and the actual in equal measure. This means that both conclusions, *ab esse ad posse* and *ab necesse*

---

[15] Loc. cit., 76.
[16] Loc. cit., 71.
[17] Loc. cit., 70f.
[18] Loc. cit., 82.

*ad posse*, are equally valid.[19] What is not possible cannot become actual either, and what is impossible cannot be necessary.

### 8. *Formal and ontological impossibility*

The converse, on the other hand: *what is not necessary is not possible*, is not true, since the actual is not necessary either. In order to take this into account, however, it is not sufficient to state it more precisely as: *what is not necessary and not actual is impossible*, since the possible, too, can be non-actual. Rather, one must state even more precisely: *what is not merely not necessary, but necessarily is not, is impossible.* The possible, the actual, the non-actual and the impossible can all be not necessary. The non-actual is either possible or impossible and is therefore not a problem in itself. Again, that something is *not necessary and that it is not* excludes only the actual, not the possible. In order to exclude the actual *and* the possible, something must be not only *not necessary*, but must also *necessarily not* be. Only that which not only is not, but also cannot be, is impossible.

---

[19] Strictly speaking, there is no conclusion to be drawn here, only attention to something implicit: being-possible is implicit in both being-actual and being-necessary. Moreover, the reverse (*a posse ad esse*) can only be ruled out in theory, not in practice. In human activity the path frequently leads *a posse ad esse*, as F. MAUTHNER has rightly pointed out, *Wörterbuch der Philosophie*, Vol. 1, Leipzig $^{2}$1923, 2–4. The "sportsman, the virtuoso, the ingenious inventor actually achieve their aims, *because* they seem impossible. 'I love the one who yearns for the impossible.' So if a genius has demonstrated the possibility of a new path by an unheard of example, he will find imitators in his normal environment. The ascent of Mont Blanc has become an everyday event, *because* it was possible. It proved possible for a Napoleon Buonaparte to become Emperor; little Louis Napoleon did indeed become Emperor. For human activity posse paves the way for esse."

The first or *formal concept of impossibility* therefore construes the relationship between the impossible and the necessary from the perspective of the negation of possibility: *what is not possible, cannot be necessary either*. The second or *ontological concept of impossibility*, on the other hand, construes the relationship between the impossible and the necessary from the perspective of the negation in principle of what is actual: *what necessarily is not, cannot be possible either*. It is not only that *which is not possible* that is impossible, but also that *which necessarily is not*.

Both concepts of impossibility would thus be extensionally equivalent only if that which necessarily is not were the same as that which is not possible. But this is not the case. As Leibniz recognised, it is not only that which is not possible, but also the possible that can necessarily not be, if there is no possible world in which it could be actual along with something else. In that case, it would not be self-contradictory *per se* (as the formally impossible is); but it would prove to be incompossible in any possible combination with anything other, as the ground of incoherence and contradictoriness. That water boils and that water freezes are both possibilities. But for the same litre of water both to boil and to freeze at the same place and time and in the same respect is impossible. Likewise God is not a self-contradictory idea, and nor is a world, in which God does not exist. But the idea that there is such a world is incompatible with the idea that God exists. If God exists, then there is necessarily not a world without God. In this sense the ontological concept of impossibility is stronger than the formal: it covers everything which the latter includes, but even more.

## *9. Limits of being and truth*

Modal concepts are traditionally understood as determinations of being which are merely properties of something that is, but do not constitute its being.[20] If something does not exist, then neither can it be possible, necessary or actual (contingent). If something is designated *not necessary* or *non-actual*, its mode of being is negated, but not its being.[21] If, on the other hand, it is designated *impossible*, it is not only the mode of its being that is questioned, but its being itself: what is impossible does not merely not exist in a certain way, it does not exist at all. Impossibility is not a modal determination of a being, but the boundary concept which excludes the application of modal determinations, since there is no being to which they could be applied.

This is reiterated in the alethic form of modality. Here modal concepts are understood as *modal operators*, which indicate, not something's modes of being, but *categories of truth* or *the validity of propositions.*[22] *Possible* propositions are those whose categorical negation is not necessarily true, i. e. those for which there is at least one possible world in which they are true; *necessary* propositions are those of which it is impossible that their negation be true, i. e. those for which there is no possible world in which they

[20] This is why in the Aristotelian modal tradition possibility is interpreted *temporally*: 'p is possible' expresses that p was actual, is actual or will be actual.

[21] Or at any rate, it does if one does not restrict *being* to contingent *being-actual*.

[22] By 'proposition' I mean the bearer of a truth value: whatever can be expressed in English by means of a that-clause specifying a propositional content, that is, which says something which can be true or false, and can be connected with a truth value predicate (' – is true', ' – is false'), is a proposition. Accordingly, propositions are meaningless if their content cannot be either true or false, so that they have no propositional content. No position is adopted with regard to the controversial ontological status of propositions. Here propositions are only of interest as bearers of a truth value – whether this is expressed verbally, mentally, pictorially, or using other means of symbolisation, in the context of speech acts such as confessing, asserting, denying, commanding or propositional attitudes such as wishing, doubting, hoping, believing and so on. Cf. W. P. Alston, *A Realist Conception of Truth*, Ithaca / London 1996, 17 ff.

are not true; *contingent* propositions are those which are just as possible as their negations, i.e. for which there is both a possible world in which they are true, and also one in which they are not true; *impossible* propositions, on the other hand, are those which are necessarily not true, i.e. for which there is no possible world in which they would be true. Here too, the concept of impossibility acts as a boundary concept marking the limit beyond which the truth predicate can no longer be applied positively or negatively, so that it does not make sense to either assert or deny that such propositions are true. The world in which something can be true or false has boundaries, as does the world in which something is like this or like that. Only thus are they each a *determined* world – whether in the factual sense as *this world* or in the logical (formal) and metaphysical (actual) sense as a possible world among the totality of possible worlds. Both are marked out by the modal boundary concept of impossibility.

### *10. The ambiguity of boundaries*

In pursuing our examination of the concept of boundaries we must, however, ensure that we have a clear appreciation of the following. It is well-known that the world is as complex as the most complex of our thoughts about it.[23] Less attention is paid to the fact that any world which we might be able to know in its entirety would not be complex enough to contain anyone who could know it.[24] The possibility of a *complete* knowledge of the world is ruled out by the impossibility of a complete *knowledge* of the world. To that extent therefore that the world in which we

---

[23] Cf. D. Henrich, *Fluchtlinien. Philosophische Essays*, Frankfurt a.M. 1982, 125.

[24] But cf. J.D. Barrow, *Impossibility. The Limits of Science and the Science of Limits*, Oxford 1998, 3.

live, think, know and understand is characterised by the modal dimensions, not only of the actual, the possible and the necessary, but also of the impossible.

Now, worlds are systems, systems draw boundaries and boundaries not only include, they also exclude. No system can encompass everything, at any rate not in well-ordered way. Considered within the context of systems – and there is no other way we can consider anything – the necessary conditions for possibility also invariably prove to be conditions for impossibility. That applies to our understanding of alterity and externality just as much as it does to passivity, gift, or religion. If one wants to integrate everything into a single system, one inevitably pays the price of having to express what is other in the system *within the system itself* – in other words, one must take the possible into account within the actual, and the impossible within the possible.

But does this work? Or how could it work? Surely the term 'impossible worlds' is nothing but a semantic variation of the term 'impossible possibilities' and surely this in turn is simply a euphemism for 'impossibilities'? How does the problem change if we formulate it, not just modally, but temporally and construe the modalities, not purely ontologically, but historically? The necessary, according to Kierkegaard, becomes necessarily not, and thus it also becomes necessarily not other: it is timeless and is therefore always what it is. But if that is true of what is necessary (the necessary), is it also true of what necessarily is not (the impossible)? Only if we do not distinguish between formal and real impossibility. The formally impossible (and *a fortiori* strictly impossible) is always and everywhere impossible: there is no possible world in which a triangle has four corners. On the other hand, what is impossible here and now, but not necessarily there and then, is in reality (or in practice) impossible. Not everything that is impossible here and now (that right now it is midnight in Central European Time) must be or remain impossible always and everywhere as well. Sometimes such a thing could become possible because the world changes, so that not only does the possible become actual, but even the impossible becomes possible. Conversely, this means that many possible things become impossible and many actual things become such that they can no longer be. The borders between possibility and impossibility are not stable, they shift. Impossibility is not just a multiply coded, but a *dynamic* modal boundary concept.

## *11. Cultural counterworlds*

This is particularly clearly shown in the dynamic antagonisms between the necessary conditions of impossibility and impossibility, which function as the drivers of cultural evolution. A culture that did not cultivate its incompossible counterworlds would be actual, or at any rate possible, but would sooner or later lose sight of the horizon of its impossible possibilities. There would then be little left to hope for, since only the calculably possible would be anticipated, and no longer the incalculable impossible. But then the determination of the limited would be lost along with the determination of the limit: there would still be the possible, but no key to unlock the nature of its possiblity. Leibniz and Kierkegaard recognised that it is only the delimitation of the impossible which reveals the character of the possible as its drive and momentum to become actual, rather than remaining non-actual. This has a double meaning: it consists, not just of the transition from *non-being to being*, but first and foremost of that from *being to becoming*, not to non-being or no-longer-being. For only thus is what *is* carried forward to what *can*, *should* and *will be*. It is precisely this momentum of the possible which remains hidden until we relocate the possible away from its correlated background, the impossible, and view it from the perspective of this delimitation and relocation. But this requires us expressly to thematize something which normally remains non-thematic: that which is impossible in relation to the possible, actual and necessary.

If we thematize it, however, we must pay methodical heed to the dialectic of boundary concepts into which this leads us. Since the impossible does not occur as such, but only ever *for someone in relation to* the possible, the actual and the necessary, and since the possible only ever occurs *for someone in relation to* the actual,[25] semantically the thematization of the impossible is the *representation of the unthinkable*, rhetorically it is the *communication and communicability of the non-communicable* and hermeneutically it is the *comprehensibility of the incomprehensible.* In other words, it affords the opportunity to understand that which, given the possibility conditions of our understanding, can only be understood as that which cannot be understood.

But this is an ambiguous formulation. It leaves the question open as to whether we have here nothing comprehensible or something incomprehensible. Either could be the case. But how should this be understood specifically? There are various answers, which is why we need to draw the distinction: it is one thing to understand nothing, but it is quite another to understand that nothing can be understood. But does one understand that one understands nothing because there is nothing to be understood, or because what one is seeking in vain to understand is something incomprehensible? In order to be able to assert the second option, it is not sufficient to invoke one's incomprehension and simply to argue that one understands nothing. The comprehension of incomprehensibility must, rather, be derived precisely from that which cannot be understood, so it must be grounded in the incomprehensible itself and not merely in the

[25] This is the basis of Kant's argument in *The Only Possible Argument in Support of a Demonstration of the Existence of God* (1763): "The proof of the existence of God which we give is merely built on the fact that something is possible", A 47, AA II, 91. For if it is true that 'the possible exists', then God exists.

one who understands nothing. Only then does one have grounds for asserting a difference between the argument that there is nothing which can be understood and the argument that there is something which cannot be understood.

### *12. Religion as the locus of the impossible*

Playing with this difference has, from time immemorial, been the domain of religion. However while in general we focus on the rational, or more reservedly, the plausible, or even more cautiously, the possible, not least when it comes to matters of religion, the cultural code of religious communication is characteristically that of metaphor and paradox. This is demonstrated in various well-known (albeit greatly differing) Christian affirmations, such as 'Jesus is the Son of God', 'God became human', 'The one who was crucified, died and was buried has been raised and is alive with God', 'The justified sinner is *simul iustus et peccator* ' and 'The church is *communio sanctorum* and *magna peccatrix*'. All of these assert something which is factually not possible but rather impossible; yet as such it is nonetheless counterfactually possible and thus not impossible; indeed, in theological terms it is actual. Such metaphors and paradoxes are versions of a communication of and with the unthinkable that is not necessary, nor is it merely possible; it is actual in such a way that it oscillates permanently between two determinations which cannot be sublated into or put to rest in a third. On the one hand, from the perspective of the experientially accessible actual, it appears as impossible (a factual impossibility); on the other hand, and in critical contrast to the experienceable actual, it can be contemplated and determined counterfactually as possible (counterfactual possibility). The two determination lines of the factually impossible and the counterfactually possible overlap in such a way as to result in a multiple coding of religious phenomena which cannot be represented and contemplated without also having to represent and contemplate that which is other than themselves. When we seek to describe these phenomena, their other invariably appears as impossible in comparison with them, even though that other must be preserved as possible precisely in order to prevent the phenomena themselves from becoming impossible.

The differential relationship between possible and impossible, actual and non-actual, necessary and non-necessary is therefore not to be understood, in a dubious ontologization, as a description of two worlds which exclude or complement each other, but, on the contrary, as *overlapping determinations of one and the same world*. Only then does the actual complexity of our world come into view: not only does it embrace a wide variety of phenomena, but the phenomena of the world can be described, not in just one way, but in different, often incompatible and paradoxical ways. The world is intrinsically overdetermined, holding in itself an inexhaustible added value of meaning which can only ever be described in approximate terms and the depths of which can never be plumbed. To pursue it right down into its fundamental paradoxical processes is the passion of the thinker, as Kierkegaard well knew. For only when one takes seriously the problem, not of the contradictory, but of the systematic avoidance of the contradictory, is one close to tracking down the impossibility of the impossible.

It is true that the impossible is far from being a phenomenon: it is at most a boundary phenomenon, that is, something occurring with and in relation to phenomena or, more precisely, with and in relation to the possibility of phenomena. However, in relation to sign-events it appears semiotically in different contexts and thus in systematically differentiated ways. This sets the direction for an exploration of meaning following the trails of paradox and contradiction and for an identification of boundaries of meaning. If the impossible only ever becomes apparent in relation to the possible, then the method we should use in approaching the impossible is predetermined: attention to the sign structure of the phenomena.

### *13. Differentiated impossibilities*

Every sign-event, as I emphasised above, is linked, through its four fundamental semiotic relationships (syntactic, semantic, pragmatic and medial), to *four horizons of possibility* and *three dimensions of reality*. These also systematically differentiate that which we term 'impossible'. The boundary concept of possible signs is formed by *impossible signs* (syntactic impossibility), the boundary concept of the signifiable by *that which is impossible to signify* (semantic impossibility), the boundary concept of the experienceable by *that which is impossible to experience* (medial impossibility) and the boundary concept of possible communities of interpretation by *impossible interpreters* (pragmatic impossibility).

Three of these impossibilities, however, overlap with the three non-actualities which appear as the negation of the three dimensions of reality: that which is *not experienced*, in the natural sphere, that which is *not used as a sign*, in the cultural sphere, the *community of interpretation which does not use signs – or does not use certain signs* – in the social sphere. Only *that which is impossible to signify* appears strictly and exclusively impossible, but it is precisely here that the distinction between the *nothing* and the *impossible* breaks down. That which is impossible to signify is to be separated into the *contradictorily signifiable* (which is impossible) and the *non-signifiable* (which is nothing). In all other cases there is a risk that we may confuse the *impossible* with the *non-actual*, thus making a boundary of the possible (impossibility) into a contra-determination of the actual (non-actuality). Yet the *non-experienced* is not the same as the *non-experienceable*, that which is *not used as a sign* is not the same as an *impossible sign*, and the *community of interpretation which does not use signs – or does not use certain signs* is not the same as an *impossible interpreter.* Reifying interpretations of the impossible reverse its boundary character in such a way that the impossible becomes the manifestation of a counter-actuality. Such interpretations are always present where the negation found in the horizon of possibility is confused or deliberately equated with negation in the dimension of reality. However the *non-experienced* is not the same as *that which is impossible to experience.* In the first, one can attempt to overcome the negation, that is, to experience what had not been experienced up to now. In the second, however, that is not a meaningful strategy: that which is impossible to experience cannot possibly be experienced. The introduction of a difference in time, place, point of reference or point of view can only ever make it possible to experience the non-experienced, not the non-experienceable. It is a strategy that applies to the reality dimensions of sign-events, not their horizons of possibility.

Where we really have the *impossible* – i. e. not just the *concrete* impossible – no change in time, in place or in the point of reference or point of view is of any help: the impossible is still impossible, *because, like 'horizon', it is* a *boundary concept, not something categorial which can therefore be positively determined.* Yet for this very reason it is indispensable to orientation in the world: those who do not orient themselves to the impossible will not explore the possible, with the result that they will remain stranded in the actual behind the possible. To that extent, Che Guevara's advice is good advice: "Soyez réaliste, demandez l'impossible". An orientation to the impossible must, however, regard it as a *boundary concept* and not misconstrue it as a pointer to a non-existent realm beyond the possible. The impossible is interesting *because of the possible*, not in itself and for its own sake.[26] Taken

[26] It only *exists* as the negation of the possible, not as an 'actuality' in itself.

on its own, there is no impossible. But without the impossible there is nothing, and the impossible is not the same as nothing, which is neither possible nor impossible. To orient oneself by the difference between impossibility and possibility is therefore a philosophical maxim which is not content with establishing what is actual, but wants to follow it through creatively into its possibilities and to understand it critically in the light of its possibilities. Only those who orient themselves by the impossible will have the measure of the horizon of the possible, and only those who make the possible the yardstick of the actual, rather than making the actual the yardstick of the possible, are the true realists.

The true realism is thus not the sciences, which attempt to relate one actuality back to other actualities, nor religion and the religions, which seek to measure the possible against experienced reality, but faith and a life determined by faith, in which the actual is appraised in the light of the possible, rooted in ultimate actuality or in ultimate presence. Faith is the orientation of one's life by a transcendence which is not purely the basis of the fact that anything is possible and actual at all, but which, as the ground of everything possible, and indeed the ground of unforeseeable possibilities, is present in the immanence of the actual. This creative transcendence is the ultimate presence beyond which one cannot go back and which is implicit in every changing present as its non-retractable requirement. It makes the possible into a gift for a life that cannot give itself reality, but receives its reality as gift, just as much as its goodness and righteousness and truthfulness. It is only these gifts that make our own life's actions possible, and indeed necessary. For everything that comes to us as gift is intended to be handed on, because it is only in passing it on that we are it and possess it. We become it by receiving it, and we have it by giving it away. Just as life has its meaning when it is passed on, so the good, the right and the true find their meaning as we set the good free, do what is right and make what is other to be true. These are the ways in which transcendence transforms life in such a way that it becomes transparent to transcendence, with the result that life in all its facets becomes the sounding board of transcendence. This is precisely what gives added value to the meaning of life, because it is only in the impossible in its various aspects that life finds its boundaries. In a secular world faith reminds us of this, and this is the point of every life which orients itself with the aid of the distinction between transcendence and immanence, whether it is lived in a religious or a non-religious way.

## H. Orientation to Transcendence. The point of making distinctions

### *1. The avoidability and inevitability of the orientation to transcendence*

In a secular world the orientation to transcendence is an option one is able to avoid: no one must consciously orient his life by it, but anyone who is capable of orienting himself can do so. But why should one do this? Not because the grounds for doing so are better than those for not doing so, but because one cannot do otherwise. Such grounds always appear too late and only explicate what has already been decided in one's life up to that point – either positively or negatively. Someone who is not merely considering orienting his life to transcendence, but who actually does so, is not doing so because there are no alternatives, but because there are no alternatives for him. What may be a mere possibility in the realm of thought becomes unavoidable in life once it becomes plain that to ignore or reject this option is just another way of responding to transcendence. If this option is not the result of a human search, which can always come to nothing because humans can think up many things they would like to be associated with (ideals), but is instead activated by the self-presentation of transcendence (as the *divine)* through its self-differentiation from immanence (as the *worldly*), then orientation to transcendence is an option that one cannot evade and towards which, in practice, each of us adopts a position through our manner of life. No one can live life without responding de facto to the presence of transcendence – whether negatively in non-belief or unfaith, or positively in faith.

### *2. The priority of the divine / worldly distinction*

Neither the one nor the other must occur in a form that can be identified as religious. One can lead a secular life, in that one has faith and rejects idolatry, or one can lead a religious life even though one does not have faith but feels at home in religious forms of life. For faith, superstitious belief is a form of unfaith, while for unfaith, faith is a form of superstitious belief. Someone who lives secularly can be doing so for contradictory reasons, as can one who lives religiously. So when one speaks of human attitudes to the self-presentation of transcendence, there is a distinction that must be drawn. Each of us orients our life according to the *divine / worldly* distinction, in that we live *in practice* by reference to the self-differentiation of transcendence from immanence in the self-presentation of the ultimate presence in all that is present, past and future. But not everyone does this consciously. Not everyone who does it consciously is orienting themselves by the *religious / secular* distinction. And not everyone who orients themselves by this distinction does so in the same sense or for the same reasons.

What is decisive for Christian life – and equally for Jewish and Muslim life – is the preservation, not of the *religious / secular* distinction, but of the *divine / worldly* distinction: God is God and the world is the world, and any kind of mixing and blurring is to be avoided if life is not to descend into chaos. But God's transcendence is quite different from the transcendence of the world or transcendences in the world. In whatever direction we transcend in the world, we will never reach God, but will remain within the horizon of the world and the worldly. But there would be no world, nor could we transcend anywhere within it, if God were not so transcendent in relation to the world that he is distinct from it as his creation and allows it to exist as other than himself by drawing near and remaining near to it, but without being absorbed into it or becoming part of it and thus suspending the distinction between transcendence and immanence. Only by becoming accessible *as* transcendence in immanence can God become the orientation point for human life. This is exactly what he does by making himself present as the ultimate presence. Without God there is no world, but without God's presence there is no orientation to God in the world. God's transcendence can only become the goal and orientation point of our transcending because, and to the extent that, as the ultimate presence in our changing presents, it becomes present in such a way that, not only can we orient ourselves by it, we actually do so by the manner in which we live our lives.

### *3. Distinctions of order and of location*

If this orientation to the ultimate presence is undertaken consciously in the light of the fundamental distinction between transcendence and immanence, it will take place in such a way that one draws distinctions so as to orient oneself – *distinctions of order*, by which one determines the horizon of the world perspective within which one is seeking to orient oneself, and *distinctions of location*, by which one localises oneself, together with what is other, in the world perspective thus opened up. This begins with the symbolisation of the fundamental distinction between transcendence and immanence as *divine* and *worldly, God* and *world, creator* and *creation, ultimate presence* and *changing present* and so on (order), and the corresponding distinction between *faith* and *unfaith* as the two basic modes of human existence in relationship to the ultimate presence of transcendence in one's life (location). And this continues in a multiplicity of further distinctions, each of which, in its own way determines and measures the horizon which opens up when one draws the distinction between the divinity of God and the worldliness of the world and follows the processes by which these two horizons of reference are mutually determined, contoured, given their emphasis and more precisely specified.

Some of the central distinctions of this life orientation to the ultimate presence have been analysed in the preceding chapters. They may be summed up as the fundamental characteristics of a grammar of Christian life orientation to the ultimate presence. This grammar explicates the context of meaning of the practice of Christian orientation by clarifying *as what* this ultimate presence is understood (as God's creative presence), *as what* we are understood (as God's creatures, closer to him than all others) and *as what* our world is understood (as God's creation). Thus God's presence, towards which Christian life is oriented, is understood as the presence of creative love, the source and ground of all the good gifts which enter one's life in its changing moments and in different degrees, but which life cannot create or sustain itself: the gift of *being* (being-possible, being-actual, being-necessary) as distinct from *non-being* (being-impossible, being non-actual, being non-necessary i.e. being contingent), of *being good* as distinct from *being evil*, of *being true* as distinct from *being false*, of *being loved* as distinct from *being unloved*, of *being right* as distinct from *being wrong*, of *being beautiful* as distinct from *being ugly*, of *being powerful* as distinct from *being powerless*, of *being alive* as distinct from *being dead*. All these distinctions are not determinations of being, but orientational distinctions of human life in its orientation to God's creative transcendence. They all display specific attributes: they are distinctions drawn *in respect of* the possible, *through* negativity and *for* human life in the world; they occur in respect of the possible within the horizon of the impossible; they use differentiating negativity as their orientation process; and they are undertaken from a standpoint which is located in what is other than transcendence and understands itself as being posited by transcendence. Life has come to be and is constantly in the process of becoming, but it is not self-enabled or self-posited and is only to a limited extent self-made. It becomes what it is within the scope of that which is possible for it. These possibilities are, on the one hand, those which are accessible to it from its contingent standpoint within immanence: it is in itself capable of becoming such and such, or it can acquire this capability. But they include, on the other hand, whatever is meted out to it by transcendence through others and through what is other, altering the scope of available possibilities: It is possible for it to become such and such, even though it is not capable of this in itself, nor can it make itself capable. We do not always have these possibilities already, and we do not bring them about by our own decision, but we can decide for or against them, if and to the extent that they are meted out to us – from others or that which is other within immanence, and from transcendence via others or what is other within immanence. They invariably enrich our present and expand the scope of possibilities available to our future. But they are always bound to the ultimate presence without which we could not be or become anything that we are able to be and become.

### *4. Becoming more than we can*

We can become more than we are able to become of ourselves for the very reason that it is not we who have made ourselves what we are, nor indeed could we have done so. We live although we might not have lived. We live as human beings, even though we often do not live humanely. And we are God's neighbours, even though we have no grounds for this. Our existence, our humanness and our integration into God's life are not the result of anything we are or have done. We cannot help existing, but we are responsible for the way we live. This responsibility acquires its real substance from our understanding of ourselves and how we therefore aspire to live together with other human beings. A creature which understands itself as an animal among animals will perceive its responsibility differently from one who understands himself or herself as a human among humans or as one of God's neighbours. We cannot make ourselves God's neighbours, but as God's neighbours we are more than we can become of ourselves. We lay claim to the increased possibilities allotted to us when we orient ourselves to the ultimate presence to whom we owe all being, all goodness, trueness, rightness and humanness. And we squander these possibilities if we do not do so.

So it is not a matter of course that we should orient our lives by the distinction between transcendence and immanence or one of their religious or theological nomenclatures (creator / creation; ultimate presence / changing presents). We need to be mindful of the fact that the world and our own lives could be more than they generally appear to be. And this can only take place *in* life, changing it from the ground up. Where it takes place, it shakes up everything we have taken for granted as being typical of our normal life in the world. When we become mindful of the ultimate presence and orient ourselves with the aid of the distinction between transcendence (creator) and immanence (creation), we locate ourselves on the immanence side, and experience and understand ourselves and everything else in relation to the bedrock of transcendence. In this way, life and the world acquire increased meaning, making it possible to see through this life to a life beyond to which this life owes its very existence and because of which it can, despite its fragmentariness, become true and whole and good.

But this cannot happen without a conversion of one's habitual orientation practices. This takes place when transcendence discloses itself within immanence as the ultimate presence and as the normative point of reference for one's life orientation. Then it is no longer our own place in the world and our own experience which are decisive for the understanding of our life and of the world in which we live together with others, but the presence of transcendence, which always precedes, underlies and follows our own life and experience. It is this fundamental before and after which enables it to function as the benchmark and criterion of the goodness, wholeness and truth of a human life that will always be fragmentary. Once we catch sight of human life in its relatedness to this ultimate presence as the source of its possibilities, it reveals itself to be more than it had appeared to itself or to others. It acquires an increased meaning which could not have been discerned from within it, but which accrues to it as it is understood against the background of the presence of transcendence as the creation of that transcendence. The truth, goodness and wholeness of a life is thus not to be sought within itself, but in that which is granted to it by the ultimate presence of transcendence. It is what it is and can be, both for and from that transcendence, not merely what it appears to be to itself and others.

It is therefore not one's own experience that determines the truth, goodness, rightness and wholeness of one's life, but that in which all life and experience is embedded: the transcendence whose self-differentiation from immanence enables finite life, and whose creative presence in every created present completes what, in a life within the immanence of the world, remains fragmentary. Life is a gift which cannot be understood in and of itself, but it is also a gift to understand, experience and live life as a gift. Neither of these is self-evident, and either can always be called in question or disputed. This is why it is a discovery one must make in life itself. But if this happens to us in our lives, our understanding of life changes radically.

## *5. Added meaning*

Recalling this discovery and enabling others in other eras to make such discoveries is a core function of Christian tradition and practice. It has its rightful place in a secular world, too. It is a fundamental characteristic of modern secular society to respect the right of every human being to orient his or her life in a religious or non-religious way. There is no prescribed life orientation for anyone. Nor is there a prohibition on discussing life orientations openly or on criticising or caricaturing them, so long as the dignity of all participants and affected persons is preserved. The framework of applicable legislation requires everyone to tolerate this, even though there may be a question mark over the way in which this dictate of tolerance is applied. A secular society is one in which religion is not state-regulated and which does not pass judgement on it, but ensures that religious and non-religious views, positions and practices may be discussed openly and critically, while preserving the human dignity of all. Everyone ought to be able to form his or her own assessment of the meaning, difficulties and benefits of an orientation to transcendence within the immanence of the secular world. And this only works when one can openly live by, represent and question different viewpoints and orientations.

It has to be said, however, that it is one thing to be familiar with a variety of religious and non-religious life orientations, but it is quite another to decide in favour of one of them – whether temporarily, tentatively and experimentally (hypothetically), or because one cannot do other than live in such a way (categorically) even though it would be perfectly possible not to do so. Where there is a concrete form of orientation to transcendence in the immanence of the secular world, life is placed within a new horizon of understanding and acquires a meaning which could not have been deduced from it, and which no one would have prescribed for themselves. The fact that we are God's creatures and neighbours, destined and empowered for life together with the creator in the diversity of the creation, cannot be demonstrated from any one trait of human life, nor yet from all of them combined. It wholly exceeds all that we are able to deduce from our own experience, including that which we experience in negative and indeterminate terms as a 'something' we lack and long for. Through retrospective self-interpretation, however, one may perhaps recognise this as an expression of the unconscious search for transcendence, the divine or God, as Augustine did in his *Confessions*, which, not by chance, are addressed to God. Where the meaning of the gift of life in the presence of God is disclosed to an individual, it appears as an alien possibility which one can either ignore and suppress, or can accept and allow to take effect as an unexpected and unmerited gift. The world is then wholly other because one has oneself become wholly other, in that one has a fresh understanding of oneself, others and all that is other. In the light of the fundamental distinction between transcendence (the divine, God, the creator) and immanence (the worldly, the world, creation) it is not only that some things are different; rather, everything has been redefined, because one has a fresh understanding of oneself. The world is understood as creation and thus stands in a relationship of contrast with God. And God is understood as creator and thus stands in a relationship of contrast with the world. Both of these denote, not a reciprocal relationship of determination between God and the world, but an asymmetrical relationship of determination between the creator and the creation. For the world cannot be understood as creation from its own perspective, but only from God's perspective, and therefore by one who understands themselves from God's perspective as a creature. Similarly, God cannot be understood as the creator from the world's perspective, but only from his perspective, and thus by one to whom God has disclosed himself as God. For the orientation of one's life to the ultimate presence, God is first and last, whereas the world is second and next-to-last. For someone who orients themselves within the immanence of the world to the transcendence of God, God is neither a world behind nor a world above the world in which we live and which we experience, but is the one without whom the world and we ourselves could not be what we can be. He is the ultimate presence without which nothing else could be present, past or future. To orient oneself to this presence means to understand the world and one's own life in relationship to God, and thus in a sphere over which one has no control but in which one finds oneself without having anything to do with it. We live in the immanence of the creation. But we do not constitute it. We can live in this immanence in a religious or a non-religious way. But we only orient ourselves in the immanence of the world to the transcendence of God if we draw a distinction between the world and God, and understand and treat the world as world and God as God, behaving as creatures towards God as creator and towards the world as God's creation.

### *6. Orientation to God in a secular world*

The distinction between God and the world is just one of the fundamental distinctions on our path towards a secular world. In order to understand the historical dialectic of secularisation, one must relate it to the basic double model of secularisation: vertical and horizontal. In the first, the world is oriented towards the world in distinction from God, and faith is oriented transcendentally towards God. In the second, the distinction is made within the world between the religious and the secular: worldliness is treated as secular and religion becomes a private matter within a secular world.

This does not mean that religions are irrelevant from a public point of view, nor that they have to be inaccessible to reason. If we only call rational that which can be represented without being associated with a particular standpoint (i.e. neutral) and in disregard of all particularistic interests (i.e. universal) before the critical eyes and ears of all (i.e. publicly), so that we define religion categorically as particular, positional and private, then it cannot (by definition, rather than on the grounds of objective examination) satisfy the rationality criteria of public reason. However, religions differ: not every religion is to be judged in every respect like all other. Consequently, each religion, indeed each religious position, should be subjected to a critical analysis, not passed off indiscriminately as meaningless or meaningful. The privacy of religion in the legal and political sense (religion may be practised freely and is outside the regulatory competence of the state) does not mean that religious people are exempt from accountability in the public sphere for their religious convictions and beliefs, or from exposing themselves to critical discussion concerning the content of their religion and its practical consequences for the ordering of their lives. A secular society needs places where this discussion will be conducted. It cannot leave religions to their own devices if it wishes to remain secular. Even less so, if it wishes neither to remain secular nor to revert to being religious, but instead to be truly *post-secular*.[1]

We can argue over whether the persistence of religion in our secular society is merely the reverberation of a vanishing epoch or the expression of an anthropological or social necessity. As far as we know, only humans have religious needs, whatever Montaigne intended to say about the piety of elephants. But do all human beings have this need? Humans can live only a short time without drinking and a little longer without eating, but they can live their whole lives without praying. Even if one defines the concept of religion very broadly, it is beyond dispute that humans can live and die without religion, and, indeed, no less respectably than their fellow humans.

Although it contradicts the spirit of the age, Christian theology therefore does well to place the emphasis of its thought and

---

[1] And, indeed, not merely in the imprecise sense outlined by M. BREUL in his *Religion in der politischen Öffentlichkeit. Zum Verhältnis von religiöser Überzeugung und öffentlicher Rechtfertigung*, Diss. Phil., Catholic Theology, University of Cologne, 2014, 126 f.

argument, not on religion, but on *God*. Religion is avoidable, God is not.[2] Naturally, one can call any life orientation religion, or a religious equivalent. However, it is less plausible to impute religion to those who expressly protest against it and who do not live by it or anything like it. If the phenomenological substance of the concept of religion is not to evaporate in the transcendental, religion must be something other than the necessary condition for human beings living religiously *or* not religiously. *One has no religion if one does not live religiously.* Religion has to appear in a life if that life is to be religious, and its *non*-appearance is not a religious phenomenon.

With God it is different: one does not have to believe in God for God to be present. Rather, God is involved even when one ignores or disputes this. Yet 'God' does not mean one phenomenon among phenomena, nor one aspect of the world alongside or among others, but the presence of a reality without which the world would not simply be other, but would not exist at all, and without which we could not be what we can be and become. If, however, one cannot live – either in faith in God or without believing in God – without God's presence, then there is no human life which is not conducted in relation to the presence of God, whether it is lived religiously or non-religiously.

One does not have to be religious, but one cannot live without God. As long as human beings have to get their bearings in a

[2] This truth is misconstrued if one attempts to fix it anthropologically as a religious position: "This law stands: Every finite spirit believes either in God or in idols." Max Scheler, quoted from D. Bell, *Die Zukunft der westlichen Welt. Kultur und Technologie im Widerstreit*, Frankfurt a. M. 1979, 202. Just because every human has to do with God, it does not follow that he believes either in God or in idols. Religion is a life phenomenon, while the localisation of life before God is an existential phenomenon. One can negate the first by not living religiously. The second can only be negated when one no longer lives – and even then it is not cancelled, as is underlined by the Christian faith in the presence of God even in death.

world which never fully reveals itself to them, they are compelled to ask whether what they perceive with their senses and their understanding is the whole of reality. In every age this has worried some people more and others less. Some have reacted religiously and others non-religiously; some have wondered at those with faith, others at unfaith.

Even one who thinks that human beings are designed for religion must admit that not all human beings live according to this design. But no one who thinks humans cannot live without God can deny that, in general, human beings live exactly as if this were possible. It is thus with good reason that Christian theology speaks not only of God, but of *sin*: not because it is fixated on a negative image of the human being, but because it is true of the real situation of human life in the presence of God that all human beings live *etsi deus non daretur.* They are so preoccupied with themselves that they do not care that they are living *coram deo*, in the presence of God's love.

## *7. Faith and theology in secular society*

Even in a secular world, it is true that Christian faith ceases to be recognisable as faith if it does not openly and publicly draw a distinction between itself and non-faith, unfaith, misbelief and idolatry Similarly, Christian theology ceases to be recognisable as such if it does not openly and publicly take accountability for this faith and for its own activity. Theology in all its disciplines is the *thinking elucidation of and reasoning responsibility for the Christian faith*. This exists only where there is concrete thinking, debate and communication – where, therefore, there is open discussion of opinions and convictions, of grounds for and against these opinions and convictions and of criteria for the evaluation of those grounds. It will be a discussion in which everyone can, potentially, participate, in which the important thing is not who says something, but what is being said and on what grounds, which thrives, therefore, not on external authority, but purely on the weight of the issues discussed, the cogency of the answers, the persuasiveness of the arguments and the clarity and relevance of the distinctions it draws.

It is also necessary that, at a crucial point, theological discourse distinguishes between itself and that which it seeks, by its thinking, to justify: *faith*. It is true that there would be no theology without faith, and there is no faith that does not reflect on itself. Nevertheless, it is one thing to reflect on faith, but quite another to *live by faith*. Non-faith, heresy and superstitious belief are not mistaken thinking, rather – in Christian judgement – they are erroneous life orientations. They cannot be corrected theologically by better thinking, but solely by a different way of life.

In secular society, the discursive public sphere of theological thinking must therefore be distinguished from the practical, life-based public sphere of faith. Where faith is concerned, *each of us can only believe on our own account*, and *none of us either can or will believe of our own accord*. One who believes has faith in God. One who has faith in God believes despite the history of his unfaith in him, and, for this very reason, has faith in God as the one to whom alone he owes his faith. God is God, precisely in that he does not leave human beings to themselves in the immanence of their lives. Rather, he becomes and remains present to them as the one who transcends himself towards them as his neighbours, in order to enable them to transcend themselves towards him to whom, one and all, they owe the fact that they are God's neighbours. He gives them life, and he gives them the gift of understanding and experiencing their lives as gift, and of living in love for God and their neighbours. The only convincing proof of God known to faith is thus God himself: *because there is faith, there is God*. Without God there would be no faith, but neither would there be any possibility of living without having faith. Lived faith and lived unfaith prove, each in its own way, the reality of God's presence in the ways in which his love is made actual – faith proves the presence of his love as grace towards human beings and as anger over their unfaith, while unfaith proves the presence of his love as patience with human beings in spite of his anger over their unfaith.

Thus faith is *God's gift of life to the godless human being* who does not realise what has come his way as God's good gift. Yet faith, too, is happenstance and fortuity in the same strict sense as life is: no one obtains life for himself, either as a possibility or a reality. The fact that we can and do live is not the result of our own efforts, but of the efforts of others, and through and beyond them, of God. Similarly, none of us comes to faith of our own accord: rather, faith comes to us as God's presence reveals itself in such a way that we can no longer ignore it as the ultimate presence of our own life and of all life. The one who believes can do no other, and the one who recites the *Credo* is confessing a faith which possesses him rather than him possessing it.

## *8. Renewal of existence*

The change from unfaith to faith is thus not a cognitive acquisition of knowledge, nor an increase in subjective assurance, nor a moral improvement in one's life – all these are at most its consequences. Rather, it is, in a fundamental sense, a *transition from death to life*, from a *life leading towards death* to a *life leading out of death towards God.*

The theologically normative model for the understanding of this change is the resurrection of the crucified one. Just as the crucified Jesus was raised, not by himself but by God, and, precisely because of this, though he was dead, is now alive with God, instead of remaining dead, so faith is a change which is brought about solely by God, and which therefore transplants people from their finite lives leading to death into the eternal presence of life with God. In faith God becomes present to godless human beings, whose concern with themselves leaves them no time to care about God, in such a way that they remain present to him, who cares unceasingly about them, in life and in death.

In faith, therefore, no one can be represented by another (e.g. children by their parents or godparents), since faith itself is the representation of one's own existence by God: the renewal of one's existence by God's presence, which makes a new life orientation possible. One who believes has faith in God, and Christians have faith in God as he revealed himself in Christ and declared himself in the word of the cross: as the one who does not leave the godless to themselves and hence to death, but instead, of his own free will, takes the death of the godless upon himself and bestows upon them his divine life. In faith in the promise of the presence of God's creative love in the word of the cross, God comes to human beings as the one who dies the death of the godless in order that they can live God's life. This is the existential change that finds expression in faith. This is why faith is gift from beginning to end, and only thus is faith what makes human beings true and human life right.

In the change from unfaith to faith, what takes place in the life of each individual is thus what took place in the raising of the crucified one to eternal life with God (Easter) or – putting it the other way round – in God's taking of human form in Christ (Christmas): God himself becomes present in human life in the same way as he became present in Christ – as the one who draws them into in his eternal life and the actual presence of his renewing love. Viewed in this way, faith is the *concrete drawing of a human being into the divine love in Jesus Christ:* or, in other words, the *concrete realisation of the incarnation in the life of a human being* who establishes his identity before God by appropriating the identity of Christ. In this way, human beings become more than they are in themselves. They acquire a new being and increased meaning which defines them not merely as animals among animals or humans among humans, but as neighbours, heirs and children of God, who transcend everything they could become of their own accord or which they could make themselves as human beings.

One cannot make oneself God's neighbour; one can only become God's neighbour if God himself brings this about. As God's neighbours, therefore, humans are what God makes them of his own free will by becoming present to godless human beings through his word and his Spirit in such a way that, despite their godlessness, they can remain present to him and can orient their lives to his presence. Faith means having the confidence to accept this and to live as God's neighbour in orientation to his presence. To have such faith is a gift of God, and the same applies to that towards which this faith is directed: God's life-renewing presence. Through his Spirit, God becomes present and, through his Word, intelligible, to godless humans as the one who takes upon himself even their godlessness, with its deadly consequences, and imputes to them his divine life, so that even in death they remain present to him. By faith in this Word, which bestows upon them their new being as God's neighbour, Christians allow God to be represented to them wholly by Christ and his Spirit (they only know God as he has become intelligible to them in Christ and through his Spirit: as creative love), and they allow themselves to be represented before God by Christ and his Spirit (they are only known by God as he knows them in Christ and through his Spirit: as the self-chosen neighbours of his love). This is the only representation that Christians know. And in accordance with this, their faith in God finds expression as a confession of Christ – in Trinitarian terms: an open, public acknowledgement of God's presence in Christ as the presence of God's love in their lives and all life, mediated by the Spirit of God.

### 9. *The public character of faith*

The public character of faith is not the extraversion of believers' inwardness, as a romantic perception of confessions that misunderstands them as the expressive acts of subjects making their inner life of faith accessible to others. Faith is not an inwardness which only becomes external and public when it is confessed. Rather believers' faith is concealed from them, no less than it is from others. It is their standing before God, from the point of view of which they see and understand themselves and everything else, but which they themselves cannot see as such, but can only perceive indirectly through the medium of the modal resonances it calls forth in others. Believers do not have privileged access to their faith; indeed it is they who know that they depend on outward assurance through word and sacrament. In faith I am, so to speak, not wholly present to myself, but am in fact, just the opposite, wholly *extra me* present to God, the father of all, since as *my* God (God-for-me) and *our* father (God-for-us) he is wholly present to me.

So assurance of faith does not mean that one is subjectively unwavering and free from doubt, but that one relies on God in and through God's presence. Indeed there is double sense in which one abandons oneself (placing no confidence in oneself and one's own trustfulness), and abandons oneself wholly and entirely to God's presence (placing all one's confidence in it). But assurance of faith is not found in searching one's own unfathomable inner depths, but rather in the place where God's presence can be openly perceived, heard and tasted, and where, in the form of his love, it is communicated to humans as his freely chosen neighbours: in word and sacrament. Anyone who looks for faith in his own status as a believer will find little else apart from his own doubt, inability to believe and unbelief. Our gaze is to be directed towards God, not ourselves, and God can only be seen at the place where he has openly made himself knowable as the creative love which transcends itself all the way down into the remote realms of death without ceasing to be that creative love which allows the possible to emerge from the impossible and the new to emerge from the old: in the word of the Cross.

The public character of the creed is therefore to be understood not in a romantic sense, but *theologically*: It is not the believing subject turning his inwardness outwards, but God's making himself present in faith that creates this public character, which enables the mystery of faith to be openly perceived, confessed and lived. Faith does not have to be 'published', since it is always already public; nor does it have to be 'verbalized', since it is always already capable of being understood verbally. God's revelation takes place neither before nor behind, but *in* speech. It is not concealed, but public, manifest, an "open secret" (1 Tim 3:16).

### *10. Ultimate presence*

Believers must render account to each and every human being concerning this open secret (1 Peter 3:15). That is to say, they must openly make clear the nature of the public sphere in which we all live: the open realm of God's presence. This is fundamentally different from all other public spheres of our life, which are constituted by *communication between human beings*. In these we always act, not merely as *participants*, but also simultaneously as *observers*. We see what it is that we are saying and communicating, and how, to whom and as whom we are saying it. This means that we can disassociate ourselves from our public image, present ourselves in one way or another, or portray ourselves falsely or in a way that conceals everything significant.

The open realm of God's presence is fundamentally different. It completely excludes the perspective of an observer in relation to God. In it there are no observers, but only participants, since no one can understand God, unless he or she does so from God's point of view and through him. No one is an observer where God is concerned, no one is in a position to withhold or conceal an aspect of himself from God. God is no alien other, with whom we stand face to face; rather, God's presence is the place in which we live, and faith, or its alternative, unfaith, are the modes of existence of this life. In the presence of God, not only is everything so open that it could not be more open; what is more, everything that is only exists at all because it exists in the openness of God's presence. It is the ultimate presence for all life and the ultimate normative open realm for all humans.

This is not the case because Christians hold it to be so. It would be the case even if no one held it to be so. It is normative because in this ultimate presence nothing is subject to human opinion; rather, everything is subject to God's judgement. Here it is God alone who judges: we are the judged. It is not our judgement of God and how he is to answer before the forum of human reason which is the decisive question for our lives; rather, it is God's judgement of us and consequently our responsibility before God.

This raises a lot of questions, but one thing is not in question: since Easter, God's judgement of us is no longer an open question; it is the "open secret" (1 Tim 3:16) which the Christian faith proclaims and to which it owes its existence. Whatever their godlessness, those who, before God, place their confidence not in themselves but wholly and exclusively in God's judgement of them, will live. This is what the Christian community proclaims and celebrates openly and publicly in its acts of worship, by presenting in word and sacrament the presence in which all human life is lived, both privately and publicly: *the presence of the creative love of God.*

The openness of the presence of this love is constituted, not by us, but solely by God. It is thus fundamentally different from the open public spheres which owe their existence to communication between human beings. These depend on the active participation of those who constitute them, and because this constantly raises the question as to who holds the power and the right to participate actively, there is inherent strife over the participation and exclusion of those who do not have access to the mechanisms of power governing participation in this public sphere. It is different in the presence of God, from which no one is excluded and from which no one can withdraw. We live in this ultimate presence, and not only when we begin to consciously orient ourselves to it and participate actively in it. Those who do not pray are also living before God. The mere fact *that* we live, whether in faith or in unfaith, means that we are living in it, since there is no one living to whom God is not present. God's presence is the ultimate presence in the life of every human being.

Believers are distinguished from others by the fact that they do not ignore God's presence as the ground and horizon of their lives, but orient themselves explicitly to the presence of God, in whose openness all life is lived. In its light, not only the church, but the whole of human life, proves to be *semper reformanda*: it could be better, more human, more open to the possibilities God sends its way and more sensitive to the needs of others, if it were truly to be lived as what it is: life in God's presence.

It is the task of theology to point this out. Its goal is not the adequate substantiation of faith before the forum of a watching public, but to give concrete reminders of the fact that we are all participants and thus human beings who live in God's presence, enacted and revealed as the self-communication of God's love. God is present to every present, even if we are all living *etsi deus non daretur*. For even that would not be possible if God were not present. He is the ultimate presence for all that is, all that will be and all that is no longer. This presence transcends the world, time and life. To orient ourselves to it means orienting ourselves to the one without whom nothing could exist – nothing present, past or future – not even in a secular world.

# Index of Names